UNDERSTANDING ISLAM THROUGH HADĪS

Understanding Islam through Hadīs

Religious Faith or Fanaticism?

RAM SWARUP

VOICE OF INDIA
New Delhi

First US edition, 1983
First Indian reprint, 1984

Reprint 2022

All passages pointed out as objectionable material by the Government of Delhi in their letter dated 17 April 2001 have been deleted in this fourth edition in keeping with our statement submitted to the High Court of Delhi on 11 May 2001

The following order was passed by full bench of the High Court of Delhi pursuing to our above referred statement:

11-05-2001

Present: Mr. Alok Kumar for petitioner
Mr. Ekram Ali Ansari for Ms. Mukta Gupta for State.

+ CM(M) No. 1705/91

Heard. During the course of hearing of the petition, learned counsel for petitioner brought to our notice a communication received by the petitioner from the Government of NCT of Delhi, Home Department dated 17th April, 2001. The same relates to certain materials which were thought to be objectionable by the Government in the book titled "Understanding Islam through Hadis". Learned counsel for the petitioner states on instructions that petitioner has no objection to delete these materials from the Book so that the part considered objectionable by the state shall not remain.

Learned counsel for the State states that if these portions are deleted then there shall not be any objection to the circulation of the book.

Petition disposed of.

sd/-
CHIEF JUSTICE

ISBN: 978-81-85990-73-6 (pbk)

Published by Voice of India, New Delhi
Printed at Replika Press Pvt. Ltd.

Contents

Introduction

Islam is not merely a theology, or a statement about Allah and his relationship with His creatures. Besides containing doctrinal and creedal material, it deals with social, penal, commercial, ritualistic, and ceremonial matters. It enters into everything, even into such private areas as one's dress, marrying, and mating. In the language of the Muslim theologians, Islam is a "complete" and "completed" religion.

It is equally political and military. It has much to do with statecraft, and it has a very specific view of the world peopled by infidels. Since most of the world is still infidel, it is very important for those who are not Muslims to understand Islam.

The sources of Islam are two: the Qurān and the *Hadīs* ("Sayings" or "Traditions"), usually called the *Sunnah* ("customs"), both having their center in Muhammad. The Qurān contains the Prophet's "revelations" (*wahy*); the *Hadīs*, all that he did or said, or enjoined, forbade or did not forbid, approved or disapproved. The word *Hadīs*, singular in form (pl. *ahādīs)*, is also used collectively for all the traditions taken together, for the whole sacred tradition.

Muslim theologians make no distinction between the Qurān and the *Hadīs*. To them both are works of revelation or inspiration. The quality and degree of the revelation in both works is the same; only the mode of expression is different. To them, the *Hadīs* is the Qurān in action, revelation made concrete in the life of the Prophet. In the Qurān, Allah speaks through Muhammad; in the *Sunnah*, He acts through him. Thus Muhammad's life is a visible expression of Allah's utterances in the Qurān. God provides the divine principle, Muhammad the living pattern. No wonder, then, that Muslim theologians regard the Qurān and the *Hạdīs* as being supplementary or even interchangeable. To them, the *Hadīs* is *wahy ghair matlū* ("unread revelation," that is, not read from the Heavenly Book like the Qurān but inspired all the same); and the Qurān is *hadīs mutwātir*, that is, the Tradition considered authentic and genuine by all Muslims from the beginning.

Thus the Qurān and the *Hadīs* provide equal guidance. Allah with the help of His Prophet has provided for every situation. Whether a believer is going to a mosque or to his bedroom or to the toilet, whether he is making love or war, there is a command and a pattern to follow. And according to the Qurān, when Allah and His Apostle have decided a matter, the believer does not have his or her own choice in the matter (33:36).

And yet situations do arise when the guidance is lacking. It is said of Imām ibn Hanbal (b. A.H. 164, d. A.H. 241 = A.D. 780-855) that he never ate watermelons, even though he knew that the Prophet had done so, because he did not know his manner of eating them. The same story is related even of Bāyazid Bistān, a great Sufi, whose mystical teachings went against orthodox Qurānic theology.

Though the non-Muslim world is not as familiar with the *Sunnah*, or *Hadīs*, as with the Qurān, the former even more than the latter is the most important single source of Islamic laws, precepts, and practices. Ever since the lifetime of the Prophet, millions of Muslims have tried to imitate him in their dress, diet, hair-style, sartorial fashions, toilet mores, and sexual and marital habits. Whether one visits Arabia or Central Asia, India or Malaysia, one meets certain conformities, such as the veil, polygamy, ablution, and *istinjā* (abstersion of the private parts). These derive from the *Sunnah*, reinforced by the Qurān. All are accepted not as changing social usages but as divinely ordained forms, as categorical moral imperatives.

The subjects that the *Hadīs* treats are multiple and diverse. It gives the Prophet's views of Allah, of the here and the hereafter, of hell and heaven, of the Last Day of Judgment, of *īmān* (faith), *salāt* (prayer), *zakāt* (poor tax), *sawm* (fast), and *hajj* (pilgrimage), popularly known as religious subjects; but it also includes his pronouncements on *jihād* (holy war), *al-anfāl* (war booty), and *khums* (the holy fifth); as well as on crime and punishment, on food, drink, clothing, and personal decoration, on hunting and sacrifices, on poets and soothsayers, on women and slaves, on gifts, inheritances, and dowries, on toilet, ablution, and bathing; on dreams, christianing, and medicine, on vows and oaths and testaments, on images and pictures, on dogs, lizards, and ants.

The *Hadīs* constitutes a voluminous literature. It gives even insignificant details of the Prophet's life. Every word from his lips, every nod or shake of his head, every one of his gestures and mannerisms was important to his followers. These are remembered by them as best as they could and passed on from generation to generation. Naturally those who came into greater contact with the Prophet had the most to tell about him. 'Āisha, his wife, Abū Bakr and 'Umar, his aristocratic followers, Anas b. Mālik, his servant for ten years, who died at the ripe age of 103 in A.H. 93, and 'Abdullah b. 'Abbās, his cousin, were fertile sources of many *ahādīs*. But another most prolific source was Abū Huraira, who is the authority for 3,500 traditions. He was no relation of the Prophet, but he had no particular work to do except that he specialized in collecting traditions from other Companions. Similarly, 1,540 traditions derive from the authority of Jābir, who was not even a Quraish but belonged to the Khazraj tribe of Medina, which was allied to Muhammad.

Every *hadīs* has a text (*matn*) and a chain of transmission (*isnād*). The same text may have several chains, but every text must be traced back to a Companion (*as-hāb*), a man who came into personal contact with the Prophet. The Companions related their stories to their successors (*tābiūn*), who passed them on to the next generation.

At first the traditions were orally transmitted, though some of the earliest narrators must have also kept written notes of some kind. But as the Companions and the Successors and their descendants died, a need was felt to commit them to writing. There were two other reasons. The Qurānic injunctions were probably sufficient for the uncomplicated life of the early Arabs, but as the power of the Muslims grew and they became the masters of an extended empire, they had to seek a supplementary source of authority to take into account new situations and new customs. This was found in the *Sunnah*, in the practice of the Prophet, already very high in the estimation of the early Muslims.

There was an even more pressing reason. Spurious traditions were coming into being, drowning the genuine ones. There were many motives at play behind this development. Some of these new traditions were merely pious frauds, worked up in order to promote what the fabricators thought were elements of a pious life, or what they thought were the right theological views.

There were also more personal motives at work. The traditions were no longer mere edifying stories. They were sources of prestige and profit. To have one's ancestors counted among the Emigrants or Helpers, to have them present at the Pledge of al-Aqabah or included among the combatants at the Battles of Badr and Uhud—in short, to have them mentioned in any context of loyalty and usefulness to the Prophet—was a great thing. So Traditionists who could get up right traditions were very much in demand. Traditionists like Shurahbīl b. Sa'd utilized their power effectively; they favored and blackmailed as it suited them.

Spurious traditions also arose in order to promote factional interests. Soon after Muhammad's death, there were cutthroat struggles for power between several factions, particularly the Alids, the Ummayads, and later on the Abbasides. In this struggle, great passions were generated, and under their influence new traditions were concocted and old ones usefully edited.

The pious and the hero-worshipping mind also added many miracles around the life of Muhammad, so that the man tended to be lost in the myth.

Under these circumstances, a serious effort was made to collect and sift all the current traditions, rejecting the spurious ones and committing the correct ones to writing. A hundred years after Muhammad, under Khalīfa 'Umar II, orders were issued for the collection of all extant traditions under the supervision of Bakr ibn Muhammad. But the Muslim world had to wait another hundred years before the work of sifting was undertaken by a galaxy of traditionists like Muhammad Ismāīl al-Bukhārī (A.H. 194–256 = A.D. 810–870), Muslim ibnu'l-Hajjāj (A.H. 204–261 = A.D. 819–875), Abū Īsā Muhammad at-Tirmizī (A.H. 209–279 = A.D. 824–892), Abū Dā'ūd as-Sajistani (A.H. 202–275 = A.D. 817–888) and others.

Bukhārī laid down elaborate canons of authenticity and applied them with a ruthless hand. It is said that he collected 600,000 traditions but accepted only 7,000 of them as authentic. Abū Dā'ūd entertained only 4,800 traditions out of a total of 500,000. It is also said that 40,000 names were mentioned in different chains of transmission but that Bukhārī accepted only 2,000 as genuine.

As a result of the labor of these Traditionists, the chaotic mass was cut down and some order and proportion were restored. Over a thousand collections which were in vogue died away in due course, and only six collections, the *Sihāh Sitta* as they are called, became authentic *Sahīs*, or collections. Of these, the ones by Imām Bukhārī and Imām Muslim are at the top—"the two authentics," they are called. There is still a good deal of the miraculous and the improbable in them, but they contain much that is factual and historical. Within three hundred years of the death of Muhammad, the *Hadīs* acquired substantially the form in which it is known today.

To the infidel with his critical faculty still intact, the *Hadīs* is a collection of stories, rather unedifying, about a man, rather all too human. But the Muslim mind has been taught to look at them in a different frame of mind. The believers have handled, narrated, and read them with a feeling of awe and worship. It is said of 'Abdullah ibn Mas'ūd (died at the age of seventy in A.H. 32), a Companion and a great Traditionist (authority for 305 traditions), that he trembled as he narrated a *hadīs*, sweat often breaking out all over his forehead. Muslim believers are expected to read the traditions in the same spirit and with the same mind. The lapse of time helps the process. As the distance grows, the hero looms larger.

We have also chosen the *Sahīh Muslim* as the main text for our present volume. It provides the base, though in our discussion we have often quoted from the Qurān. The Qurān and the *Hadīs* are interdependent and mutually illuminating. The Qurān provides the text, the *Hadīs* the context. In fact, the Qurān cannot be understood without the aid of the *Hadīs*, for every Qurānic verse has a context which only the *Hadīs* provides. The *Hadīs* gives flesh and blood to the Qurānic revelations, reveals their more earthly motives, and provides them with the necessary locale.

To clarify certain points, we have also quoted here and there from the Prophet's traditional biographies, which are no more than ordered traditions arranged chronologically around events in the life of the Prophet. Apart from several *maghāzī* books (books about the Prophet's campaigns) which went before, almost the very first definitive biography was that of Ibn Ishāq, who was born in Medina in A.H. 85 and died in A.H. 151 (A.D. 768) in Baghdad. Other biographers of note who succeeded him and who amply made use of his labors were Al-Wāqidī, Ibn Hishām, and At-Tabarī. An English translation of Ishāq's *Sīrat Rasūl Allāh* by A. Guillaume is available under the title *The Life of Muhammad* (Oxford, 1958).

Until now only partial English translations of some *Hadīs* collections were available. Therefore, we must thank Dr. Abdul Hamīd Siddīqī for filling up this gap and giving us a full-scale translation of the *Sahīh Muslim* (Lahore: Sh. Muhammad Ashraf). The translation of an Eastern text by an Eastern mind has one advantage: it retains the flavor of the original. It may not be in the Queen's English and may seem rather exotic to those whose mother tongue is English, but it is faithful and reproduces the atmosphere of the original.

Dr. Siddīqī has done more than translate the original work. He has provided copious explanatory notes. In a *Sahīh* containing 7,190 *ahādīs*, he provides 3,081 footnotes. In addition to clarifying obscure points and references, the notes give us an authentic taste of traditional Muslim scholarship. In fact, because the notes are set in a well-established scholarly lore, they could be an important subject of treatment in their own right. They show that the role of scholarship in Islam is secondary—that it is the handmaid of the Qurān and the *Hadīs*, unmotivated by any seeking of its own, but capable of cleverness and even brilliance within its self-chosen role of justifying and defending. Here and there, we have also quoted from the notes—about forty-five times—to give the reader a sampling of Islamic scholarship.

Now a word about how the present volume came to be written. When we read Dr. Siddīqī's translation, we felt that it contained important material about Islam which should be more widely known. Islam, having been dormant for several centuries, is again on the march. Even before the Europeans came on the scene, the Muslims had their own variation of the "white man's burden" of civilizing the world. If anything, their mission was even more pretentious for it was commanded by Allah Himself. Muslims wielded their swords to root out polytheism, dethrone the gods of their neighbors, and install in their place their own godling, Allah. That they received plunder and established an empire in the process is another matter. These were accidental terrestrial rewards for disinterested celestial labors.

Thanks to the new oil wealth of the Arabs, the old mission is being revived. A kind of "Muslim Cominform" is taking shape in Jidda. The oil-rich Arabs are assuming responsibility for Muslims everywhere, looking after their spiritual needs as well as their more temporal interests. Their money is active throughout the Muslim world, in Pakistan and Bangladesh, in Malaysia, Indonesia, and even India, with a large Muslim population.

The Arabs are still militarily weak and dependent on the West, but the full fury of their interference is to be seen in countries of Asia and Africa which are economically poor and ideologically weak. Here they work from the bottom as well as from the top. They buy local politicians. They have bought the conversion of the presidents of Gabon and the Central African Empire. They have adopted the Muslim minorities of *Daru'l Harb*, i.e., infidel countries which have not yet been fully subdued by Muslims. They are using these minorities to convert these countries into *Daru'l Islam*, or "countries of peace," i.e., countries where Islam dominates.

Even in the best of circumstances, it is difficult to assimilate Muslim minorities into the national mainstream of a country. Arab support has made the task still more difficult. It was this support which was behind the rebellion of the Moro Muslims in the Philippines. In India, there is a continuing Muslim problem that refuses solution despite the division of the country. Arab interference has complicated matters still further.

A new fundamentalism is sweeping over the Muslim world, throwing up leaders like Khomeini and Mu'ammar Qaddafi. Wherever it triumphs, dictatorship comes in its wake. Fundamentalism and authoritarianism are twins.

According to some thinkers, this fundamentalism is nothing but a search by Muslims for self-identity and self-assertion. It is a weapon of self-defense, derived from the available symbols of their culture, against the materialist and bourgeois values of the West. But on calm reflection, it is also something more; it is also their dream of recapturing the grandeur of their old imperial days. Islam is by nature fundamentalist; and this fundamentalism in turn is aggressive in character. Islam claims to have defined human thought and behavior for all time to come; it resists any change, and it feels justified in imposing its beliefs and behavior patterns on others.

Whether this fundamentalism is considered resurgence or reversal and the threat of the reappearance of an old imperialism will depend on one's point of view. But anything that throws light on any aspect of the problem will be a great contribution.

This we find the *Hadīs* literature most fitted to do. It gives a living picture of Islam at its source and of Islam in the making, providing an intimate view of the elements that constitute orthodox Islam in their pristine purity. Indeed, it is these very elements of Islam that Muslims find most fascinating, and thus, motivated by a compulsive atavism, they repeatedly appeal to them and revert to them.

For this purpose, we have chosen as our guide the *Sahīh Muslim*, which has the advantage of being available in an English translation. Since most *Hadīs* collections contain the same core material, this self-limitation is no great disadvantage. On the other hand, it fruitfully defines the field of our study and inquiry.

It has one drawback, though, both of commission and omission. While we have in this way touched on many points, we have discussed none in full. And, similarly, since we have followed the lead of the *Sahīh Muslim*, some matters quite important in themselves remain undeveloped and even untouched because they are not treated in the *Sahīh*. This problem was unavoidable, but we have tried to overcome it here and there by going beyond the confines of this particular *Sahīh*.

In spite of the limitations of the procedure we have adopted, the *Sahīh Muslim* remains a very comprehensive and informative source on Islamic beliefs and behavior, and we have quoted extensively and faithfully from it. It gives us 7,190 traditions divided into 1,243 chapters. In many instances the same text is reported in several chapters with only minor variations but with different chains of transmission. Therefore, in many cases, one *hadīs* stands for a number of *ahādīs*, and to quote one *hadīs* is really to quote a whole chapter. In this volume, we have quoted about 675 individual *hadīs* having this representative character. Another 700 of the *ahādīs* we have quoted are group *ahādīs* or their summaries. Portions that deal with mere rituals and ceremonies and have no particular importance to non-Muslims we omitted altogether, but we readily included anything that had a deeper ring, although such instances are rather rare. For example, in the long "Book of Pilgrimage" (*Kitāb al-Hajj*), containing 583 traditions, there is not a single one that remotely suggests the idea of the "inner pilgrimage" about which mystics speak so much. Similarly, in the "Book of Jihād and Campaigns," comprising 180 traditions, there is hardly anything that would suggest the sentiment of *jihād'l-akbar*, "the greater warfare" directed against one's own lower nature (*nafs*). Most of the discussion lacks inwardness.

The *Sahīh Muslim*, like other *Hadīs* collections, also gives very intimate glimpses of the life of the Prophet, an impressionistic view that makes him seem more a living, breathing person than the portrayals given in his more formal biographies. Here one comes to know him, not through his pompous deeds and thoughts, but through his more workaday ideas and actions. There is no makeup, no cosmetics, no posturing for posterity. The Prophet is caught as it were in the ordinary acts of his life—sleeping, eating, mating, praying, hating, dispensing justice, planning expeditions and revenge against his enemies. The picture that emerges is hardly flattering, and one is left wondering why in the first instance it was reported at all and whether it was done by his admirers or enemies. One is also left to wonder how the believers, generation after generation, could have found this story so inspiring.

The answer is that the believers are conditioned to look at the whole thing through the eyes of faith. An infidel in his fundamental misguidance may find the Prophet rather sensual and cruel—and certainly many of the things he did do not conform to ordinary ideas of morality—but the believers look at the whole thing differently. To them morality derives from the Prophet's actions; the moral is whatever he did. Morality does not determine the Prophet's actions, but his actions determine and define morality. Muhammad's acts were not ordinary acts; they were Allah's own acts.

It was in this way and by this logic that Muhammad's opinions became the dogmas of Islam and his personal habits and idiosyncrasies became moral imperatives: Allah's commands for all believers in all ages and climes to follow.

In regard to the title of the book, the *Hadīs* gives such a spontaneous and realistic view of the Prophet that it could most faithfully be called "Muhammad in the Words of *Hadīs* (*Sahīh Muslim*)"; but since a good deal of Islam is Mohammadism, it could equally justly be called "Islam in the Words of *Hadīs*."

In devout Islamic literature, whenever the name or the title of the Prophet is mentioned, it is accompanied by a standard blessing, "may peace be upon him." A similar formula, "may Allah be pleased with him," accompanies the mention of any of his more important Companions. In our quotations from this literature, we have omitted these formulas in the interest of smoother reading.

Diacritical marks are necessary in specialist works, but they do not have the same usefulness in books of a more general nature. Therefore, in order to avoid them as far as possible, we have rendered the letters of the Arabic alphabet by their nearest English equivalents in sound-value.

For example, the Arabic alphabet's *se*, *sīn*, and *swād* have been uniformly rendered by the English *s*; *te* (soft dental) and *toe* by *t*; *zāl*, *ze*, and *zwād* by *z*. We have also used two diacritical marks: a macron over a vowel sound to indicate that it is long, and an apostrophe ('). The apostrophe generally is used to render another sound called *hamza*, but we have made it do also for another sound, *ain*; both have to be learned by ear, but these could be disregarded by non-Arabian readers, for they do not affect the substance of the book.

Shri L. C. Jain, Dr. Sisir Kumar Ghose, Shri A. C. Gupta, Shri Kaidar Nath Sahani, and Mrs. Francine Ellison Krishna read the manuscript in that order and suggested many improvements. Shri H. P. Lohia and Shri Sita Ram Goel were associated with the manuscript at every stage of its writing. The present edition is due entirely to two Indian friends, one from Bengal and the other from

Andhra Pradesh, now both resident in America; they have preferred to remain anonymous. Shri P. Rajappan Achary typed out the manuscript. I thank them all gratefully. I also thank the editors and publishers of Exposition Press for their appreciation and cooperation from the very beginning and for bringing out a very presentable edition of this book.

RAM SWARUP

UNDERSTANDING ISLAM THROUGH HADĪS

1
Faith (*Īmān*)

The very first book of the *Sahīh Muslim* is the "Book of Faith" (*Kitāb al-Īmān*). It contains 431 traditions (*ahādīs*) divided into ninety-two chapters. It discusses questions regarding faith. Someone comes to Muhammad from a great distance, yet without any sign of fatigue, and says: "Muhammad, inform me about *al-Islam*." The Messenger of Allah replies: "*Al-Islam* implies that you testify that there is no god but Allah and that Muhammad is the Messenger of Allah, and you establish prayer, pay *Zakāt*, observe the fast of *Ramzān* [Ramadan] and perform pilgrimage." Later on, when the inquirer is gone, Muhammad tells 'Umar: "He was Gabriel. He came to you in order to instruct you in matters of religion"(1).* This is the very first *hadīs* narrated by 'Umar, the future Khalīfa, through several chains of narrators.

This theme runs through hundreds of *ahādīs*. *Al-Islam* is faith in Allah, faith in Muhammad as His Messenger, faith in His Book, in His angels, in the resurrection, in the hereafter, and in the payment of the poor tax (*zakāt*) and the observance of fast (*Ramzān*) and pilgrimage.

Allah Is Not Enough

Belief in Allah alone in not sufficient. It must be accompanied by belief in the apostleship of Muhammad. A delegation of the tribe of Rabī'a visits Muhammad. He tells the delegates: "I direct you

*All traditions in the *Sahīh* are serially numbered. So also are the notes and comments of the translator. In quoting them, we give their numbers in parentheses.

to affirm belief in Allah alone," and then asks them: "Do you know what belief in Allah really implies?" Then he himself answers: "It implies testimony to the fact that there is no god but Allah, and that Muhammad is the Messenger of Allah." Other things mentioned are prayer, *zakāt*, *Ramzān*, and "that you pay one-fifth of the booty"(23). We shall hear more about war booty in its proper place.

In the same vein, Muhammad tells Mu'āz, whom he sends out as governor of Yemen: "First call them to testify that there is no god but Allah, that I [Muhammad] am the Messenger of Allah; and if they accept this, then tell them that Allah has made *Zakāt* obligatory for them" (27).

There is a still clearer statement of Muhammad's mission. "I have been commanded to fight against people till they testify that there is no god but Allah, that Muhammad is the Messenger of Allah, and they establish prayer, and pay *Zakāt* and if they do it, their blood and property are guaranteed protection on my behalf" (33).

Muhammad retails the word "Allah" profusely, but there are times when even Allah occupies a backseat. "None of you is a believer till I am dearer to him than his child, his father and the whole mankind," Muhammad tells the believers (71).

Allah and his Messenger—rather, Muhammad and his God—prayer, *zakāt*, *Ramzān*, and pilgrimage are sometimes called the "five pillars" of Islam, but there are other beliefs and institutions no less important which recur again and again in the *Hadīs*. These are, to name the more important ones, Paradise, Hell, Doomsday, *jihād* (holy war against polytheists,) *jizyā* (the poll tax paid by polytheists), war booty (*ghanīmah*), and *khums* (the holy one-fifth). These are the staples of the religion preached by Muhammad. Allah becomes concrete in His threats and punishments of Hell, and in His promises and rewards of Paradise. Similarly, in the history of Islam, *jihād* and war booty have played a more important role than even pilgrimage or *zakāt*. All of these concepts will come up for review in this study in their proper places.

GOOD AND EVIL DEEDS

What are good deeds and what are bad deeds? These questions have been the concern of many religions, many philosophies, and many teachers. Islam too has provided its characteristic answers. It tells us that good deeds are not a matter of indifference but must be coupled with the choice of the right religion. Abdul Hamīd Siddīqī, the translator of the *Sahīh Muslim*, gives the Islamic view in the following words: "The good deeds performed in the state of ignorance (outside the fold of Islam) are indicative of the fact that a man is inclined towards piety. But to be truly pious and virtuous it is quite essential to have the correct understanding of the Will of God. This can be confidently known only through the Prophets and is embodied in Islam. Thus without having faith in Islam we cannot serve our Master and Lord according to His Will. . . . The acts of virtue may be good in their own way but it is by coming within the fold of Islam that these become significant and meaningful in the eyes of the Lord" (note 218).

In the eyes of Muhammad, a wrong theology is worse than wicked deeds. When asked, "Which sin is the gravest in the eyes of Allah?" he replies: "That you associate a partner with Allah." To kill your child and to commit adultery with the wife of your neighbor are second and third in gravity according to Muhammad (156).

In fact, only a wrong theology can keep a Muslim out of Paradise. But no morally wicked act—not even adultery and theft—can prevent his entry. Muhammad tells us: "Gabriel came to me and gave me tidings: Verily he who died amongst your *Ummah* [sect, nation, group] without associating anything with Allah would enter paradise." In clarification, Abū Zarr, the narrator of the *hadīs*, asks Muhammad whether this is true even if the man committed adultery and theft. Muhammad replies: "Yes, even if he committed adultery and theft" (171). The translator clarifies the point further: He says that adultery and theft "are both serious offences in Islam . . . but these do not doom the offender to the eternal hell," but polytheism or associating any god "with the Lord is an unpardonable crime and the man who commits it is doomed to Hell" (notes 169 and 170).

If polytheism is the worst of crimes, monotheism, by the same token, is the best of virtues. Muhammad is asked about "the best of deeds." He replies: "Belief in Allah." "What next?" he is asked. "*Jihād*," he replies (148). In Muslim theology the formula "belief in Allah" of course means "belief in Allah and His Messenger."

Once one accepts the theological belief in Allah and His Messenger, one's past crimes are obliterated, and future ones hold no great terror. Muhammad gave this assurance to some polytheists who "had committed a large number of murders and had excessively indulged in fornication," but who were ready to join him. To another person who felt a sense of guilt about his past, Muhammad said: "Are you not aware of the fact that Islam wipes out all the previous misdeeds?" (220).

MORAL VALUES

Muhammad's religion is predominantly theological, but moral values are not altogether neglected. The pre-Muslim Arabs believed in many moral values common to all mankind. Muhammad retained these values but gave them a sectarian twist. A Muslim owes everything to the *ummah*, very little to others. He has no obligations, moral or spiritual, toward non-Muslims as part of the human race, except to convert them by sword, spoils, and *jizyā*. For example, sincerity is a universal human value, and we should exercise it in our relations with one another irrespective of creed and nationality. But in Islam, it is limited to Muslims. Muhammad at one place defines *al-din* ("*the* religion," i.e., Islam) as "sincerity and well-wishing," which should be a good definition for any religion. But on being asked, "Sincerity and well-wishing for whom?" he replies: "For Allah, His Book, His Messenger and for the leaders and general Muslims" (98). Jarīr b. 'Abdullah reports that he "pledged allegiance to the Apostle of Allah on sincerity and well-wishing for every Muslim" (102).

Again, other moral values are given the same twist, and the universal is turned into the sectarian. Muhammad tells his followers: "Abusing a Muslim is an outrage and fighting against him is unbelief" (122).

THEOLOGY DISTORTS MORALS

No wonder that such a sectarian and preponderantly theological approach should now and then teach us topsy-turvy morals. Thanks to this approach, despoiling a whole people is meritorious if they are polytheists, but stealing booty once it is in the possession of Muslims is a mortal sin. A slave of Muhammad died in a holy war, thus automatically earning a place in Paradise as a martyr. But Muhammad saw "him in the Fire for the garment or cloak that he had stolen from the booty." On hearing this, some people were greatly perturbed. One of them who had presumably committed a similar act of pilfering, came to Muhammad "with a lace or two laces and said: Messenger of Allah, I found them on the day of Khaibar [name of a battle]. The Holy Prophet remarked: This is a lace of fire or two laces of fire" (210). This means, as another text puts it, that like the two pieces of lace the man had stolen, there will be two columns of fire like unto these waiting for him in the hereafter.

To rob a whole people is piety, but to remove a paltry something from a looted treasure is moral depravity of a magnitude that deserves eternal fire. Men driven by ordinary temptations indulge only in petty crimes and small lapses, but committing real enormities needs the aid of an ideology, a revelation, a God-ordained mission.

The Pre-Muslim Arabs

Muslim theologians and writers are in the habit of painting a very dark picture of pre-Islamic Arabia. They describe it as morally depraved and utterly lacking in any sense of chivalry and generosity, referring to this period of history as the "state of ignorance or barbarism" (*jahilīyya*). Everything good began with Muhammad. But there are many *ahādīs* which prove the contrary. We are told that one Hakīm b. Hīzam did "many deeds of religious purification . . . in the state of ignorance" (222). Another *hadīs* tells us that he "freed one hundred slaves and donated one hundred camels" in this state (225).

Ordinarily such good acts do not avail a polytheist; but if he embraces Islam, it is a different story, and the whole complexion of his acts is changed. They are no longer wasted; they become fruitful and are credited to his account. Muhammad assures Hakīm: "you have accepted Islam with all the previous virtues that you had practised" (223).

EVIL THOUGHTS AND EVIL DEEDS

A Muslim is Allah's prodigal son as well as His spoiled child. His past is forgotten unless it is good, his future is assured, and many things are permissible for him that are not permissible for a polytheist or even for a Jew or a Christian, the Peoples of the Book. Jesus spoke of "lusting with the eyes" regarding it as bad as lust in its more visible form. But Muhammad gave greater latitude to his followers: "Verily Allah forgave my people the evil promptings which arise within their hearts as long as they did not speak about them or did not act upon them" (230). This idea is expressed with less partiality and in more universal terms in the Indian spiritual tradition. God knows that man is weak and forgives his lapses and failure but supports his strength and multiplies his good. The less theistic but not less exalted yogic systems would put this idea somewhat differently and in more psychological terms—we should not harp too obsessively on our lapses, but should dwell more lovingly on the Divine within us.

MUHAMMAD HAS THE LARGEST FOLLOWING ON THE DAY OF JUDGMENT

Muhammad tells us that he "will have the greatest following on the Day of Resurrection" (283). And understandably so, for the hellfire is on his side. The hellfire will be busy consuming the opponents of Muhammad, and there will be no one left for Paradise to receive except the Muslims.

Muhammad tells us: "He who amongst the community of Jews and Christians hears about me, but does not affirm his belief in that with which I have been sent and dies in this state of disbelief, he shall be but one of the denizens of Hell-Fire" (284). The Jews and Christians will suffer in hell not only for their own unbelief in Muhammad, they will also act as proxies for any Muslims who happen to be sent there. "There would come people amongst the Muslim on the Day of Resurrection with as heavy sins as a mountain, and Allah would forgive them and he would place in their stead the Jews and the Christians," Muhammad tells us (6668). This would also, incidentally, solve the problem of space in heaven: "Space in paradise would be provided by Christians and Jews being thrown into Hell-Fire," the translator tells us (note 2967).

Another important segment of the infernal population is made up of women. Muhammad says, "O womenfolk . . . I saw you in bulk amongst the dwellers of Hell." When a woman asks him why it should be so, Muhammad tells her: "You curse too much and are ungrateful to your spouses. I have seen none [like them] lacking in common sense and failing in religion but robbing the wisdom of the wise." The "proof of the lack of common sense" in them is the fact that in Allah's law promulgated by Muhammad himself, "the evidence of two women is equal to one man"; and the proof of their failing in religion, as he tells them, is that "you spend some nights and days in which you do not offer prayer and in the month of *Ramzān* you do not observe fast" (142). Women sometimes abstained from voluntary fasts because the Prophet had commanded that it was more meritorious for them to do their duty by their husbands than to fast. 'Āisha, the Prophet's wife, did not observe some fasts "due to the regards for the Apostle of Allah" (2550). But, it seems, the very merit of women turns into its opposite: predestined damnation.*

*A woman's social and legal disabilities, and even her differential biological constitution and functions, are interpreted in terms of her moral inferiority for which Allah has rightly punished her. In his *Counsel for Kings*, Al-Ghazzālī (A.D. 1058-1111), a famous Arab divine of his time, says that "Allah, He be praised, punished women with eighteen things": (1) menstruation; (2) childbirth; (3) separation from parents and marriage to a stranger; (4) pregnancy; (5) not having control over her own person; (6) a lesser share in inheritance; (7) her liability to be divorced and inability to divorce; (8) its being lawful for men to have four wives, but for a woman to have only one husband; (9) the fact that she must stay secluded in the house; (10) the fact that she must keep her head covered inside the house; (11) the fact that two women's testimony has to be set against the testimony of one man; (12) the fact that she must not go out of the house unless accompanied by a near relative; (13) the fact that men take part in Friday and feast day prayers and funerals while women do not; (14) disqualification for rulership and judgeship; (15) the fact that merit has one thousand components, only one of which is attributable to women, while nine hundred and ninety-nine are attributable to men; (16) the fact that if women are profligate they will be given only half as much torment as the rest of the community at the Resurrection Day; (17) the fact that if their husbands die they must observe a waiting period of four months and ten days before remarrying; (18) the fact that if their husbands divorce them they must observe a waiting period of three months or three menstrual periods before remarrying (Nasīhat Al-Mulūk, London: University of Durham Publications, 1971; pp. 164-165).

THE DAY OF JUDGMENT

The Day of Judgment (*qiyāmat*), the Last Day (*yaumu'l-ākhir*), is an indispensable prop of Muslim theology. In the Qurān, the word *qiyāmat* appears seventy times and in addition has seventy-five synonyms, as shown by Mirza Hairat in his *Mukaddma Tafsīru'l Furqan.** Along with its attendant concepts, Paradise and Hell, it pops up from practically every page of the *Hadīs* too. The dreaded day (*yaum*), colorfully described as the day of "reckoning" (*hisāb*), or of "separation" (*fasl*), or of "standing up" (*qiyāmah*), is mentioned over three hundred times in the Qurān.

The arrival of the Last Day will be announced by many signs. "When you see a slave woman giving birth to her master—that is one sign; when you see barefooted, naked, deaf and dumb as the rulers of the earth—that is one of the signs of Doom. And when you see the shepherds of the black camels exult in buildings—that is one of the signs of Doom" (6). In short, when the poor and the deprived inherit the earth, that is the end of it according to Muhammad.

There is a vivid account of the Day of Resurrection in eighty-two *ahādīs* at the end of the "Book of Faith." Muhammad tells us that on this day, Allah "will gather people," a "bridge would be set over the hell," and "I [Muhammad] and my *Ummah* would be the first to pass over it" (349).

Unbelievers, of course, will be thoroughly miserable on this day but even the Jews and the Christians—the Peoples of the Book—will fare no better. For example, Christians will be summoned and asked, "What did you worship?" When they reply, "Jesus, the son of Allah," Allah will tell them, "You tell a lie; Allah did not take for Himself either a spouse or a son." Then they will be asked what they want. They will say: "Thirsty we are, O our Lord! Quench our thirst." They will be given a certain direction, and Allah will ask: "Why don't you go there to drink water?" When they go there, they will find that they have been misguided; the water is no more

*All these synonyms are reproduced in *Qurān Parichaya*, a work in Hindi (author and publisher, Deva Prakash, Ratlam, India).

than a mirage, and it is really hell. Then they will "fall into the Fire" and perish (352).

On this day, no other prophet or savior will avail except Muhammad. People will come to Adam and say: "Intercede for your progeny." He will reply: "I am not fit to do this, but go to Ibrāhīm, for he is the friend of Allah." They will go to Ibrāhīm, but he will reply: "I am not fit to do this, but go to Moses, for he is Allah's Interlocutor." They will go to Moses, but he will reply: "I am not fit to do this, but you go to Jesus, for he is the Spirit of Allah and His Word." They will go to Jesus, and he will reply: "I am not fit to do this; you better go to Muhammad." Then they will come to Muhammad, and he will say: "I am in a position to do that." He will appeal to Allah, and his intercession will be granted (377).

In many *ahādīs* (381-396), Muhammad tells us that among the apostles he has a special intercessory power, for "no Apostle amongst the Apostles has been testified as I have been testified" (383). If this is true, it gives substance to his claim that among the apostles he "would have the largest following on the Day of Resurrection" (382). Thanks to his special role, "seventy thousand persons of [my] *Ummah* would enter Paradise without rendering an account" (418), and Muslims "would constitute half the inhabitants of Paradise" (427). Considering that unbelievers, infidels, and polytheists are strictly kept out, and that the entry of Jews and Christians also is prohibited, one wonders who will be the other half of the population of Paradise.

How did Muhammad acquire this special intercessory power? Muhammad himself answers this question: "There is for every Apostle a prayer which is granted, but every prophet showed haste in his prayer. I have, however, reserved my prayer for the intercession of my *Ummah* on the Day of Resurrection" (389). The translator makes this statement clearer for us. He says: "The Apostles are dear to Allah and their prayers are often granted. But with every Apostle there is one request which may be called decisive with regard to his *Ummah*, and with it is decided their fate; for example, Noah in a state of distress uttered: 'My Lord! leave not any one of the disbelievers in the land' (*al-Qurān* 71.26). Muhammad reserved his prayer for the Day of Resurrection and he would use it for the salvation of the believers" (note 412).

We have no means of knowing about the curse of Noah, but this kind of cursing is quite in Muhammad's line. For example, look at his curse against several tribes: "O Allah! trample severely Muzar and cause them a famine . . . O Allah! curse Lihyān, Ri'l Zakwān, Usayya, for they disobeyed Allah and His Messenger" (1428).

In any case, when the disbelievers are being hurled into the Fire, Muhammad will not intercede even when he knows that no other intercession would avail: "Thou shalt not damn thy enemies, but needst not go out of your way to save them."

The Prophet's Father and Uncles

We must admit, however, that Muhammad was consistent. He reserved his power for saving his *ummah*, those who believed in Allah to the exclusion of Allāt and 'Uzzā, and in his own apostleship. He did not use it to save even his dearest and nearest ones like his father and uncle. Regarding his father, he told a questioner: "Verily, my father and your father are in the Fire" (398). But he was somewhat more kind to his uncle, Abū Tālib, who brought him up and protected him but who did not accept his religion. About him, Muhammad tells us: "I found him in the lowest part of the Fire and I brought him to the shallow part" (409). But even this shallowest part must have been roasting the poor uncle. Muhammad assures us that "among the inhabitants of the Fire Abū Tālib would have the least suffering, and he would be wearing two shoes of Fire which would boil his brain" (413). Would you call that much of a relief?

Though Muhammad took pride in "establishing ties of relationship," he himself repudiated all ties with the generations of his forefathers and their posterity. "Behold! the posterity of my fathers . . . are not my friends," declares Muhammad (417). On the Day of Resurrection, their good works will not avail them. 'Āisha, the Prophet's young wife, reports: "I said: Messenger of Allah, the son of Jud'ān [a relation of hers and one of the leaders of the Quraish] established ties of relationship, fed the poor. Would that be of any avail to him? He said: it would be of no avail to him" (416).

God's mind is made up with regard to the polytheists; therefore, a true believer should not even seek blessing on their behalf. As the

Qurān says: "It is not meet for the Prophet and for those who believe, that they should beg pardon for the polytheists, even though they were their kith and kin, after it had been known to them that they were the denizens of Hell" (9:113).

Muhammad's Night Journey to Heaven

Various other matters, such as Muhammad's night journey to Jerusalem, and the coming of Dajjāl and Jesus before the Day of Resurrection, are also discussed in the "Book of Faith." These are quite important in Islamic lore.

One night, riding on al-Barāq, "an animal white and long, larger than a donkey but smaller than a mule," Muhammad was taken to the Temple in Jerusalem and from there to the different regions, or "circles" (as Dante called them), of heaven, on the way meeting different apostles. Adam he met in the first heaven, Jesus in the second, Moses in the sixth, and Abraham in the seventh. Then he met Allah, who enjoined on the Muslims fifty prayers a day. But on the advice of Moses, Muhammad made a representation to Allah and the number was reduced to five. "Five and at the same time fifty"—one prayer will now count for ten—for "what has been said will not be changed" (313). So nothing was really lost in efficacy, and five will do the work of fifty.

The more mystic-minded explain this journey spiritually, but Muhammad's Companions and later on most Muslim scholars believe that the journey or ascension (*mi'rāj*) was physical. Many in his day scoffed at Muhammad and called his journey a dream. But our translator argues that precisely because it was not believed, it was not a dream! For "had it been only a dream, there would have been no occasion for such a reaction about it. Visions like this can flit across the imagination of any man at any time" (note 325).

Jesus

Muhammad had a belief of a sort in Jesus. In fact, this belief, along with his belief in the apostleship of Moses and Abraham, is often cited as a proof of Muhammad's liberal and catholic outlook.

But if we look at the matter closely, we find it was more a *motivated* belief, meant partly to prove his own apostolic pedigree, and partly to win converts from among the Jews and the Christians. In any case, his opinion of Jesus does not amount to much. He turned Jesus into a *mujāhid* (crusader) of his entourage. When Jesus returns in the Second Coming, no more than a pale copy of Muhammad, he will be waging war against the Christians as well as others: "The son of Mary will soon descend among you as a just judge. He will break crosses, kill swine, and abolish *Jizya*," Muhammad proclaims (287). How? The translator explains: "Cross is a symbol of Christianity. Jesus will break this symbol after the advent of Muhammad. Islam is the *dīn* (religion) of Allah and no other religion is acceptable to him. Similarly, the flesh of the swine is a favorite dish of the Christians. Jesus will sweep out of existence this dirty and loathsome animal. The whole of the human race would accept Islam and there would be no *zimmīs* left, and thus *Jizya* would be automatically abolished" (notes 289-290). Jesus is regarded as a just Judge, but this only means that he will judge according to the *sharī'ah* of Muhammad. For, as the translator explains, "the *Sharī'ah* of all the earlier prophets stands abrogated with the advent of Muhammad's Apostleship. Jesus will, therefore, judge according to the law of Islam" (note 288).

2

Purification (Tahārah)

The next book is the "Book of Purification." It deals with such matters as ablution, defecation, and abstersion. It relates not to inner purity but to certain acts of cleanliness, physical and ritualistic, that must be performed before reciting the statutory daily prayers. The main topics discussed in Muslim *fiqh* (canon law) under this heading are: (1) *wuzū*, minor ablution of the limbs of the body, prescribed before each of the five daily prayers and omitted only if the worshipper is sure that he has not been polluted in any way since the last ablution; (2) *ghusl*, the major, total ablution of the whole body after the following acts which make a person *junub*, or impure: coitus (*jimā*), nocturnal pollution (*ihtilām*), menses (*hayz*), and childbirth (*nifās*); (3) *tayammum*, the minor purification with dust in the place of water; (4) *fitra*, literally "nature," but interpreted as customs of the previous prophets, including acts like the use of the toothpick (*miswāk*), cleansing the nose and mouth with water (*istinshāq*), and abstersion (*istinjā*) with water or dry earth or a piece of stone after evacuation and urination; (5) *tathīr*, the purification of objects which have become ritualistically unclean.

Some broad injunctions on the subject of purification are given in the Qurān (e.g., verses 4:43 and 5:6), but they acquire fullness from the practice of the Prophet.

Ablution (*Wuzū*)

Muhammad emphasizes the need for bodily cleanliness. He tells his followers that "cleanliness is half of faith" (432) and that their prayer will not be accepted in a state of impurity till they "perform ablution" (435). But *impurity* here has a strictly ritualistic meaning.

Muhammad was a Unitarian in his theology but a Trinitarian in his ablution. He performed his ablution like this: "He washed his hands thrice. He then rinsed his mouth and cleaned his nose three times. He then washed his face three times, then washed his right arm up to the elbow three times, then washed his left arm like that, then wiped his head, then washed his right foot up to the ankle three times, then washed his left foot," and so on. Muhammad said that "he who performs ablution like this ablution of mine . . . and offered two *rak'ahs* [sections] of prayer . . . all his previous sins are expiated" (436). This became the standard ablution. According to Muslim canon scholars, this is the most complete of the ablutions performed for prayer. There are twenty-one *ahādīs* repeating Muhammad's practice and thought on the subject as given above (436–457).

CLEANSING THE NOSE

The nose should be properly cleansed. Muhammad says: "When any one of you awakes from sleep . . . he must clean his nose three times, for the devil spends the night in the interior of one's nose" (462).

CLEANING THE TEETH (*Miswāk*)

Muhammad loved toothpicks and used them often. "Were it not that I might overburden the believers—I would have ordered them to use the toothpick at every time of prayer," he said (487).

THE FIVE ACTS (*Fitra*)

There are nine *ahādīs* (495–503) on five acts natural to man and proper to Islam: circumcision, shaving the pubes, cutting the nails, plucking the hair under the armpits, and clipping the moustache.

About the moustache and the beard, the Prophet said: "Act

against the polytheists, trim closely the moustache and grow beard" (500). The next *hadīs* substitutes the word "fire-worshippers" for "polytheists." The translator provides the rationale for this injunction: "Islam created a new brotherhood on the basis of belief and good conduct. . . . For the identification of faces, the Muslims have been ordered to trim the moustache and wear the beard, so that they may be distinguished from the non-Muslims who grow a moustache and shave beard" (note 471).

Bodily Functions

Now Muhammad takes us to the toilet. He forbids his followers "to face the *qibla* [i.e., toward the mosque at Mecca] at the time of excretion or urination, or cleansing with right hand or with less than three pebbles" (504).

Cleansing after excretion must be done an "odd number of times" (460), and one must not use "dung or bone" (505) for this purpose. There is a story explaining why the use of bones and dung is forbidden. Muhammad once spent a night with *jinns* (genii) reciting the Qurān to them. When they asked him about their provision of food, he told them: "Every bone on which the name of Allah is recited is your provision. The time it will fall in your hand it would be covered with flesh, and the dung of the camels is fodder for your animals." He therefore told his followers: "Don't perform *istinjā* with these things for these are the food of your brothers" (903).

He also tells his followers: "When anyone amongst you enters the privy, he must not touch the penis with his right hand" (512).

'Āisha tells us that the "Messenger of Allah loved to start from the right-hand side in his every act, i.e., in wearing shoes, in combing, and in performing ablution" (515).

Tathīr

Muhammad enjoins that "when the dog licks the utensil, wash it seven times, and rub it with earth the eighth time" (551).

DON'T EXPOSE YOUR PRIVATE PARTS

Muhammad says that "a man should not see the private part of another man," nor should men lie together "under one covering" (667). In this connection, he also tells us that the Jews used to take their baths naked and looked at each other's private parts, but Moses took his bath alone. Instead of feeling ashamed for not following their leader's example the Jews taunted him. They said he refrained from exposing his private parts because he suffered from scrotal hernia. But God vindicated him. Once, while taking his bath, Moses put his clothes on a rock, but the rock moved away. "Moses ran after it crying: O stone, my clothes; O stone, my clothes." The Jews then had a chance to see Moses' private parts, and said: "By Allah, Moses does not suffer from any ailment" (669).

SOILED CLOTHES

'Āisha tells us that the "Messenger of Allah washed the semen, and then went out for prayer in that very garment and I saw the mark of washing on it" (570). There is another *hadīs* of similar import, but it also narrates some material of Freudian significance. A guest who was staying at 'Āisha's house had a nocturnal seminal emission. Next day he dipped his clothes in water for washing. A maidservant observed this and informed 'Āisha. She asked the guest: "What prompted you to act like this with your clothes?" He replied, "I saw in a dream what a sleeper sees." Then 'Āisha asked him: "Did you find any mark of fluid on your clothes?" He said: "No." She said: "Had you found anything you should have washed it. In case I found that semen on the garment of the Messenger of Allah dried up, I scratched it off with my nails" (572).

BATHING AFTER A SEMINAL EMISSION

There are a dozen *ahādīs* (674–685) on the subject of bathing after a seminal emission. Once Muhammad called out an *ansār* who was in the midst of sexual intercourse. "He came out and water was trickling down from his head. Muhammad said: perhaps we put you to haste. The man said yes. The prophet said: When you made haste and semen is not emitted, bathing is not obligatory for you, but ablution is binding" (676). In another *hadīs*, Muhammad says that when a man leaves his wife in the midst of an intercourse without having experienced orgasm, "he should wash the secretion of his wife, and then perform ablution and offer prayer" (677). But when there is a seminal emission "bath becomes obligatory" (674).

Once there was a controversy on this point between some *muhājirs* ("Emigrants" or "Refugees") and some *ansārs* ("Helpers"). One of them came to 'Āisha for clarification, asking: "What makes a bath obligatory for a person?" She answered: "You have come across one well-informed." Then she reported what Muhammad had said on the subject: "When anyone sits amidst fore parts of the woman, and the circumcised parts touch each other a bath becomes obligatory" (684). And on yet another occasion, a man asked Muhammad whether a bath is obligatory for one who parts from intercourse with his wife without having had an orgasm. The Prophet, pointing to 'Āisha, who was sitting by him, replied: "I and she do it and then take a bath" (685).

Tayammum

If water is not available, you can take to *tayammum*, i.e., wiping your hands and feet and forehead with earth, and that should be as good as ablution with water. The translator explains why. He says that "the main purpose behind ablution and bathing is a religious one and the hygienic one is a matter of secondary importance. . . . Allah has directed us to perform *tayammum* in case water is not available . . . to retain the spiritual value of ablution as a means of directing us from the mundane activities of life and directing us to the presence of the Lord" (note 579). There is a verse in the Qurān and eight *ahādīs* (714–721) on this subject. "And if you be ailing or on a journey or one comes from the privy, or you have touched women, and you find no water, then betake yourself to clean earth and wipe your faces and your hands therewith" (Qurān 4:43).

One *hadīs* tells us of the words of 'Āmmār to 'Umar: "Do you remember, O Commander of the Faithful, when I and you were in a military detachment and we had had a seminal emission and did not find water for taking bath and you did not say prayer, but as for myself I rolled in dust and said prayer, and when it was referred to the Apostle, he said: 'It was enough for you to strike the ground with your hands and then blow the dust and then wipe your face and palms' " (718).

FOOD AND ABLUTION

Muhammad enjoined that "ablution is obligatory for one who takes anything touched by fire" (686). But later on this command was abrogated. "The Messenger of Allah took meat of goat's shoulder and offered prayer and did not perform ablution" (689).

Ablution is necessary after leaving the privy if you are going to pray but not if you are going to eat. "The Apostle of Allah came out of the privy, and he was presented with some food, and the people reminded him about ablution, but he said: Am I to say prayer that I should perform ablution?" (725).

MENSTRUATION (*HAIZ*)

The third book is on menstruation. The subjects of this book and the previous one overlap, for both have to do with ritualistic purity. Therefore, some cross-reference is inevitable. This chapter too, in fact, does not have very much to say on menstruation as such but a great deal on ritualistic ablution and bathing after sexual intercourse.

On the subject of menstruation, Muhammad's practice appears, in some respects, different from what was enjoined by the revelation in the Qurān. The Qurān uses rather strong language on the subject: "They ask thee concerning women's courses. Say: They are a hurt and a pollution. So keep away from women in their course, and do not approach them until they are clean" (2:222).

But perhaps *approach* here means to have sexual intercourse, for except for coitus all other contacts were permitted by the Prophet. Maimūna tells us: "The Messenger of Allah used to lie with me when I menstruated, and there was a cloth between me and him" (580).

Umm Salama reports the same (581). 'Āisha says: "When anyone amongst us menstruated, the Messenger of Allah asked her to tie a waist-wrapper over her and then embraced her" (577).

Other *ahādīs* make the same point, besides throwing interesting sidelights on some of the more intimate habits of the Prophet. 'Āisha reports: "The Messenger of Allah would recline in my lap when I was menstruating, and recite the *Qurān*" (591). Rather an unlikely place for *svādhyāya*, or scriptural studies.

Carrying the same sexual overtones taught by Freud, 'Āisha again reports: "I would drink when I was menstruating, then I would hand over the vessel to the Apostle and he would put his mouth where mine had been, and drink, and I would eat flesh from a bone when I was menstruating, then hand it over to the Apostle and he would put his mouth where mine had been" (590).

The Prophet would also allow 'Āisha to comb his hair when she was menstruating and he was supposed to be observing *i'tikāf*, technically segregating oneself and staying in a mosque for a certain number of days, especially during the last ten days of the month of Ramzān. "The Messenger of Allah put out from the mosque his head for me as he was in *i'tikāf* [her room opened on the mosque], and I washed it in the state that I was menstruating," 'Āisha reports (584).

All this was opposed to the Jewish practice, which forbade not only sexual intercourse but also kissing and all other forms of physical contact during menstruation. Some Muslims wanted to go whole hog in their opposition to Jewish practice and suggested to Muhammad that he should permit sexual intercourse too since the Jews forbade it. But Muhammad did not go that far.

Sexual Pollution and Ablution

'Āisha reports: "Whenever the Messenger of Allah had sexual intercourse and intended to eat or sleep, he performed the ablution of prayer" (598). The commentator explains that this was done "so that the soul of man may be transported from the urges of the flesh to its original spiritual domain" (note 511).

Muhammad enjoined the same on his followers. For example,

'Umar once went to the Prophet and told him that "he became *junbi* [unclean] during the night. The Messenger of Allah said to him: Perform ablution, wash your sexual organ and then go to sleep" (602). The same advice was conveyed to 'Alī, who as his son-in-law was shy in putting this question to Muhammad directly. His problem was *mazi* (prostatic fluid) and not *manī* (semen). "Ablution is obligatory in such a case," he was told (593).

Ablution was also necessary if one wanted to repeat the intercourse. In the words of Abū Bakr, the narrator of this *hadīs*, "between two acts, there should be an ablution" (605).

BATH (*Ghusl*)

For the exercise of prayer, the whole body must be washed to absolve it from uncleanliness after certain acts: menses, puerperium, coitus, and *pollutio nocturna*. This practice is derived from the Qurānic verse: "If you are polluted, then purify yourselves" (5:6).

There are over two dozen *ahādīs* on the subject of Muhammad's own custom in this regard. 'Āisha says: "When Allah's Messenger bathed because of sexual intercourse, he first washed his hands; he then poured water with his right hand on his left hand and washed his private parts . . ." (616).

Muhammad's practice was that after the sexual intercourse, "sometimes he took a bath and then slept, and sometimes he performed ablution only," postponing the bath till the end of the night before the morning prayer. When 'Āisha reported this to the narrator of this *hadīs*, his pious reaction was: "Praise be to Allah Who has made things easy" for the believers (603).

The same obligation lay on women. One Umm Sulaim went to Muhammad and asked him: "Is bathing necessary for a woman when she has a sexual dream?" Muhammad replied: "Yes, when she sees the liquid [vaginal secretion]." Muhammad's wives were scandalized when they learned that Umm Sulaim had put a question to the Prophet which suggested that a woman too could have a sexual dream. "You humiliated the women," they told her (610, 611).

Single Bath for Multiple Coitus

Unlike ablution, the bath need not be repeated after each act of intercourse. Anas reports that "the Messenger of Allah used to have sexual intercourse with his wives with a single bath" (606); or in the colorful language of Tirmizī: "with one bath, the Apostle walked over all his women" (vol. I, *hadīs* 124). The translator explains: "The holy prophet did not take a bath after every intercourse; he simply performed ablution and took a bath at the end" (note 514).

Bathing Together

Many *ahādīs* narrate how the Prophet and his wives used to bathe together after sexual intercourse. 'Āisha reports: "The Messenger of Allah took a bath from the vessel [which contained 15 to 16 pounds of water]. And I and he [the Prophet] took a bath from the same vessel" (625). She reports the same idea with more details in another *hadīs*: "I and the Messenger of Allah took a bath from one vessel and our hands alternated into it in the state that we had sexual intercourse" (629).

Two other wives of Muhammad, Umm Salama and Maimūna, also report that they and Muhammad took their baths together (581, 631).

The translator feels that the practice of the Prophet needs defense from the likely attacks of hostile critics. He tells us that this bath was quite a modest act. There were no glaring lights; and though the Prophet and his wives on occasion took a bath from the same vessel, it was not a tub-bath where a couple sit together; moreover, they took their bath in pitch darkness, and thus there was no question of their seeing each other's bodies (note 538).

Conserving Body Heat

If one lost too much body heat during the bath, it could be regained by lying again in the embrace of one's wife. According to a *hadīs* quoted by Tirmizī, 'Āisha reports: "On many occasions it happened that the apostle of Allah came back to me after the bath of purification with the intention of warming up. I 'wrapped' him up round me even though I myself had not taken bath [and was therefore in a state of impurity]'' (vol. I, *hadīs* 108).

Notwithstanding all these rules and regulations, Muhammad was not bound by them. He had his Apostle's privilege, which, in this case, he shared with 'Alī. According to Abū sa'īd, Muhammad told 'Alī: ''O 'Alī! It is not lawful for anyone except me and thee to go to a mosque in a state of sexual defilement'' (Tirmizī, vol. II, *hadīs* 1584).

3

Prayer (Salāt)

The fourth book is the "Book of Prayer" (*Salāt*). It is the longest, with 1,398 *ahādīs* divided into 203 chapters. But in all these pages, one looks in vain for any reference to such problems as self-exploration and self-knowledge, problems of enduring concern for the spirituality of the Indian tradition. There is not even a remote hint of different men endowed with different natures taking different paths toward a divinity differently figured. As there is one Allah, one Guide, one Book, there is also one Prayer, caught and fixed in a single formula.

From the titles of the 203 chapters this book contains, one can see that they all relate to the externals: *azān* (the call to prayer), postures like bowing, prostrating and rising, the number and times of the different prayers, the place of *imām* in the system of prayers, the merits of prayers at different times, the prayer for rain, the prayer for protection against windstorms and other calamities, the prayer relating to the dead, and so on.

Azān

We are told how the institution of *azān* began. In the beginning, in Medina, people forgathered in the mosque without knowing when they were to pray. As a means of calling people to prayer at fixed times, some suggested using a bell, as the Christians did; others a horn, as the Jews did. Some even suggested that a fire should be lighted. All these methods were ruled out. To make the Muslim practice different from that of the Jews, the Christians, and the Fire-worshippers, the system of the human voice was introduced. Bilāl, who was very loud-throated, and 'Abdullah b. Umm Maktūm, who later became blind, were the first *mu'azzin* (callers) (735, 737, 741).

Azān is very effective. "When Satan hears the call to prayer, he runs away to a distance like that of Rauhā," a distance of 36 miles from Medina (751).

ATTACKS ON NON-MUSLIMS

Azān became a great indicator. Where it was heard, it meant that everything was not *kufr* (infidelity). "The Messenger of Allah used to attack the enemy when it was dawn. He would listen to the *Azān*; so if he heard an *Azān*, he stopped" (745). This the commentator finds greatly virtuous in Muhammad. "The greatest contribution made by the Holy Prophet in the sphere of warfare is that he elevated it from the surface of reckless murder or slaughter to the level of humanized struggle for the uprooting of evil in society. The Holy Prophet, therefore, did not allow his Companions to take the enemy unawares under the cover of darkness of night" (note 600).

BLESSINGS FOR MUHAMMAD

When men hear the *mu'azzin*, they should repeat what he says and invoke blessings on Muhammad. They should "beg from Allah *al-Wasīla* for me, which is a rank in Paradise fitting for only one of Allah's servants. If any one who asks that I be given the *Wasīla*, he will be assured of my intercession," says Muhammad (747).

In a variation on this theme, if a man who hears a caller responds by testifying that he is "satisfied with Allah as my Lord, with Muhammad as Messenger, and with Islam as *dīn* [religion] his sins would be forgiven" (749).

In seeking blessings for himself, Muhammad does not forget his wives and progeny. "Apostle of Allah, how should we bless you?" Muhammad is asked. He replies: "O Allah! bless Muhammad, and his wives and his offspring. . . . He who blesses me once, Allah would bless him ten times" (807, 808).

Posture during Prayer

Muslim prayer is not carried on in one tranquil posture, sitting or standing; it is accompanied by many bodily movements. These have been codified on the basis of the practice and precepts of Muhammad. There are many *ahādīs* on the subject. One narrator saw Muhammad "raising his hands opposite the shoulders at the time of beginning the prayer and before bowing down and after coming back to the erect position after bowing, but he did not raise them between two prostrations" (758). Another saw his "hands lifted opposite to ears." He also saw that the Prophet "then wrapped his hands in his cloth and placed his right hand over his left hand. And when he was about to bow down, he brought out his hands from the cloth, and then lifted them. . . . And when prostrated, he prostrated between the two palms" (792).

Muhammad was commanded by Allah that "he should prostrate on the seven bones and he was forbidden to fold back the hair and clothing." The seven bones are: "The hands, the knees, and the extremities of the feet and the forehead" (991). But he asked his followers to "observe moderation in prostration" and not to stretch out [their] forearms on the ground like a dog" (997).

Originally the practice had been to put one's hands together, palm to palm, and then to put them between one's thighs. But later on this practice was abrogated and the followers were "commanded to place them [hands] on the knees" (1086–1092).

Another precaution: "People should avoid lifting their eyes towards the sky while supplicating in prayer, otherwise their eyes would be snatched away" (863).

The Imām

Muslim prayer is mostly group prayer. It should be led by an *imām*. Muhammad enjoins that "when there are three persons, one of them should lead them" (1417).

Muhammad exhorts his followers to follow their *imām*. "When he prostrates, you should also prostrate; when-he rises up, you should also rise up," he tells them (817). He also forbids them to bow and prostrate themselves ahead of the *imām*: "Does the man who lifts his head before the *imām* not fear that Allah may change his face into that of an ass?" (860). Also, those who are being led in prayer are required to keep pace with the *imām* and are forbidden to recite so loudly as to compete with him. When someone once did this, Muhammad told him: "I felt as if [you were] disputing with me . . . and taking out from my tongue what I was reciting" (783). The *imām* is authorized to appoint anyone as his deputy, when there is a valid reason for doing so, just as Muhammad appointed Abū Bakr during his last illness (832–844).

We see here that European imperialism with all its rationalizations and pretensions was anticipated by Islamic imperialism by a thousand years. In Islam we find all the ideological ingredients of imperialism in any age: a divine or moral sanction for the exploitation of the barbarians or heathens or polytheists; their land considered as a *lebensraum* or held as a mandate; they themselves regarded as the wards and special responsibility (*zimma*) of the civilizing masters.

Another *hadīs* mentions Muhammad's power of "intercession" on the Day of Judgment, which other prophets lack (1058). Other *ahādīs* mention other points. "I have been helped by terror.* . . . and while I was asleep I was brought the keys of the treasures of the earth," says Muhammad. This wealth the followers of the Apostle "are now busy in getting them," adds Abū Huraira, the narrator of this *hadīs* (1063).†

*That is, my enemies hold me in such terror and awe that they surrender without fighting. This resulted from Muhammad's terroristic methods: his assassinations and killings and the constant marauding raids by the Muslims. For example, the beheading of eight hundred members of the tribe of Quraiza in cold blood in the market of Medina must have sent a chill of terror down the spine of everyone, foe or friend.

†Abū Huraira should know. He lived long enough (surviving Muhammad by twenty-five years) to see the nascent Muslim state grow into an empire and the tribute pour into the coffers of Medina. Immediately after Muhammad's death during the two years of Abū Bakr's caliphate, the share of every Meccan and Medinan Muslim in the tithes received was only 9 dirhams for the first year and 20 dirhams for the next year. But within two decades everything changed, thanks to the enormous revenues received from the outlying colonial regions in the neighborhood of the Arabian peninsula. The *diwān*, or Civil List, established by 'Umar specified that each of Muhammad's widows was to receive 12,000 dirhams a year; each of the more than three hundred veterans of the Battle of Badr, 5,000 dirhams a year; everyone who had converted to Islam before that date, 4,000 dirhams a year, and their children, 2,000 dirhams a year. Every Muslim had a place in this classification. Officers of the Arab occupation armies in the different cantonment areas of the empire received yearly from 6,000 to 9,000 dirhams; and every boy born in these military quarters received from his birth 100 dirhams annually. For a fuller account of the Civil List, refer to the *Tārīkh Tabarī*, vol. II., pp. 476–479.

WOMEN AND MOSQUES

Women can go to the mosque but they "should not apply perfume" (893), a privilege not denied to men who can afford it. They were also told not to precede men in lifting their heads from prostration. The translator explains that this *hadīs* relates to a period when the Companions were very poor and could not afford proper clothing. The instruction was meant to give them time to adjust their clothing before the women lifted their heads (*hadīs* 883 and note 665).

Muhammad commanded the believers to "take out unmarried women and purdah-observing ladies for *'Id* prayers, and he commanded the menstruating women to remain away from the place of worship of the Muslims" (1932). But in a footnote explaining the standpoint of the Islamic *sharī'ah* with regard to women joining men in prayer, the translator says: "The fact is that the Holy Prophet deemed it preferable for women to say their prayers within the four walls of their houses or in the nearest mosque" (note 668).

DOS AND DON'TS

There are many dos and don'ts. For example, to wear shoes while praying is permissible (1129–1130), but clothes having designs and markings on them are distracting and should be avoided (1131–1133). The Prophet commanded the believer that while praying "he should not spit in front of him, for Allah is in front of him when he is engaged in prayer" (1116). According to another tradition, he "forbade spitting on the right side or in front, but it is permissible to spit on the left side or under the left foot" (1118).

To eat onion or garlic is not *harām* (forbidden), but Muhammad found their odors "repugnant" (1149) and therefore forbade coming to the mosque after eating them, "for the angels are harmed by the same things as men" (1145).

CURSE ON THE JEWS

It is meritorious to build a mosque, for "he who builds a mosque for Allah, Allah would build for him a house in Paradise"

(1034). But it is forbidden to build mosques on graves and to decorate them with pictures. 'Āisha reports that when the Prophet "was about to breathe his last . . . he uncovered his face and said in this very state: 'Let there be curse upon the Jews and the Christians that they have taken the graves of their Apostles as places of worship' " (1082).

Dinner before Prayer

This rule may seem to lack piety but in some ways it is realistic. The believer is told to prefer supper to prayer. "When the supper is brought and prayer begins, one should first take food," says Muhammad (1134). First things first.

Prayer in Time of Danger

According to Muslim jurists, there are different forms of prayer for sixteen specific dangerous situations. For example, during a war, one group prays while the other one fights (1824–1831).

Friday Prayer

Friday is a special day. "On it Adam was created, on it he was made to enter Paradise, on it he was expelled from heaven" (1856).

Every *ummah* was given the Book before the Muslims. But though Muslims "are the last," they "shall be the first on the Day of Resurrection." While the Jews and the Christians observe Saturday and Sunday as their respective days, Muslims were fortunate to have Friday as their day, the day prescribed by Allah Himself for them. "We were guided aright to Friday, but Allah diverted those who were before us from it" (1863).

An interesting story is reported in this connection. One Friday, when the Prophet was delivering a sermon, a caravan with merchandise from Syria arrived. People left the Prophet and flocked toward the caravan. Then this verse was revealed: "And when they see merchandise or sport, they break away to it and leave you standing" (1877; Qurān 62:11).

MUHAMMAD AS A PREACHER

Jābir b. 'Abdullah draws for us a pen-portrait of Muhammad delivering a sermon. He reports: "When Allah's Messenger delivered the sermon, his eyes became red, his voice rose, and his anger increased so that he was like one giving a warning against the enemy and saying: 'The enemy has made a morning attack on you and in the evening too.' He would also say: 'The Last Hour and I have been sent like these two,' and he would join his forefinger and middle finger (just as there is no other finger between these two, similarly there will be no new Prophet between Muhammad and the Day of Resurrection) and would further say: 'The best of the speech is embodied in the Book of Allah, and the best of guidance is the guidance given by Muhammad. And the most evil affairs are their innovations; and every innovation is error' " (1885).

There are other eyewitness accounts of Muhammad's sermons. One report says: "Allah's Messenger stood up [to pray] and we heard him say: 'I seek refuge in Allah from thee,' Then said: 'I curse thee with Allah's curse three times,' then he stretched out his hand as though he was taking hold of something." When asked to throw light on this unusual behavior, he replied: "Allah's enemy *Iblīs* came with a flame of fire to put it in my face." But even though cursed, he did not retreat. "Thereafter, I meant to seize him. I swear by Allah that had it not been for the supplication of my brother Sulaimān he would have been bound, and made an object of sport for the children of Medina" (1106).

MUSIC, DANCE, AND SPORTS

'Āisha reports: "The Messenger of Allah came in my apartment while there were two girls with me singing the song of the Battle of Bu'ās. He lay down on the bed and turned away his face. Then came Abū Bakr and he scolded me and said: Oh! this musical instrument of the devil in the house of the Messenger of Allah. The Messenger of Allah turned towards him and said: Leave them alone. And when he became unattentive I hinted them [the girls] and they went out, and it was the day of *Īd*" (1942). Muhammad added:

"Abū Bakr, every people have a festival and it is our festival [so let them play on]" (1938).

This is the only *hadīs* that can be construed as an instance of Muhammad's approving of music. In a large measure he was indulging his child-wife 'Āisha, but the sufi schools of Islam, in which music plays an important role, make the most of this *hadīs*.

On the same occasion, Muhammad, with 'Āisha's head resting on his shoulder, was watching some Abyssinians engage in a mock armed fight. 'Umar came and wanted to drive them away by throwing pebbles at them. But Muhammad told him: " 'Umar, leave them alone" (1946).

Prayers for Different Occasions

There are prayers for rain, prayers for protection against windstorms or terrible dark clouds, prayers to be recited at the time of a solar eclipse (1966–1972). However, Muhammad had no friendly eye for nature. He regarded clouds and winds with terror. "When there was on any day windstorm or dark cloud its effect could be read on the face of the Messenger of Allah, and he moved forward and backward in a state of anxiety," 'Āisha tells us. She further says: "I asked him the reason of this anxiety and he said: I was afraid that it might be a calamity that might fall on my *Ummah*" (1961).

Muhammad deals with the problem with the help of an incantation. 'Āisha tells us: "Whenever the wind was stormy, the Apostle of Allah used to say: O Allah! I ask Thee for what is good in it, and the good which it contains, and the good of that which it was sent for. I seek refuge with Thee from what is evil in it, what evil it contains, and the evil of that what it was sent for" (1962).

Prayers for the Dead

There are also prayers for the dead and the dying. The dying must be treated to a bit of theology. "Exhort to recite, 'There is no god but Allah,' to those who are dying," says the Prophet (1996).

When you visit the sick or the dead, supplicate for good, because "angels may say amen to whatever you say." Umm Salama tells us: "When Abū Salama died, I went to the Apostle of Allah and said: Messenger of Allah, Abū Salama has died. He told me to recite: 'O Allah! forgive me and him [Abū Salama] and give me a better substitute than he.' So I said this, and Allah gave me in exchange Muhammad, who is better for me than him [Abū Salama]" (2002).

Umm Salama was the widow of Abū Salama, to whom she had borne many children. He died at Uhud, and Muhammad married her four months later.

WEEPING OVER THE DEAD

Muhammad discouraged weeping over the dead: "The dead is punished because of his family's weeping over it" (2015). He also taught haste in the disposal of dead bodies. "If the dead person was good, it is a good state to which you are sending him on: but if he was otherwise it is an evil of which you are ridding yourself" (2059).

Muhammad himself wept over the death of his loyal followers. Weeping over the dying Sa'd b. Ubāda, he said: "Allah does not punish for the tears that the eye sheds or the grief the heart feels, but He punishes for this [pointing to his tongue], meaning loud lamenting" (2010).

4
The Poor Tax (Zakāt)

The fifth book is on *al-zakāt* (charity or poor tax). Every society preaches and to some extent practices charity toward its less-fortunate brothers. Muhammad too stresses the importance of charity, or *zakāt*, an old Arab practice. But with him it became a tax, an obligatory payment made by the Muslims to the new state that was forming, and to be spent by its representatives. In this form, those who paid *zakāt* were resentful, and those who spent it actually acquired a new source of power and patronage.

Much of the "Book of *Zakāt*" is concerned with the question of power. In the beginning, Muhammad had many followers who were needy, and most of them, being migrants, depended a great deal on the goodwill and charity of the people of Medina. Perhaps the rhetoric on charity emanates largely from this situation. There was as yet no universal fellowship as such for a brother in distress, no sense of a larger human brotherhood. *Zakāt* was solely meant for the brothers in faith, and everyone else was excluded on principle. This has been the Muslim practice ever since.

Uses of Zakāt Funds

According to the Qurān, the *zakāt* funds are meant for "the poor and the paupers [*fuqarā* and *miskīn*], for those in bondage and debt, and for the wayfarers." All these are conventional recipients of charity. The funds are also to be used for the "bureaucracy," those who collect and administer the funds. But two other items are also mentioned which deserve special attention. The funds are to be used in "the service of Allah" (*fīsabīli'llāh*) and for "gaining over [or reconciling, or inclining] the hearts [*muallafa qulūbuhum*]'' to Islam (Qurān 9:60).

In the technical vocabulary of Islam, the first phrase, ''in the service, or way, of Allah,'' means religious warfare, or *jihād*. *Zakāt* funds are to be spent on buying arms, equipment, and horses. The second phrase, ''gaining over, or reconciling, hearts,'' means ''bribes'' in unadorned language. The faith of new converts should be strengthened with the help of generous ''gifts,'' and that of adversaries should be subverted by the same means. This was an important limb of the Prophet's religious offensive and diplomacy, and as the Qurānic verse shows, it had for the Prophet, as it still has for his followers, a heavenly sanction.

EXEMPTIONS AND INCENTIVES

There was a lower exemption limit. ''No *Sadaqa* [*zakāt*] is payable on five *wasqs* of dates or grain [1 *wasq* = about 425 pounds], on less than five camel heads and on less than five *uqiyas* of silver [1 *uqiya* = about 10 *tolas*, or ¼ pound]'' (2134). Also, ''No *Sadaqa* is due from a Muslim on his slave or horse'' (2144). There was no tax on horses meant for use in a *jihād*. ''The horse which is used for riding in *jihād* is exempted from the payment of *zakāt*'' (note 1313).

AN UNPOPULAR TAX

There is an interesting *hadīs* which shows that the *zakāt* tax was unpopular even with the highest. 'Umar was appointed the collector. When he reported that Khalīd b. Walīd (who later became a famous Muslim general) and even the Prophet's own uncle, 'Abbās, had refused to pay the tax, Muhammad replied: ''You are unjust to Khalīd, for he reserved the armours and weapons for the sake of Allah; and as for 'Abbās, I shall be responsible. . . . 'Umar, bear in mind, the uncle of a person is like his father'' (2148).

The resentment against *zakāt* was general. It was particularly strong among the non-Medinan Arab tribes, who shared the burden of the tax but not its benefits. The Bedouins complained to the

Prophet that the "collectors of *Sadaqa* come to us and treat us unjustly. Upon this the Messenger of Allah said: Please your collectors" (2168).

But things were rougher and not as easily settled as this *hadīs* seems to suggest. After the conquest of Mecca, when the power of Muhammad became supreme, the collection of the tithe became aggressive. In the beginning of the ninth year of the Hijra (Hegira), parties of collectors were sent out in different directions to realize the tax from the Kilāb, Ghifār, Aslam, Fazār, and several other tribes. It seems that the opposition of a section of the tribe of Banū Tamīm to the collection was somewhat forceful. So Muhammad sent a punitive force consisting of fifty Arab horsemen, who took the tribe by surprise and brought fifty men, women, and children back to Medina as hostages. They had to be ransomed, and after this the tax collection became smoother.

The Qurān itself is an eloquent witness to the Arab resentment against the tax. Allah warns Muhammad: "Some of desert Arabs look upon their payments as a fine, and they wait a turn of fortune against you; but against them shall a turn of evil fortune be; for God both hears and knows" (9:98).

In fact, the resentment was so great that as soon as Muhammad died, the Arab tribes rose in revolt against the infant Muslim state and had to be reconquered. Their opposition ceased only when they became partners in the growing Muslim imperialism and their *zakāt* obligation was drowned in the immense gains derived from military conquests and colonization abroad.

Divine Sanctions

The divine punishment for not paying the poor tax is more gruesome than any secular punishment devised by a human agency. "If any owner of gold or silver does not pay what is due on him, when the Day of Resurrection would come, plates of fire would be beaten out for him; these then would be heated in the Fire of Hell and his sides, forehead and his back would be cauterized with them. And when these cool down, the process is repeated during a day the extent of which would be fifty thousand years." And for someone who owns camels and does not pay, "a sandy plain would be set for him, as extensive as possible," and his camels "will trample him with their hoofs and bite him with their mouths . . . during a day the extent of which would be fifty thousand years." The same fate awaits the tax-defaulting owner of cows and sheep: "They will gore him with their horns and trample him with their hoofs" for the same period (2161).

CHARITY SHOULD BEGIN AT HOME

There was a lot of uncoerced charity in its nontax version among the Arabs of pre-Muhammad days. For example, the Arabs of that time would take their camels to a pond every six or seven days and there milk them and distribute the milk among the needy (note 1329).

Muhammad's response to this generosity was positive. But he taught, and in some ways wisely, that charity should begin at home. This point is brought out in many *ahādīs* (2183–2195). The order in which one should spend his wealth is this: First on one's own self, then on one's wife and children, then on relatives and friends, and then on other good deeds.

Following a common practice, an Arab once willed that his slave was to be freed after his death. When Muhammad heard this, he called him and asked him if he had any other property. The man replied no. Muhammad then sold the slave for 800 dirhams, gave the money to the owner, and told him: "Start with your own self and spend it on yourself, and if anything is left, it should be spent on your family, and if anything is left it should be spent on your relatives."

There is another story that makes the same point. A lady set her slave-girl free. When informed about it, Muhammad told her: "Had you given her to your maternal uncle, you would have a greater reward" (2187).

So the morality that Muhammad taught on the question was not particularly heroic, but it agrees with the general practice. Nor was it really revolutionary. The emancipation of slaves was not a matter of justice but only of charity. And even then it should not conflict with the well-being of the family of the believer.

DEEPER ASPECTS

Rather unusual for the *Hadīs*, charity in its deeper aspect is also mentioned in some *ahādīs* (2197–2204). People who cannot pay in money can pay in piety and good acts. "Administering of justice between two men is also a *Sadaqa*. And assisting a man to ride upon his beast, or helping him load his luggage upon it, is a *Sadaqa*; and a good word is a *Sadaqa*; and every step that you take towards prayer is a *Sadaqa*, and removing of harmful things from the pathway is a *Sadaqa*" (2204).

There are some other passages of equal beauty and insight. Among those whom God affords protection is one "who gives charity and conceals it so that the right hand does not know what the left hand has given" (2248). In the same vein, Muhammad tells us that "if anyone gives as *Sadaqa* the equivalent of one date . . . the Lord would accept it with His Right Hand" (2211).

And in another *hadīs*: "In every declaration of the glorification of Allah* [i.e., saying *Subhān* Allah], there is a *Sadaqa* . . . and in man's sexual intercourse [with his wife—the omission is supplied by the translator], there is a *Sadaqa*" (2198).

URGINGS AND PLEADINGS

Muhammad makes an eloquent plea for alms-giving. Everyone should give charity even if it is only half a date. Abū Mas'ūd reports: "We were commanded to give charity though we were coolies" (2223).

One *hadīs* tells us: "There is never a day wherein servants [of God] get up at morn, but are not visited by two angels. One of them says: O Allah, give him more who spends, and the other says: O Allah, bring destruction to one who withholds" (2205). Was not the first part enough? Must a blessing always go along with a curse?

The Prophet warns believers to make their *Sadaqa* and be quick

*And, of course, Allah can only be glorified monotheistically, not polytheistically or pantheistically; and the glorification of Allah must include glorification of Muhammad too.

about it, for "there would come a time when a person would roam about with *Sadaqa* of gold but he would find no one to accept it from him." He also adds that "a man would be seen followed by forty women seeking refuge with him on account of the scarcity of males and abundance of females" (2207). What does this mean? The translator finds the statement truly prophetic. By citing the male and female population figures for postwar England and showing their disproportion, he proves "the truth of the Prophetic statement" (note 1366).

THEFT, FORNICATION, PARADISE

Some of the material included in certain discussions in the various *ahādīs* is not in fact relevant to the nominal topic of the discussion. This is true, for instance, of *ahādīs* 2174 and 2175, which both relate to *zakāt* but also treat matters that have nothing to do with charity, although in their own way they must be reassuring to believers. For example, Abū Zarr reports that while he and Muhammad were once walking together, Muhammad left him to go some other place, telling him to stay where he was until he returned. After a while Muhammad was out of sight but Abū Zarr heard some sounds. Although he was apprehensive of some possible mishap to the Prophet, he remembered his command and remained where he was. When Muhammad returned, Abū Zarr sought an explanation for the sounds. Muhammad replied: "It was Gabriel, who came to me and said: He who dies among your *Ummah* without associating anything with Allah would enter Paradise. I said: Even if he committed fornication or theft? He said: Even if he committed fornication or theft" (2174).

CHARITY AND DISCRIMINATION

There is a *hadīs* which seems to teach that charity should be indiscriminate. A man gives charity, with praise to Allah, first to an adulteress, then to a rich man, then to a thief. Came the angel to him and said: "Your charity has been accepted." For his charity might become the means whereby the adulteress "might restrain herself from fornication, the rich man might perhaps learn a lesson and spend from what Allah has given him, and the thief might thereby refrain from committing theft." One may suppose that the man's acts of charity had these wonderful results because they were accompanied by "praise to Allah" (2230).

Zakāt Not for Muhammad's Family

Zakāt was meant for the needy of the *ummah*, but it was not to be accepted by the family of Muhammad. The family included 'Alī, Ja'far, 'Aqīl, 'Abbās, and Haris b.'Abd al-Muttalib and their posterity. "*Sadaqa* is not permissible for us," said the Prophet (2340). Charity was good enough for others but not for the proud descendants of Muhammad, who in any case needed it less and less as they became heirs to the growing Arab imperialism.

But though *sadaqa* was not permitted, gifts were welcome. Barīra, Muhammad's wife's freed slave, presented Muhammad with a piece of meat that his own wife had given her as *sadaqa*. He took it, saying: "That is *Sadaqa* for her and a gift for us" (2351).

War Booty

Within a very short period, *zakāt* became secondary, and war spoils became the primary source of revenue of the Muslim treasury. In fact, the distinction between the two was soon lost, and thus the "Book of *Zakāt*" imperceptibly becomes a book on war spoils.

Khums, the one-fifth portion of the spoils of war which goes to the treasury, has two aspects. On the one hand, it is still war booty; but on the other, it is *zakāt*. When it is acquired, it is war booty; when it is distributed among the *ummah*, it is *zakāt*.

Muhammad regards war booty as something especially his own. "The spoils of war are for Allah and His Messenger"(Qurān 8:1). They are put in his hands by Allah to be spent as he thinks best, whether as *zakāt* for the poor, or as gifts for his Companions, or as bribes to incline the polytheists to Islam, or on the "Path of Allah," i.e., on preparations for armed raids and battles against the polytheists.

'Abd al-Muttalib and Fazl b. 'Abbās, two young men belonging to Muhammad's family, wanted to become collectors of *zakāt* in order to secure means of marrying. They went to Muhammad with their request, but he replied: "It does not become the family of Muhammad to accept *Sadaqa* for they are the impurities of the people." But he arranged marriages for the two men and told his treasurer: "Pay so much *Mahr* [dowry] on behalf of both of them from the *khums*" (2347).

DISSATISFACTION

Most of the properties abandoned by the Banū Nazīr were appropriated by Muhammad for himself and his family. Other funds at his disposal for distribution were also increasing. This new money was hardly *zakāt* money but war booty. Its distribution created a lot of heart-rending among his followers. Many of them thought they deserved more—or at any rate that others deserved less—than they got. Muhammad had to exercise considerable diplomacy, combined with threats, both mundane and celestial.

"GAINING HEARTS" BY GIVING GIFTS

The principle of distribution was not always based on need, justice, or merit. Muhammad had other considerations as well. "I give [at times material gifts] to persons who were quite recently in the state of unbelief, so that I may incline them to truth," says Muhammad (2303).

To gain hearts (*mullafa qulūbhum*) for Islam with the help of gifts is considered impeccable behavior, in perfect accord with Qurānic teaching (9:60). Muhammad made effective use of gifts as a means of winning people over to Islam. He would reward new converts generously but overlook the claims of Muslims of long standing. Sa'd reports that "the Messenger of Allah bestowed gifts upon a group of people. . . . He however left a person and did not give him anything and he seemed to me the most excellent among them." Sa'd drew the Prophet's attention to this believing Muslim, but Muhammad replied: "He may be a Muslim. I often bestow something on a person, whereas someone else is dearer to me than he, because of the fear that he [the former] may fall headlong into the fire'' (2300), that is, he may give up Islam and go back to his old religion. The translator and commentator makes the point very clear by saying that it was ''with a view to bringing him nearer and making him feel at home in the Muslim society that material gifts were conferred upon him by the Holy Prophet'' (note 1421).

There are other instances of the same type. 'Abdullah b. Zaid reports that ''when the Messenger of Allah conquered Hunain he distributed the booty, and he bestowed upon those whose hearts it was intended to win'' (2313). He bestowed costly gifts on the Quraish and Bedouin chiefs, many of them his enemies only a few weeks before. Traditions have preserved the names of some of these elite beneficiaries, like Abū Sufyān b. Harb, Safwān b. Umayya, 'Uyaina b. Hisn, Aqra' b. Hābis, and 'Alqama b. Ulasa (2303-2314). They received a hundred camels each from the booty.

Muhammad did the same with the booty of some gold sent by 'Alī b. Abū Tālib from Yemen. He distributed it among four men: 'Uyaina, Aqra, Zaid al-Khail, ''and the fourth one was either 'Alqama b. 'Ulāsa or Āmir b. Tufail'' (2319).

Pacification

But this course was not without its problems. It created quite a lot of dissatisfaction among some of his old supporters, and Muhammad had to use all his powers of diplomacy and flattery to pacify them. ''Don't you feel delighted that [other] people should go with riches, and you should go back with the Apostle of Allah,'' he told the *ansārs* with great success when, after the conquest of Mecca, they complained about the unjust distribution of the spoils. They had grumbled: ''It is strange that our swords are dripping with their blood, whereas our spoils have been given to them [the Quraish]'' (2307).

Muhammad added other words of flattery and told the *ansārs* that they were his ''inner garments'' (i.e., were closer to him), while the Quraish, who had received the spoils, were merely his ''outer garments.'' To cajolery, he added theology, telling them that they "should show patience till they meet him at *Hauz Kausar*," a canal in heaven (2313). The *ansārs* were happy.

MUHAMMAD RUFFLED

According to another tradition, Muhammad gave a hundred camels each to Abū Sufyān, Safwān, 'Uyaina, and Aqra, but less than his share to 'Abbās b. Mirdās. 'Abbās told Muhammad: "I am in no way inferior to anyone of these persons. And he who is let down today would not be elevated." Then Muhammad "completed one hundred camels for him" (2310).

In other cases when similar complaints were made, Muhammad could not always keep his temper. One man complained that "this is a distribution in which the pleasure of Allah has not been sought." On hearing this, Muhammad "was deeply angry . . . and his face became red"; he found comfort in the fact that "Moses was tormented more than this, but he showed patience" (2315).

THE KHWĀRIJ

'Alī sent some gold alloyed with dust from Yemen to Muhammad. In its distribution, Muhammad showed favoritism. When some people complained, Muhammad demanded: "Will you not trust me, whereas I am a trustee of Him Who is in the heaven? The news comes to me from the heaven morning and evening." This silenced the men, but one of them, a man with deep-sunken eyes, prominent cheekbones, thick beard, and shaven head, stood up, and said: "Messenger of Allah, fear Allah and do justice." This angered Muhammad, and he replied: "Woe be upon thee, who would do justice if I do not do justice?" 'Umar, who was present, said to Muhammad: "Messenger of Allah, permit me to kill this hypocrite." Though the man was spared, he and his posterity were denounced. Muhammad said: "From this very person's posterity there would arise people who would recite the Qurān, but it would not go beyond their throat; they would kill the followers of Islam but would spare the idol-worshippers. . . . If I were to find them I would kill them like 'Ād [a people who were exterminated root and branch]" (2316-2327).

These men, who later on were called the *khwārij*, took some of the slogans of Islam seriously. It was about them, according to 'Alī, that Muhammad said: "When you meet them, kill them, for in their killing you would get a reward with Allah on the Day of Judgment" (2328). These were the anarchists and purists of the early days of Islam. The injunction about them was: "Pursue them as they are routed and kill their prisoners and destroy their property."

5

Fasting and Pilgrimage (Sawm and Hajj)

The sixth and seventh books relate respectively to fasting (*al-sawm*) and pilgrimage (*al-hajj*). Both of these practices are accounted among the "pillars" of Islam.

Fasts

There are many kinds of fasts in Islam, but the fast during the month of *Ramzān* (Ramadan) is considered the most important. Enjoined in the Qurān, it is compulsory. "When there comes the month of *Ramzān*, the gates of mercy are opened, and the gates of Hell are locked and the devils are chained" (2361).

Fasting in the Muslim tradition is rather different from fasting in many other religious traditions. In Islam, there is no uninterrupted fasting (*saum wisal*), because Muhammad forbade this practice (2426–2435) "out of mercy" for his Companions (2435). During fasts eating is prohibited in the daytime but permitted at night. This has its disciplinary role, but nonetheless there is an attempt to make things easy. One is advised to eat as late as possible before sunrise, and to break the fast as soon as possible after sunset. "Take meal a little before dawn, for there is a blessing in taking meal at that time" (2412); and "the people will continue to prosper as long as they hasten the breaking of the fast" (2417).

This approach distinguished the Muslims from the Jews and the Christians, who ate early and broke their fasts late, waiting for the stars to appear. "The difference between our fasting and that of the People of the Book is eating shortly before dawn," says Muhammad (2413). The translator explains the advantages that accrued to the *ummah* from maintaining this difference. It "distinguishes the *Ummah* of the Islam from other *Ummahs*," and "hammers" into its consciousness the sense of "its separate entity which is the first step towards prosperity of any nation." In addition, "taking a meal late in the dawn and breaking fast early at the sunset indicate the fact that one feels the pangs of hunger. . . . This feeling inculcates in one a spirit of humility rather than of stoic pride" (note 1491).

SEXUAL INTERCOURSE ALLOWED DURING RAMZĀN

The Prophet softens the rigor of the fast somewhat by proclaiming that "eating and drinking in forgetfulness does not break the fast" (2575). Kissing and embracing too are permissible (2436–2450). 'Āisha, Hafsa, and Salama, Muhammad's wives, all report that the Prophet used to kiss them and embrace them while fasting. 'Āisha narrates: "The Messenger of Allah kissed one of his wives while he was fasting, and then she ['Āisha] smiled" (2436).

The translator elucidates: "It is one of the great favours of Allah upon humanity that He has guided us in every sector of our life through his Prophet Muhammad. Prior to Islam, the man observing fast separated himself completely from his wives. Islam did not approve this practice" (note 1502).

Sexual intercourse is also permitted during the night of the fast. It has a divine sanction. "It is made lawful for you to go to your wives on the night of the fast," says the Qurān (2:187). In fact, even if one gets up in a state of seminal emission and the dawn overtakes him without giving him time for the ordained bath, he should still go on with his fast. The state of *janabah* (in which one is "unclean" and cannot perform a religious act or join in religious assemblies) does not break the fast. 'Āisha and Salama, Muhammad's wives, report: "The Messenger of Allah at times got up in the morning in a state of *Junub* on account of having a sexual intercourse . . . in the month of *Ramzān*, and would observe fast" (2454). There are other *ahādīs* on the same subject (2451–2456).

This *hadīs* was checked and rechecked by Abū Bakr himself. At first Abū Huraira thought differently, but when the matter was clarified by 'Āisha and Salama, he said, "They have better knowledge," and retracted his previous position (2451).

Sexual intercourse during the daytime in the month of *Ramzān* could be atoned for either by freeing a slave or, failing that, by observing a two-month fast or, failing that, by feeding sixty poor men—but during the Prophet's lifetime, a poor man who violated this prohibition got his expiation at no cost to himself. Muhammad gave him a basket of dates and told him: "Go and give it to your family to eat" (2457).

Missed fasts could be completed later on at any time of the year. Women do not fast during the days of menses but are required to complete the fast the following year before the commencement of the next *Ramzān* (in the month of Sha'bān).

Fasting Not Obligatory under Certain Circumstances

Under certain circumstances fasting was optional. For example, a fast during a journey could be broken. "Fast if you like and break it if you like," Muhammad told a questioner on the subject (2488).

There is even a reward for not observing the fast if you are engaged in the "Way of Allah," i.e., in the act of *jihād*. "You are going to encounter the enemy in the morning and breaking of the fast would give you strength, so break the fast," Muhammad tells the believers (2486).

Women sometimes abstained from fasts so that they could perform their duties to their husbands unhindered. 'Āisha reports: "I had to complete some of the fasts of *Ramzān*, but I could not do it . . . due to my duties to the Messenger of Allah" (2549). 'Āisha reports the same about Muhammad's other wives. "If one amongst us had to break fasts [of *Ramzān* due to natural reasons, i.e., menses] during the life of the Messenger of Allah, she could not find it possible to complete them so long as she had been in the presence of Allah's Messenger till *Sha'bān* [the eighth month] commenced" (2552). The translator explains that every wife of Muhammad was "so much devoted to him that she avoided fasting lest it should stand in her way in the performance of her duty as a wife to him" (note 1546).

It was not only from devotion but also because of Muhammad's injunction that the wives did not fast. "No woman should observe fast when her spouse is present [in the house] but with his permission. And she should not admit any *mahram* in his house, while the husband is present, but with his permission" (2238). A *mahram* is a near relative with whom it is unlawful to marry. A woman can feel free in his presence and thus need not observe *purdah*.

The translator gives us the rationale for this injunction. "Such is the regard which Islam gives to the natural instinct of man that it enjoins upon women not to observe (voluntary) fasts, and not to admit even those relatives of theirs in their apartments who are *maharam* to them so that they may not stand in the way of the husbands to satisfy their sexual urge" (note 1387).

OTHER FASTS

Several other fasts are mentioned. One is the *Ashura* fast, observed on the tenth day of Muharram. The *Ashur* day "was one which the Jews respected and they treated it as *'Īd*" (2522), and in the pre-Islamic days, "Quraish used to fast on this day" (2499); but after Muhammad migrated to Medina he made it optional for his followers. Other voluntary fasts are mentioned, but we need not go into them here.

One interesting thing about these fasts is that one could declare one's intention of observing them in the morning but break them without reason in the evening. One day, Muhammad asked 'Āisha for some food, but nothing was available. Thereupon Muhammad said: "I am observing fast." After some time, some food came as gift, and 'Āisha offered it to Muhammad. He asked: "What is it?" 'Āisha said: "It is *hais* [a compound of dates and clarified butter]." He said: "Bring that." 'Āisha further narrates: "So I brought it to him and he ate it"; and then he said: "This observing of voluntary fasts is like a person who sets apart *Sadaqa* out of his wealth. He may spend it if he likes, or he may retain it if he so likes" (2573).

The Merits of Fasting

There are many merits in observing the fasts. "The breath of the observer of fast is sweeter to Allah than the fragrance of musk," Muhammad tells us. On the Day of Resurrection, there will be a gate called *Rayyān* in Paradise, through which only those who have fasted will be allowed to enter—and when the last of them has entered, "it would be closed and no one would enter it" (2569).

The recompense of one who combines fasting with *jihād* will be immense. "Every servant of Allah who observes fast for a day in the way of Allah, Allah would remove, because of this day, his face from the Fire of Hell to the extent of seventy years' distance" (2570).

PILGRIMAGE

The book on *hajj* ("setting out") is full of ceremonial details which have little interest for non-Muslims. Its ninety-two chapters contain minute instructions on the rites and rituals of the pilgrimage, providing useful guidance to a *hajji* (pilgrim) but of dubious value to a traveler of the Spirit.

An Idolatrous Idea

Considered from the viewpoint of Muslim theology, the whole idea of pilgrimage to Mecca and the Ka'ba is close to being idolatrous. But it has great social and political importance for Islam. Even the very first Muslim pilgrimage to Mecca under the leadership of Muhammad was perhaps more of a political demonstration and a military expedition than a religious congregation.

In the sixth year of the Hijra, Muhammad started out for Mecca to perform the *'umrah* ceremony (the lesser pilgrimage), the very first after coming to Medina. He headed a pilgrim force of fifteen hundred men, partially armed. In order to swell the number, he had appealed to the desert Arabs to join him, but their response was lukewarm, for no booty was promised and they thought, as the Qurān puts it, that "the Apostle and the believers would never return to their families" (48:12).

Even so, fifteen hundred was an impressive number, and anyone could see that this was hardly a band of pilgrims. The Meccans had to enter into a treaty with Muhammad, called the Treaty of Hodeibia. Muhammad regarded this as a victory for himself, and a victory it turned out to be. Two years later, by a kind of delayed action, Mecca succumbed. In this year of victory, pilgrimage, or *hajj*, was declared one of the five fundamentals of Islam.

Two years later, in March A.D. 632, Muhammad undertook another pilgrimage; it turned out to be his last and is celebrated in the Muslim annals as the "Farewell Pilgrimage of the Apostle." Great preparations were made for the occasion. It was meant to be more than an assembly of believers. It was to be a demonstration of the power of Muhammad. "Messengers were sent to all parts of Arabia inviting people to join him in this great Pilgrimage."

After the fall of Mecca, Muhammad's power was unrivaled, and the Bedouin tribes understood that this summons was more than an invitation to a pilgrimage of the type they had formerly performed on their own, at their own convenience and for their own gods. It was also, they knew, a call to submission. Thus, unlike the last time, their response on this occasion was great. "As the caravan moved on, the number of participants swelled," until, according to some of the narrators, it reached more than 130,000 (*Sahīh Muslim*, p. 612). Everyone was in a hurry to jump on the bandwagon.

THE STATE OF IHRĀM

The "Book of Pilgrimage" deals with the pilgrim's attire and with the place where he puts on the garments of a pilgrim, entering into the state of *ihrām* ("prohibiting"), in which he is forbidden to do certain things till he has completed his worship at Mecca.

For his dress, he is forbidden to "put on a shirt or a turban, or trouser or cap" (2647). The use of perfume is disallowed during the state of *ihrām*, but not before and after. "I applied perfume to the Messenger of Allah as he became free from *Ihrām* and as he entered upon it," says 'Āisha (2683). "The best of perfume," she adds in another *hadīs* (2685).

HUNTING

Hunting too is forbidden to a *muhrim* (one in a state of *ihrām*). Somebody once presented Muhammad with the flesh of a wild ass, but he declined it, saying: "If we were not in a state of *Ihrām*, we would have accepted it from you" (2704). But if the animal is killed by a non-*muhrim*, its flesh is acceptable to a *muhrim*. The leg of a wild ass killed by a non-*muhrim* Companion was presented to Muhammad. "The Messenger of Allah took it and ate it" (2714).

Though hunting of a sort is forbidden to a *muhrim*, this does not make him a Jain or a Vaishnava. "Four are the vicious beasts" he should still kill: "kite, crow, rat and voracious dog." But "what about a snake?" somebody asks. Muhammad replies: "Let it be killed with disgrace" (2717).

CIRCUMAMBULATION AND KISSING

After a man has put on the pilgrim's robe, two seamless wrappers, he should not shave or pare his nails. He should now proceed toward Mecca singing the pilgrim's song, *"Talbiyah, Labbaika! Allāhumma!"* ("I stand up for thy service, O Allah"). After arriving in Mecca, he performs ablutions in the Masjidu'l Harām and kisses the Black Stone (*al-hajaru'l-aswad*), then makes seven circuits round the Ka'ba (*tawāf*). Muhammad himself circumambulated "on the back of his riding camel . . . so that people should see him, and he should be conspicuous" (2919). For the same reason, he touched the Corner (Black Stone) with a stick. "I saw Allah's Messenger circumambulating the House, and touching the Corner with a stick that he had with him, and then kissing the stick," reports Abū Tufail (2921).

The practice of kissing the Stone is idolatrous. 'Umar said: "By Allah, I know that you are a stone and if I were not to see Allah's Messenger kissing you, I would not have kissed you" (2912). Following the lead of Christian theologians who distinguish between *veneratio* and *adoratio*, Muslim scholars argue that the Ka'ba and the Black Stone are objects of veneration and not of worship.

Another important rite is that the pilgrim runs from the top of Mount as-Safā to the summit of Mount al-Marwah, the two "Signs of Allah," according to the Qurān (2:158). Muhammad says that "Allah does not complete the *Hajj* of a person or his *'Umra* if he does not observe *Sa'i* [i.e., run between *al-Safā* and *al-Marwa*]" (2923).

Each time the pilgrim is on the top of these mounts, he recites the following: "There is no deity but Allah. . . . He hath performed His promise, and hath aided His servant [Muhammad] and hath put to flight the hosts of infidels by Himself alone." Muhammad never relaxes. At every turn, he instills an unrelenting enmity toward the infidels.

CASTING THE PEBBLES

Another important ceremony is *ramyu'r-rijām*, the casting of the pebbles. On the tenth day, also the "Day of Sacrifice," the pilgrim throws seven pebbles at Jamrat al-'Aqaba, also known as Shaitānuu'l Kabīr, the Great Devil. While doing this, he chants: "In the name of God, the Almighty, I do this, and in hatred of the Devil and his shame." Allah and Devil are somehow inseparable in certain theologies.

This ceremony celebrates an ancient event when the Devil successively met Adam, Abraham, and Ishmael, and was driven away by the simple method which Gabriel taught them of throwing seven small pebbles. The three pillars at Minā represent the three occasions when this happened; therefore, the pilgrim casts seven stones at each of the three pillars.

There are several *ahādīs* on the merits of throwing pebbles, on their size and number, and on the best time for throwing them. The pebbles should be small—"I saw Allah's Apostle throwing stones like pelting of small pebbles" (2979). The best time for throwing them is after sunrise on the Day of Sacrifice—"Allah's Messenger flung pebbles at Jamra on the Day of *Nahr* after sunrise, and after that—on the 11th, 12th and 13th of *Dhu'l-Hijja*—when the sun had declined" (2980). Their number should be odd. "Odd number of stones are to be used for cleaning the private parts after answering the call of nature, and the casting of pebbles at the Jamrat is to be done by odd numbers (seven), and the number of circuits around *al-Safā* and *al-Marwa* is also odd (seven), and the number of circuits around the Ka'ba is also odd (seven)," says the Prophet (2982).

Animal Sacrifice

Next comes the sacrifice of the *'idu'l-azhā*. The *hājji* (pilgrim) could sacrifice a goat or a sheep, or a cow or a camel, "The Messenger of Allah sacrificed a cow on behalf of 'Āisha" (3030).

It is permissible for seven persons to join in the sacrifice of a cow or a camel (3024–3031). While sacrificing the camel, the *hājji* should not make his camel "kneel down" but slaughter it in a standing posture and in a fettered condition "according to the *Sunnah* of the Holy Prophet" (3032). Its left foreleg should be tied to its hindlegs. Cows and goats should be sacrificed after making them lie down.

One who cannot go for *hajj* can send a sacrificial animal to al-Haram and earn merit thereby. 'Āisha reports: "I wove the garlands for the sacrificial animals of Allah's Messenger with my own hands, and then he marked them, and garlanded them, and then sent them to the House, and stayed at Medina and nothing was forbidden to him which was lawful for him before" (3036).

As Muhammad's affluence increased, the scale of his sacrifices also increased. On his *'umrah* pilgrimage in the sixth year, his biographers tell us, he sacrificed seventy camels at Hodeibia. On a similar pilgrimage the next year, he sacrificed sixty camels. On the Farewell Pilgrimage in the tenth year, we are told by Jābir, "the total number of those sacrificial animals brought by 'Alī from Yemen [where he had gone on a campaign against the Bani Nakha] and those brought by the Apostle was one hundred" (2803). A little further on in the same *hadīs* we are told that Muhammad "then went to the place of sacrifice, and sacrificed sixty-three camels with his own hands. Then he gave the remaining number to 'Alī who sacrificed them. . . . He then commanded that a piece of flesh from each animal sacrificed should be put in a pot, and when it was cooked, both of them ['Alī and Muhammad] took some meat out of it and drank its soup."

To his followers, Muhammad said: "I have sacrificed the animals here, and the whole of Minā is a place of sacrifice; so sacrifice your animals at your places" (2805).

Even Jehovah, the God of the Jews, whose Temple was a veritable slaughterhouse, had declared that He "desired mercy, and not sacrifice" (Hosea 6:6); but Muhammad's Allah expresses no such sentiment. Because Islam is so preponderantly Muhammadism, one of the consequences of the Prophet's offering sacrifices is that sacrificing has become a sacred institution in Islam. Thus we find in Islam none of that generous movement of the spirit against animal sacrifice that we find in some measure in most cultures.

DRINK

Muhammad also drank water from the well of Zamzam as part of the ritual. Coming to the tribe of 'Abd al-Muttalib (also his own tribe), he said: "Draw water, O Banī 'Abd al-Muttalib; were it not that people would usurp this right of supplying water from you, I would have drawn it along with you. So they handed him a basket and he drank from it" (2803). Kātib al-Wāqidī, the Prophet's biographer, gives us one further detail which would be considered unhygienic by the impious. Muhammad took part of the content, then rinsed his mouth in the pitcher and directed that the water remaining in it should be thrown back into the well. That was his way of invoking a blessing on a well—by spitting into it. Many such wells are mentioned in the traditions (*Tabaqāt,* vol. II, pp. 241-244).

He also did not forgo his favorite beverage, *nabīz*, a soft drink. Though the *nabīz* offered him had been fouled by many hands, he took it, declining the offer of a cleaner and purer one. The orthodox pilgrims of every generation have continued the practice.

SHAVING: MUHAMMAD'S HAIR

After the sacrifice, the ceremony of pilgrimage concludes, and the *hājji* has himself shaved and his nails pared and his pilgrim garment removed. Shaving should begin from the right side. Anas reports that Allah's Messenger "went to *Jamra* and threw pebbles at it, after which he went to his lodging in Minā, and sacrificed the animal. He then called for a barber and, turning his right side to him, let him shave him; after which he turned his left side. He then gave these hairs to the people" (2991); the hairs became important Islamic relics.

Now the pilgrimage is over, but the pilgrim should spend another three days in Mecca to rest after the hectic four days of ceremony. Before leaving Mecca, he should again go round the Ka'ba seven times and throw stones at the satanic pillars at Minā seven times. Before returning home, he should go to Medina to pay his homage at the tomb of Muhammad.

Ka'ba Closed to Non-Muslims

The Ka'ba, which had been open to all in pre-Islamic times, whether they were worshippers of Al-Lāh or Al-Lāt, was closed to all except Muslims after Muhammad conquered Mecca. "After this year no polytheist may perform the Pilgrimage," it was declared on his behalf (3125). This was Allah's own command. The Qurān says: "O you who believe! those who ascribe partners to God are impure, and so they shall not approach the sacred House of worship from this year onward" (9:28).*

*There was an agreement between Muhammad and the polytheists that none should be kept back from the temple and that none should fear interference from each other during the sacred months. But a "discharge" came to Muhammad from Allah absolving him from his side of the obligation, that "Allah is free from obligation to the idolaters and so is His Messenger." Four months were given to them either to mend their ways or face death. Muslims were told that "when the sacred months are over, kill the idolaters wherever you may find them; and take them and besiege them, and prepare for them each ambush. . . . Lo! Allah is forgiving and merciful" (Qurān 9:5).

Muslims thought that if non-Muslims were disallowed to enter Mecca, their trade would be affected. So Muhammad proposed a poll tax on the Jews and the Christians "as a compensation for what you fear to lose by the closing of the markets," as Ibn Ishāq tells us (*Sīrat Rasūl Allah*, p. 620). The relevant Qurānic verses are: "If you fear poverty, Allah will enrich you from His grace. . . . Fight against such of those who have been given the scripture and believe not in Allah . . . and follow not the religion of truth, until they pay the tribute with willing submission and be as little ones" (9:28, 29).

Most religions build houses or temples for their gods out of their own labor, but Islam conquered one for its god, Allah, from others. The difference is striking. A worthy habitation for any worthwhile god is the one built by his devotees with the love of their hearts and the labor of their hands. Any other house is a monument of imperialist greed and aggrandizement and is not acceptable to the gods of the purified spirit.

6

Marriage and Divorce (Al-Nikāh and Al-Talāq)

The eighth book is entitled the "Book of Marriage"; one section of it also discusses divorce (*al-talāq*).

Muhammad forbids celibacy. "Those among you who can support a wife should marry, for it restrains eyes from casting evil glances and preserves one from immorality" (3231). One of his Companions wanted to live in celibacy, but Muhammad "forbade him to do so" (3239).*

In fact, Muhammad discouraged self-denial in general. One of his Companions said, "I will not marry women"; another said, "I will not eat meat"; and yet another said, "I will not lie down in bed." Muhammad asked himself: "What has happened to these people that they say so and so, whereas I observe prayer and sleep too; I observe fast and suspend observing them; I marry women also? And who turns away from my *Sunnah*, he has no relation with me" (3236).

A woman is a great safety valve, but if even that fails and a man is aroused by some other woman, he should come home and cohabit with his wife. "Allah's Messenger saw a woman and so he came to his wife, Zainab, as she was tanning a leather and had sexual intercourse with her. He then went to his Companions and told them: The woman advances and returns in the shape of a devil, so when

*According to a tradition derived from Ibn 'Abbās and quoted by Ibn Sa'd, popularly known as Kātib at-Wāqidī, the prophet's biographer, Muhammad said: "In my *ummah*, he is the best who has the largest number of wives" (*Tabaqāt*, vol. II, p. 146).

one of you see a woman, he should come to his wife, for that will repel what he feels in his heart" (3240). We are all too ready to see the devil in others, but not in our own selves.

TEMPORARY MARRIAGE (*Mut'ah*)

Muhammad allowed temporary marriages. 'Abdullah b. Mas'ud reports: "We were on an expedition with Allah's Messenger and we had no women with us. We said: Should we not have ourselves castrated? The Holy Prophet forbade us to do so. He then granted us permission that we should contract temporary marriage for a stipulated period giving her a garment [for a dowry]." At this 'Abdullah felt happy and remembered the Qurānic verse: "The believers do not make unlawful the good things which Allah has made lawful for you, and do not transgress. Allah does not like transgressors" (3243; Qurān 5:87).

Jābir reports: "We contracted temporary marriage giving a handful of dates and flour as a dower" (3249). He told another group: "Yes, we had been benefiting ourselves by this temporary marriage during the lifetime of the Holy Prophet, and during the time of Abū Bakr and 'Umar" (3248). Iyās b. Salama reports, on the authority of his father, "that Allah's Messenger gave sanction for contracting temporary marriage for three nights in the year of Autās [after the Battle of Hunain, A.H. 8] and then forbade it" (3251).

Sunni theologians regard this form of marriage as no longer lawful, but the Shias differ and still practice it in Persia. The Shia theologians support this with a Qurānic verse: "Forbidden to you also are married women, except those who are your hands as slaves. . . . And it is allowed you, besides this, to seek out wives by means of your wealth, with modest conduct, and without fornication. And give those with whom you have cohabited their dowry. This is the law. But it shall be no crime in you to make agreements over and above the law. Verily, God is knowing, Wise" (Qurān 4:24).

PROHIBITIONS

The law appears to be quite indulgent, but it is not entirely so. There are many restrictions on grounds of number, consanguinity, affinity, religion, rank, etc. For example, a man cannot marry more than four free women at a time (Qurān 4:3)—there is no restriction on the number of slave concubines. Also, one cannot marry one's wife's father's sister nor her mother's sister (3268–3277). It is also forbidden to marry the daughter of one's foster brother, or even the sister of one's wife if the wife is alive and not divorced (3412–3413).

It is also forbidden to marry an unbeliever (Qurān 2:220–221). Later on, this restriction was relaxed, and a male Muslim could then marry a Jew or a Christian (Qurān 5:5). Under no circumstances could a female Muslim marry a nonbeliever.

Marriage is also disallowed when the parties are not equal in rank or status (*kafa'ah*), though what is rank is differently understood by different people. Generally speaking, an Arab is considered higher than a non-Arab, the Prophet's relatives being the highest. One who had committed a portion of the Qurān to memory was considered a qualified match by Muhammad himself. A woman came to him and entrusted herself to him. He "cast a glance at her from head to foot . . . but made no decision" about her. Then a Companion who was there stood up and said: "Messenger of Allah, marry her to me if you have no need for her." But the man possessed nothing, not even an iron ring for a dowry. He was turning away in disappointment when Muhammad asked him if he knew any verses of the Qurān and could recite them. The man said yes. Then Muhammad decided and said: "Go, I have given her to you in marriage for the part of the Qurān which you know" (3316).

One should also not outbid one's brother. "A believer is the brother of a believer, so it is not lawful for a believer to outbid his brother, and he should not propose an agreement when his brother has thus proposed until he gives it up" (3294).

Shighār marriage is also prohibited (3295–3301).* This is the marriage which says: Marry me your daughter or sister, and in exchange I will give you in marriage my daughter or sister.

*Is the prohibition connected with some event in the Prophet's life? When He married 'Aisha, Abū Bakr's daughter, the latter in turn waited on him for the hand of his daughter, Fātimah. But Muhammad replied: "I am waiting for a revelation." When Abū Bakr reported these words to 'Umar, the latter said: "He has rejected thy request" (Mirkhond, *Rauzat-us-Safa*, vol. I, part II, p. 269).

One should also not marry when one has put on the ritual garb of pilgrimage. "A *Muhrim* should neither marry nor make the proposal of marriage," reports Usmān b. Affān, quoting the Prophet (3281). But this point is controversial, for Muhammad himself "married Maimūna while he was a *Muhrim*" (3284).

One cannot remarry one's divorced wife unless she subsequently married someone else and the new husband had sexual intercourse with her and then divorced her (3354–3356). A divorcee married but then decided to go back to her old husband. Seeking the Prophet's permission, she told Muhammad that all the new husband possessed was "like the fringe of a garment" (i.e., he was sexually weak). The Prophet "laughed" but withheld the permission. "You cannot do that until you have tasted his [the new husband's] sweetness and he has tasted your sweetness," he told her (3354).*

THE HUSBAND'S RIGHTS

A husband has complete sexual rights over his wife. "Your wives are your tilth; go then unto your tilth as you may desire" (3363). The same idea is also found in the Qurān (2:223). Another *hadīs* in the same group tells the husband that "if he likes he may have intercourse being on the back or in front of her, but it should be through one hole" (3365), which means vagina only, as the commentators tell us.

It is the duty of a wife to be responsive to all of her husband's overtures. "When a woman spends the night away from the bed of her husband, the angels curse her until morning" (3366).

WOMEN'S RIGHTS

In return, a woman has her rights. She is entitled to a lawful maintenance (*nafaqah*); if the husband fails to provide it, she can

*We are told that this injunction was laid down to discourage divorce, which was sometimes lightly undertaken because reunion was easy. A couple must realize that the marital relationship is a serious one and must think twice (in fact, thrice) before severing it. But man is inventive, and he disposes what Allah proposes. The new dispensation led to another abuse. It gave rise to the institution of the temporary husband, hired by the first husband from among the ugly ones, to make the new contact unpleasant to the wife.

seek a divorce. She is also entitled to a dowry (*mahr*), or what the Qurān in some verses (4:24, 33:50) calls her "hire" (*ujūrat*). She can claim it when divorced.

She is also to be consulted in the choice of her partner. "A woman who has been previously married (*Sayyib*) has more right to her person than her guardian. And a virgin should also be consulted, and her silence implies her consent" (3307). Theoretically, a Muslim woman is entitled to make the marriage contract herself, but in practice it is her nearest kinsman, the guardian (*walī*), who does it. The father and the grandfather are even called "compelling *walīs*." According to some schools, a minor girl given in marriage by a guardian other than her father or grandfather can seek dissolution of the marriage when she attains her majority.

Al-'Azl

Coitus interruptus is permitted, but it is useless if the object is to prevent conception, for that is in the hand of Allah. Abū Sirma reports: "We went out with Allah's Messenger on the expedition . . . and took some excellent Arab women; and we desired them . . . but we also desired ransom for them. So we decided to have sexual intercourse with them but by observing *'azl*." They consulted Muhammad, and he advised: "It does not matter if you do not do it, for every soul that is to be born up to the Day of Resurrection will be born" (3371).

Captive Women

Adultery and fornication are punished according to Muhammad's law, but not if you commit them with the "women that your right hands possess," that is, those women, whether married or unmarried, who are captured by the Muslims in *jihād*, or holy war. A Qurānic verse fortifies this position: "Also prohibited are women already married except those whom your right hands possess" (4:24).

Ahādīs 3432–3434 tell us that this verse descended on the Prophet for the benefit of his Companions. Abū Sa'īd reports that "at the Battle of Hunain Allah's Messenger sent an army to Autās.

. . . Having overcome them [the enemies] and taken them captives, the Companions of Allah's Messenger seemed to refrain from having intercourse with captive women because of their husbands being polytheists. Then, Allah, Most High, sent down [the above verse]" (3432).

The followers had a feeling of delicacy in the matter, based on an old moral code, but Allah now gave a new one.

CAST A GLANCE AT THE WOMAN YOU WANT TO MARRY

It is permissible to cast a glance at the woman one wants to marry, from "head to foot." A believer came to Muhammad, informing him that he had contracted a marriage with an *ansār* woman and wanted him to contribute toward the dowry payment. "Did you cast a glance at her, for there is something in the eyes of the *Ansārs*," Muhammad asked. The man replied: "Yes." "For what dower did you marry her," Muhammad inquired. "For four *Ūqiyas*," the man replied. "For four *Ūqiyas*? It seems as if you dig out silver from the side of the mountain (that is why you are prepared to pay so much dower). We have nothing which we should give you. There is a possibility that we may send you to an expedition where you may get booty." The man was sent on an expedition marching against the Banū 'Abs (3315).

But this permission actually originated in a different incident. An Arab woman named 'Umra, the daughter of one Jaun, "was mentioned before Allah's Messenger." By now the Prophet was an important man in Arab politics, so he commanded an official of his named Abū Usaid to send a messenger to the woman. She was brought and she "stayed in the fortresses of Banū Sā'idah." Allah's Messenger went out until he came to her to give "her a proposal of marriage." She was "sitting with her head downcast." They saw each other, and Muhammad talked to her. She told him: "I seek refuge with Allah from you." Meanwhile the Prophet had arrived at his own conclusion. He told her: "I have decided to keep you away from me." Then Muhammad retired with his host and told him: "Sahl, serve us drink" (4981).

It is in this *hadīs* that one finds it permissible to cast a glance at the woman whom one intends to marry (note 2424).

Deportment toward One's Wives

Ticklish problems arise if one has more than one wife and if one marries often. One of the problems, for example, is how many nights one should spend with one's newly wed wife? The answer is seven days if she is a virgin, and three days if she is a widow (3443–3449).

Umm Salama, one of the wives of Muhammad, tells us that when Muhammad married her, he spent three nights with her. When he intended to leave, she "caught hold of his garment." But the Prophet told her: "If you wish I can stay with you for a week, but then I shall have to stay for a week with all my wives" (3443–3445).

Though a husband should divide his days equally among all his wives, one wife could make over her day to another. *Ahādīs* 3451–3452 tell us that when Sauda became old, she made over her day to 'Āisha. So Allah's Messenger "allotted two days to 'Āisha" (3451).

But sometimes the Prophet himself would ask a wife to forgo her day. One wife told him: "If I had the option in this I would not have allowed anyone to have precedence over me" (3499).

Eventually the rule of rotation was withdrawn altogether by a special dispensation of Allah: "Thou may defer the turn of any of them that thou pleasest, and thou may receive any thou pleasest; and there is no blame in thee if thou invite one whose turn thou hast set aside" (Qurān 33:51). Allah is very accommodating. 'Āisha, for whose benefit He really spoke, taunted Muhammad: "It seems to me that your Lord hastens to satisfy your desire" (3453).

Night Sessions

We have one important *hadīs* which provides another indulgence to the believers and also throws some light on the Prophet's sexual code. In order to be impartial, a believer should visit his wives by turn. But while he is in bed with one of them, he is allowed to have his other wives around. Anas, one of the servants of Muhammad, reports that "all the wives of the Messenger of Allah used to gather every night in the house of one where he [the Apostle] had to come. . . . It was the night in the house of 'Āisha, when Zainab came there. He [the Holy Prophet] stretched his hand towards her [Zainab], whereupon she ['Āisha] said: it is Zainab. Allah's Apostle withdrew his hand. There was an altercation between the two until their voices became loud." When the morning prayer was announced, Abū Bakr came to get Muhammad; hearing their voices, he said: "Messenger of Allah, come for prayer, and throw dust in their mouths" (3450).

ON MARRYING A VIRGIN

In other *ahādīs*, the Prophet touches upon the excellence of marrying a virgin (3458–3464). Jābir reports: "The Apostle of Allah said: 'Jābir, have you married?' I said, 'yes.' He said: 'A virgin or one previously married?' I said: 'with one previously married,' whereupon he said: 'Why did you not marry a virgin with whom you could sport?' " (3458), or "who might amuse you and you might amuse her" (3464).

TASTAHIDDA

Muhammad also made effective use of what are known in literary criticism as vulgar expressions. Once the Prophet and his party returned from an expedition rather late, and his Companions wanted to hurry to their homes. But the Prophet told them to wait till "the woman with dishevelled hair may comb it, and the woman whose husband had been away may get herself clean; and when you enter, you have the enjoyment" (3462).

The translator tells us that the Arabic word for "get herself clean" is *tastahidda*, which literally means "to remove the hairs on the private parts," but it is here used metaphorically in the sense of getting ready for the husband's company (note 1926).

THE ORIGINAL SIN

"Had it not been for Eve, woman would have never acted unfaithfully towards the husband," the Prophet tells us (3471).

MUHAMMAD'S MARRIAGES

Some incidents relating to the Prophet's marriages with Safīyya (3325–3329) and Zainab bint Jahsh are mentioned (3330–3336).

RĪHĀNA AND JUWAIRĪYA

Safīyya was no exception. Many other women, among them Rīhāna and Juwairīya, were taken in and treated as part of the war booty. Rīhāna was a Jewish girl of the Banū Quraizah. After her husband was beheaded in cold blood along with eight hundred other male members of her tribe in the genocide at Medina, Muhammad kept her as his concubine. We shall touch upon this massacre again in our discussion of *jihād*.

Juwairīya, another of these unfortunate girls, was the daughter of the chief of the Banu'l Mustaliq. She was captured in the fifth or sixth year of the Hijra along with two hundred other women. "The Messenger of Allah made a raid upon Banū Mustaliq while they were unaware and their cattle were having a drink at the water. He killed those who fought and imprisoned others. On that very day, he captured Juwairīya bint al-Hāris" (4292).

In the division of the booty, she fell to the lot of Sābit ibn Qays. He set her ransom price at nine ounces of gold, beyond the power of her relatives to pay. 'Āisha's reaction when she saw this beautiful girl being led into the presence of Muhammad is recounted in these words: "As soon as I saw her at the door of my room, I detested her, for I knew that he [Muhammad] would see her as I saw her." And indeed, when Muhammad saw Juwairīya he paid her ransom and took her for his wife. Juwairīya was at that time about twenty, and she became the seventh wife of the Prophet. The whole story is given by Ibn Ishāq, the Prophet's biographer.*

There was another girl, named Zainab, again Jewish, who had seen her father, husband, and uncle killed. She poisoned the roasted lamb she was ordered to prepare for Muhammad. Suspecting something wrong, Muhammad spat out the very first morsel. He was saved, and she was immediately put to death, according to some authorities (*Tabaqāt*, vol. II, pp. 252–255).

**Sīrat Rasūl Allah*, p. 493.

DIVORCE (TALĀQ)

Talāq literally means "undoing the knot," but in Islamic law, it now means annulment of marriage by the pronouncement of certain words.

The marriage and divorce laws of Islam derive from the Prophet's own practice and pronouncements. According to the Shias, the Prophet had twenty-two wives, two of whom were bondswomen; but that was a special divine dispensation for him alone. The other believers are allowed only four wives at a time, exclusive of slave concubines, who do not count. The total of four wives at one time cannot be exceeded, but individual wives can be replaced through *talāq*. The procedure is not difficult; once a man says the word *talāq* three times, the divorce becomes operative.

Yet there are certain restrictions. For example, it is forbidden to divorce a woman during her menstrual period (3473–3490). 'Abdullah, the son of 'Umar, the future Khalīfa, divorced his wife while she was in a state of menses. When 'Umar mentioned this to Muhammad, the latter ordered: "He ['Abdullah] should take her back, and when she is pure he may divorce her" (3485).

THREE PRONOUNCEMENTS

The word *talāq* has to be pronounced three times before *talāq* becomes operative (3491–3493). But opinions differ as to whether it has to be pronounced on three separate occasions, after three successive menses, or whether three times at one sitting is enough. According to the translator, "traditions are not lacking in which three pronouncements at one sitting were held as irrevocable divorce even during the time of the prophet'' (note 1933).

With such easy conditions of divorce, the limitation of wives to four at a time was not unduly self-denying. Wives were constantly replaced. 'Abdar-Rahmān, a senior Companion, adviser, and friend of Muhammad, Abū Bakr, and 'Umar, had children by sixteen wives besides those from concubines. Somewhat later, Hasan, the son of 'Alī and grandson of Muhammad, married seventy—some say ninety—times. People in his day called him the Divorcer.

It is no wonder that women had no sanctity. Wives could be easily disposed of by gifting or divorce. For example, on emigrating to Medina, 'Abdar-Rahmān was adopted by Sa'd, son of Rabī, as a brother in faith—in accordance with the arrangement made by Muhammad to join every Emigrant to an *ansār* in brotherhood. As they sat together at supper, the host said: ''Behold my two wives and choose one you like the best.'' One wife was divorced on the spot and gifted away.*

ZIHĀR AND ĪLĀ'

There were two other forms of separation not amounting to legal divorce prevalent among the Arabs at the time of Muhammad: *zihār* and *īlā'*. In *zihār*, the husband vowed that his wife would be unto him as the back (*zahr*) of his mother and then stayed away from her for a specified period. This was a customary vow of abstinence among the Arabs, and according to some traditions, Muslims also took it during the period of fasting. The purpose of the abstinence could be penitential or devotional, or the vow might be taken in a fit of anger. The same formula was also used as a form of divorce. Muhammad condemned divorce by *zihār* (Qurān 58:1–5) and allowed a husband who had taken the vow to go back to his wife. The broken vow could be expiated by making a *kaffārah* (literally, ''that which covers a sin''), which in this case is either a fast for two months or the feeding of sixty poor men and women.

*Kātib al Wāqidī, quoted by W. Muir, *Life of Mahomet*, vol. II, pp. 272–273.

There was another form of separation called *īlā'* ("to swear"). In this form, the husband swore an oath to abstain from sexual intercourse with his wife. In the pre-Islamic period, the Arabs regarded *īlā* as a form of divorce, but it did not fully dissolve the marriage. The oath of *īlā* was sometimes taken to penalize the wife and extort ransom from her. Muhammad forbade this (Qurān 2:226). A man who had taken such a vow was to go back to his wife without any blame to himself; if not, the marriage was ipso facto legally dissolved at the end of four months. The broken vow could be expiated. "When a man declares his wife as unlawful for himself that is an oath which must be atoned. . . . There is in the Messenger of Allah a model pattern for you" (3494–3495).

In due course, the two forms of separation died away in Islam.

MUHAMMAD'S SEPARATION FROM HIS WIVES

Īlā' is a temporary separation from one's wife. In this sense of the term, the believers are indeed fortunate in having a "model pattern" in an example provided by the Prophet.

Muhammad himself had to undergo separation from his wives for a period which lasted twenty-nine days. The *Sahīh Muslim* narrates this incident in several *ahādīs*; but before we take them up, let us provide some background information.

In visiting his numerous wives, Muhammad observed a rough-and-ready rule of rotation. In fact, the days in his life were known by the name of the wife he was visiting. One day Muhammad was supposed to be with Hafza, but instead she found him with Mary, the beautiful Coptic concubine. Hafza was furious. "In my room, on my day and in my own bed," she shouted. Muhammad, trying to pacify her, promised never to visit Mary again, but he wanted Hafza to keep the incident a secret.

Hafza, however, told 'Āisha, and very soon everybody knew about it. Muhammad's Quraish wives detested Mary and were jealous of the servile wretch, who had even given Muhammad a son. Soon the harem was filled with gossip, excitement, and jeering. Muhammad was very angry, and he told his wives that he would have nothing to do with them. He separated himself from them, and soon the news was afloat that he was divorcing them all. In fact, in the eyes of the believers this rumor was more newsworthy and significant than the reports that Medina was soon to be attacked by Ghassān (the Arab auxiliaries of Byzantium).

In a long *hadīs*, 'Umar b. al-Khattāb (Hafza's father) reports: "When Allah's Apostle kept himself away from his wives, I entered the mosque, and found the people striking the ground with pebbles and saying: Allah's Messenger has divorced his wives." 'Umar decided to find out what was actually happening. First he asked 'Āisha if she had "gone to the extent of giving trouble to Allah's Messenger." 'Āisha told him to mind his own business. "I have nothing to do with you. You should look to your own receptacle [Hafza]." 'Umar next sought out Hafza and chided her. "You know that Allah's Messenger does not love you, and had I not been your father he would have divorced you," he told her. She wept bitterly.

Then 'Umar sought permission to be admitted into the presence of Muhammad. The request was disregarded, but he insisted. "O Rahāb, seek permission for me from Allah's Messenger. I think that Allah's Messenger is under the impression that I have come for the sake of Hafza. By Allah, if Allah's Messenger would command me to strike her neck, I would certainly do that," he told Rahāb, Muhammad's doorman. He was admitted.

As 'Umar entered, he saw "the signs of anger on his [Muhammad's] face," so he tried to calm him down. He told him "how we the people of Quraish had domination over women but when we came to Medina we found people whom their women dominated. So our women began to learn from their women."

He also told him: "Messenger of Allah, what trouble do you feel from your wives, and if you had divorced them, verily Allah is with you, His angels, Gabriel, Mika'il, I and Abū Bakr and the believers are with you."

Muhammad relaxed. "I went on talking to him until the signs of anger disappeared on his face . . . and he laughed," 'Umar narrates. In this new mood, the famous verses descended on the Prophet, freeing him from his oath respecting Mary, threatening his wives with divorce, and incorporating 'Umar's assurance that all the angels and believers supported him: "O Prophet!" said Allah. "Why do you prohibit thyself what God has made lawful to you, craving to please thy wives? . . . Allah has already ordained for you the dissolution of your oaths." Allah also told the Prophet's wives in no uncertain terms that "his Lord if he divorces you will give him in exchange wives better than you." Allah warned them, particularly 'Āisha and Hafza, in the following terms: "If ye both turn repentant unto God,—for your hearts have swerved!—but if you back each other up against him, verily, Allah, He is the sovereign; and Gabriel, and the righteous of the believers, and the angels after that will back him up." Allah also told them that if they misbehaved, being the Prophet's wives would avail them nothing on the Day of Judgment. "God strikes out a parable to those who misbelieve: the wife of Noah and the wife of Lot; they were under two of our righteous servants, but they betrayed them: and they availed them nothing against God; and it was said, 'Enter the Fire with those who enter' " (Qurān 66:1-10).

The matter blew over, and they became his wives again. The Holy Prophet "had taken an oath of remaining away from them [his wives] for a month, and by now only twenty-nine days had passed, [but] he visited them." 'Āisha mischievously reminded the Prophet that it was not yet one month but only twenty-nine days, to which Muhammad replied: "At times, the month consists of twenty-nine days" (3507-3511).

Now 'Umar stood at the door of the mosque and called out at the top of his voice: "The Messenger of Allah has not divorced his wives." A verse chiding his followers for so readily believing in rumors also descended on Muhammad: "And if any matter pertaining to peace or alarm comes within their ken, they broadcast it. But if they had only referred it to the Apostle, or to those charged with authority among them, the proper investigators would indeed know it" (Qurān 4:83; *hadīs* 3507).

OPTION OF DIVORCE DIFFERENT FROM DIVORCE

It seems there were other occasions of domestic discord, some of them centering round money. These must have occurred in the early days at Medina, when Muhammad lacked funds. Once Abū Bakr and 'Umar went to Muhammad and found him "sitting sad and silent with his wives around him." He told the two fathers: "They [his wives and their daughters] are around me as you see, asking for extra money." Then Abū Bakr "got up, went to 'Āisha and slapped her on the neck; and 'Umar stood up and slapped Hafza" (3506).

On this occasion, the Prophet also gave his wives the option of a goodly departure if they "cared more for this world and its adornments than for Allah and His Apostle and the abode of the Hereafter" (Qurān 33:28–29). The wives chose the latter.

The moral of these *ahādīs* (3498–3506) as drawn by the translator is that "mere giving option to women to divorce does not make the divorce effective, but when it is really intended."

No Maintenance Allowance for a Divorcee

Fātima bint Quais was divorced by her husband "when he was away from home." She was very angry and went to Muhammad, who told her: "There is no lodging and maintenance allowance for a woman who has been given irrevocable divorce." But he mercifully helped her to find another husband. She had two suitors, Abū Jahm and Mu'āwiya. Muhammad advised against them both, for the former did "not put down his staff from his shoulder" (i.e., he beat his wives), and the latter was poor. In their place, he proposed the name of Usāma b. Zaid, the son of his slave and adopted son, Zaid (3512).

Later on a more generous sentiment prevailed. 'Umar ruled that husbands should provide their divorced wives with a maintenance allowance during the period of *'idda* on the ground that the true purpose of the Prophet's words had been misunderstood by Fātima, a mere woman. "We cannot abandon the Book of Allah and the *Sunnah* of our Apostle for the words of a woman" (3524).

'Idda is a period of waiting during which a woman cannot remarry. It normally lasts four months and ten days but ends sooner if the woman gives birth to a child. Once *'idda* has ended, the woman can contract another marriage (3536-3538).

Having to provide an allowance for four months at the most was not very difficult. Thus, since husbands had almost no fear of any future burden, and could get rid of their wives so easily, the threat of divorce hung heavily on Muslim women.

MOURNING

A woman whose husband dies must abstain from all adornment during the *'idda* period, but mourning for other relatives should not last for more than three days (3539–3552). Abū Sufyān, the father of Umm Habība, one of Muhammad's wives, died. She sent for some perfume and rubbed it on her cheeks, observing: "By Allah, I need no perfume but for the fact that I heard Allah's Messenger say, 'It is not permissible for a woman believing in Allah and the Hereafter to mourn for the dead beyond three days, but in the case of the death of the husband it is permissible for four months and ten days' " (3539).

LI'AN (INVOKING CURSE)

If a man finds his wife in adultery, he cannot kill the adulterous man, for that is forbidden; nor can he make an accusation against his wife, for unless he has four witnesses, he receives eighty stripes for making a false accusation against the chastity of a woman. But if the witnesses are not always forthcoming, which is most likely in such a case, what should he do? This was the dilemma confronting the believers. An *ansār* posed the problem to Muhammad: "If a person finds his woman along with a man, and if he speaks about it, you would lash him; and if he kills, you will kill him, and if he keeps quiet, he shall have to consume anger." Muhammad supplicated God: "Allah, solve this problem" (3564). And a verse descended on him (Qurān 24:6) which gives us the practice of *li'ān*. The word literally means "oath," but technically it stands for that particular form of oath which brings about separation between husband and wife with the help of four oaths and one curse. A husband's solitary evidence can be accepted if he bears witness four times with an oath by Allah that he is solemnly telling the truth and then invokes the curse of Allah upon himself if he is lying. Similarly, the wife can solemnly deny the accusation four times and then invoke the wrath of Allah on herself if her accuser is telling the truth. One of them must be lying, but this closes the chapter, and they are wife and husband no more (3553–3577).

EMANCIPATING A SLAVE

For some unexplained reason, a few chapters at the end of the book dealing with marriage and divorce are on slaves. This may be due to a faulty method of classification, or it may be that emancipating a slave was considered a form of *talāq*, which literally means "freeing" or "undoing the knot"; or it may be that the subject really belongs to the next book, which is on business transactions—a slave, after all, was no more than a chattel.

Modern Muslim writers trying to boost Islam as a humane ideology make much of the sayings of Muhammad on the emancipation (*'itq*) of slaves. But the fact remains that Muhammad, by introducing the concept of religious war and by denying human rights to non-Muslims, sanctioned slavery on an unprecedented scale. Pre-Islamic Arabs, even in their wildest dreams, never imagined that the institution of slavery could take on such massive proportions. Zubair, a close companion of the Prophet, owned one thousand slaves when he died. The Prophet himself possessed at least fifty-nine slaves at one stage or another, besides thirty-eight servants, both male and female. Mirkhond, the Prophet's fifteenth-century biographer, names them all in his *Rauzat-us-Safa*. The fact is that slavery, tribute, and booty became the main props of the new Arab aristocracy. Slaves continued to suffer under the same old disabilities. They were the property of their master (*saiyid*), who could dispose of them as he liked, selling them, gifting them away, hiring them out, lending them, mortgaging them. Slaves had no property rights. Whatever they acquired became the property of their masters. The master had the right to live in concubinage with his female slaves if they confessed Islam or belonged to the "People of the Book." The Qurān (*Sūra* 4:3, 4:24, 4:25, 23:6) permitted this. Slavery was interwoven with the Islamic laws of sale, inheritance, and marriage. And though the slaves fought for their Muslim masters, they were not entitled to the spoils of war according to Muslim religious law.

EMANCIPATION OF SLAVES

The emancipation of slaves was not unknown in pre-Islamic Arabia. Slaves could gain their freedom in several ways. One way, and a very common one, of course, was that they were ransomed by their relatives. Another was when a master granted his slave a free and unconditional emancipation (*'itq*). There were two other forms of emancipation: *tadbir* and *kitabah*. In the first, the master declared that on his death his slaves would be free. In the second, slaves who were not ransomed by their relatives obtained their master's permission to earn their ransom by work.

We have already seen how Hakīm b. Hizām "freed one hundred slaves" (225) even before he became a Muslim. We have also observed that it was an old custom among the Arabs of more pious disposition to will that their slaves would be freed at their death, a practice which was opposed in some cases by Muhammad because he did not want such emancipations to take place at the expense of the heirs and relatives of the masters. On the whole, however, Muhammad's response to the practice was positive, but this did not make him into a Messiah of the slaves. On the other hand, he saw the time when the meek and the lowly would inherit the earth as a portent of the approaching end of the world. "When the slave-girl will give birth to her master, when the naked, barefooted would become the chiefs of the people—these are some of the signs of Doom," according to him (4).

To Muhammad, the freeing of a slave was an act of charity on the part of the master, not a matter of justice. In any case, a slave should not seek his emancipation by running away. "The slave who fled from his master committed an act of infidelity so long as he would not return to him," says Muhammad (129).

WHICH SLAVES DESERVE EMANCIPATION?

Only a believing slave deserves freedom. Someone once slapped his maid-slave in anger and then, in contrition, wanted to free her. When Muhammad was consulted, he said: "Bring her to me." She was brought. Muhammad asked her: "Where is Allah?" She replied:

"He is in the heaven." Muhammad asked: "Who am I?" "Thou art the Messenger of Allah," she answered. Muhammad gave his verdict: "Grant her freedom, she is a believing woman" (1094).

Thus there is merit in freeing a slave. "A Muslim who emancipates a Muslim [slave], Allah will save from Fire every limb of his for every limb of the slave, even his private parts for his" (3604).

One could also emancipate a jointly owned slave to the extent of one's share in him. For the rest a fair price for the slave was to be fixed, and the slave "will be required to work to pay for his freedom, but must not be overburdened" (3582).

Who Inherits a Slave's Property?

Even if a slave's person was freed, any property he might have or come to have was inherited by the emancipator (3584–3595). 'Āisha was ready to help a slave-girl, Barīra, to purchase her freedom on the condition that "I shall have the right in your inheritance." But the owner, though ready to free her for cash money, wanted to retain the right of inheritance for himself. Muhammad gave his judgment in favor of 'Āisha: "Buy her, and emancipate her, for the right of inheritance vests with one who emancipates." Muhammad then admonished: "What has happened to the people that they lay down conditions which are not found in the Book of Allah" (3585).

Other Disabilities

A freed slave is subjected to several other disabilities. He cannot seek any new alliance, nor can he offer himself as an ally without the permission of his former owner. One "who took the freed slave as an ally without the consent of his previous master, there is upon him the curse of Allah and that of His angels and that of the whole mankind" (3600).

Slavery Has Its Own Reward

Beyond all that may be said or done, the condition of a slave is no great evil. It has its own reward. "When a slave looks to the welfare of his master and worships Allah well, he has two rewards for him" (4097).

PROPER READING FOR MUHAMMAD'S DESCENDANTS

We close the "Book of Marriage and Divorce" by quoting one of the very last *ahādīs*. It is on a different subject but interesting. 'Alī, the Prophet's son-in-law, says: "He who thinks that we [the members of the Prophet's family] read anything else besides the book of Allah and the *Sahīfa* [a small book or pamphlet that was tied to the scabbard of his sword] tells a lie. This *Sahīfa* contains problems pertaining to the ages of the camels and the recompense of injuries, and it also records the words of the prophet. . . . He who innovates or gives protection to an innovator, there is a curse of Allah and that of his angels and that of the whole humanity upon him" (3601).

7

Business Transactions, Inheritances, Gifts, Bequests, Vows and Oaths

The ninth book is the "Book of Business Transactions" *(al-Buyu')*. Let us remind ourselves that Muhammad in his pre-prophetic days was a merchant, so his views on the subject should be of interest.

Speculation Forbidden

Muhammad forbids speculation. "He who buys food grains should not sell it until he has taken possession of it" (3640). During Muhammad's own lifetime, as the control of Arabia passed into his hands, his injunctions became state policy. Sālim b. 'Abdullah reports: "I saw people being beaten during the lifetime of Allah's Messenger in case they bought the food grain in bulk and then sold them at that spot before taking it to their places" (3650).

Because of their speculative nature, Muhammad also disallowed "futures" transactions. He forbade "selling ahead for years and selling of fruits before they become ripe" (3714). Transactions with the help of documents (probably the *hundi* or bill of exchange system), were also made unlawful. The injunction was implemented with the help of the police. "I saw the sentinels snatching these documents from the people," reports Sulaimān (3652).

Outbidding

Muhammad also forbade outbidding. "A person should not enter into a transaction when his brother is already making a transaction and he should not make a proposal of marriage when his brother has already made a proposal except when he gives permission" (3618). He also forbade brokerage, "the selling of goods by a townsman on behalf of a man of the desert" (3621).

CONTRACTS

Muhammad recognized the contract system. Unless otherwise laid down in the contract, "he who buys a tree after it has been fecunded, its fruits belongs to one who sells it. . . . and he who buys a slave, his property belongs to one who sells him" (3704).

TENANCY

Muhammad also forbade the leasing of land. "He who has land should cultivate it, but if he does not find it possible, he should lend it to his Muslim brother, but he should not accept rent from him" (3719).

THE PROPHET AS A LANDLORD

Several *ahādīs* (3758-3763) show that Muhammad's own business practices could be sharp. 'Abdullah, the son of 'Umar, reports that "when Khaibar had been conquered, it came under the sway of Allah, that of his Messenger and that of the Muslims" (3763). Muhammad made an agreement with the Jews of Khaibar that they could retain the date-palms and the land on the condition that they worked them with their own wealth (seeds, implements) and gave "half of the yield to Allah's Messenger" (3762). Out of this half, "Allah's Apostle got the fifth part," and the rest was "distributed" (3761). This lends credence to the common observation that those who control the funds, whether in the name of Allah or the state or the poor, are apt to spend them first on themselves.

These acquisitions enabled Muhammad to give each of his wives 100 *wasqs* (1 *wasq* = about 425 English pounds), 80 *wasqs* of dates, and 20 *wasqs* of barley per year. When 'Umar became the Khalīfa he distributed the land and gave the wives of Allah's Apostle the option of taking the land or the yearly *wasqs*. Their reactions to this offer differed. 'Āisha and Hafza, two wives of the Prophet, "opted for land and water" (3759).

Improper Earnings

Muhammad also "forbade the charging of price of the dog, and earnings of a prostitute and sweets offered to a *Kāhin* [soothsayer]" (3803). He said that "the worst earning is the earning of a prostitute, the price of a dog and the earning of a cupper" (3805).

Muhammad had a great dislike for dogs. He said: "It is your duty to kill the jet-black [dog] having two spots [on the eyes], for it is a devil" (3813). 'Abdullah, 'Umar's son, tells us that the Prophet "ordered to kill dogs, and he sent men to the corners of Medina that they should be killed. . . . and we did not spare any dog that we did not kill" (3810, 3811). Later on, on representation, an exception was made in the case of dogs meant for hunting and for protecting the herds. With the exception of these dogs, anyone who kept a dog "lost two *qīrāt* [the name of a measure] of reward every day" (3823).

Muhammad also forbade the sale of wine, carcasses, swine, and idols. "May Allah the Exalted and Majestic destroy the Jews; when Allah forbade the use of fat of the carcass for them [see Leviticus 3:17], they melted it, and then sold it and made use of its price" (3840).

Barter Disapproved

In some matters, the Prophet was modern. He disapproved of the barter system and in its place stood for money-exchange. The collector of the revenues from Khaibar once brought Muhammad some fine dates. Muhammad asked whether all the dates of Khaibar were of such fine quality. The collector said: "No. We got one *sā* [of fine dates] for two *sās* [of inferior dates]." Muhammad disapprovingly replied: "Don't do that; rather sell the inferior quality of dates for *dirhams* [money], and then buy the superior quality with the help of *dirhams*" (3870).

RIBĀ

Muhammad also forbade *ribā,* which includes both usury and interest. He "cursed the accepter of interest and its payer, and one who records it, and the two witnesses"; and he said: "They are all equal" (3881).

Though he forbade interest, Muhammad himself sent Abū Bakr to the Qainuqā tribe of Medina with a message bidding them to "lend to God at good interest," using the very words of the Qurān, "to lend to God a goodly loan" (5:12). When they rebuffed him, their fate was sealed, and they were driven away from their homes.

INHERITANCES, GIFTS, AND BEQUESTS

The next three books are the "Book of Inheritances" *(al-fara'id)*, the "Book of Gifts" *(al-hibāt)*, and the "Book of Bequests" *(al-wasīyya)*. In some ways, they are interrelated. The laws deriving from them are complicated, and we need not go beyond mentioning them here.

GIFTS

Anything given as a gift or charity should not be taken back. 'Umar had donated a horse in the Path of Allah (i.e., for *jihād)*. He found that the horse was languishing in the hands of the recipient, who was very poor, and considered buying it back. "Don't buy it back. . . . for he who gets back the charity is like a dog which swallows its vomit," Muhammad told him (3950).

WAQF

Muhammad favored *waqf,* i.e., the dedication of the corpus of a property to Allah. 'Umar told Muhammad: "I have acquired land in Khaibar [the land of the defeated Jews, which had now been conferred on the Companions]. I have never acquired property more valuable for me than this, so what do you command me to do with it? Thereupon, Allah's Apostle said: If you like, you may keep the corpus intact and give its produce as *sadaqa*. . . . 'Umar devoted it to the poor, to the nearest kin, and to the emancipation of slaves, and in the *way of Allah* and guests'' (4006).

Two-thirds for Legal Heirs

The estate of a deceased person can be distributed after certain obligations, such as funeral expenses and debts incurred by the deceased, have been met. A person who professes a religion other than Islam cannot inherit anything from a Muslim, and vice versa (3928). Another principle of inheritance is that ''the male is equal of the portion of two females'' (3933).

Muhammad says that one can will only one-third of one's property; the remaining two-thirds must go to the legal heirs. Muhammad visited Sa'd b. Abī Waqqās, on his deathbed. Sa'd had only one daughter. He wanted to know whether he could will two-thirds or half of his property in *sadaqa* (charity). The Prophet replied: ''Give one third, and that is quite enough. To leave your heirs rich is better than to leave them poor, begging from people'' (3991).

Debts

Muhammad was scrupulous about the debts of the deceased. That was the first charge on the property of a deceased person after the funeral expenses. In cases where the property was not sufficient to meet the debt obligations, money was raised through contributions. But when Muhammad became rich through conquest, he himself met these charges. ''When Allah opened the gateways of victory for him, he said: 'I am nearer to the believers than themselves, so if anyone dies leaving a debt, its payment is my responsibility, and if anyone leaves a property it goes to his heirs' '' (3944).

Muhammad's Last Will

On a certain Thursday when his illness took a serious turn, Muhammad said: ''I make a will about three things: Turn out the polytheists from the territory of Arabia; show hospitality to the foreign delegations as I used to do." The third the narrator forgot (4014).

Muhammad also wanted to write a will in his last moments. "Come, I may write for you a document; you would not go astray after that," he said, asking for writing materials. But 'Umar, who was present, said that the people already had the Qurān. "The Book of Allah is sufficient for us," he asserted, and thus it was unnecessary to tax Muhammad in his critical state. When those who were gathered around his bed then began to argue among themselves, Muhammad told them to "get up and go away" (4016).

'Umar might have been moved by genuine concern for the dying man, but the supporters of 'Alī later claimed that Muhammad in his last will had wanted to appoint 'Alī as his successor, and that 'Umar, in league with Abū Bakr, had prevented him from doing so by a dirty trick.

VOWS AND OATHS

The twelfth and thirteenth books, on vows *(al-nazar)* and oaths *(al-aiman)*, respectively, can be treated together. Muhammad discourages taking vows, for a vow "neither hastens anything nor defers anything" (4020). Allah has no need of a man's vows. A man once took a vow to walk on foot to the Ka'ba, but Muhammad said that "Allah is indifferent to his inflicting upon himself chastisement," and "commanded him to ride" (4029).

Muhammad also forbids believers to swear by Lāt or 'Uzzā or by their fathers. "Do not swear by idols, nor by your father," says Muhammad (4043). But he allows you to swear by God, something which Jesus forbade. "He who has to take an oath, he must take it by Allah or keep quiet," Muhammad says (4038).

ABROGATION OF AN OATH

Allah Himself allowed abrogation of oaths if need be. "God has already ordained for you the dissolution of your oaths" (Qurān 66:2).

A vow which is in disobedience to Allah or which is taken for un-Islamic ends is not to be fulfilled. Muslim jurists differ as to whether a vow taken during the days of ignorance (i.e., before one embraces Islam) is binding or not. Some hold that such a vow should be fulfilled if it is not against the teachings of Islam.

An oath can be broken, particularly if the oath-taker finds something better to do. "He who took an oath, but he found something else better than that, should do that which is better and break his oath," says Muhammad (4057). Some people once asked Muhammad to provide them with mounts. Muhammad swore: "By Allah, I cannot provide you a mount." But immediately after they were gone, he called them back and offered them camels to ride. Muhammad explained: "So far as I am concerned, by Allah, if He so wills, I would not swear, but if later on, I would see better than it, I would break the vow and expiate it and do that which is better" (4044).

The "God Willing" Clause

If one includes the proviso "God willing" *(Inshā Allāh)* when taking an oath, the vow must be fulfilled. Sulaimān (Solomon) had sixty wives. One day he said, "I will certainly have intercourse with them during the night and everyone will give birth to a male child who will all be horsemen and fight in the *cause of Allah.*" But only one of them became pregnant, and she gave birth to a premature child. "But if he had said *Inshā' Allah* he would have not failed," observes Muhammad. In other *ahādīs* about the same story, the number of wives increases from sixty to seventy and then to ninety (4066-4070).

8

Crime and Punishment (Qasāmah, Qisās, Hadūd)

The fourteenth, fifteenth, and sixteenth books all relate to the subject of crime: the forms and categories of crime, the procedure of investigating them, and the punishments resultant from having committed them.

Muslim *fiqh* (law) divides punishment into three heads: *hadd, qisās,* and *ta'zīr*. *Hadd* (pl. *Hadūd)* comprises punishments that are prescribed and defined in the Qurān and the *Hadīs.* These include stoning to death *(rajm)* for adultery *(zinā)*; one hundred lashes for fornication (Qurān 24:2-5); eighty lashes for slandering an "honorable" woman *(husun)*, i.e., accusing her of adultery; death for apostatizing from Islam *(irtidād)*; eighty lashes for drinking wine *(shurb)*; cutting off the right hand for theft *(sariqah,* Qurān 5:38-39*)*; cutting off of feet and hands for highway robbery; and death by sword or crucifixion for robbery accompanied by murder.

The law also permits *qisās,* or retaliation. It is permitted only in cases where someone has deliberately and unjustly wounded, mutilated, or killed another, and only if the injured and the guilty hold the same status. As slaves and unbelievers are inferior in status to Muslims, they are not entitled to *qisās* according to most Muslim *faqīhs* (jurists).

In cases of murder, the right of revenge belongs to the victim's heir. But the heir can forgo this right and accept the blood-price *(diyah)* in exchange. For the death of a woman, only half of the blood-price is due. The same applies to the death of a Jew or a Christian, but according to one school, only one-third is permissible in such cases. If a slave is killed, his heirs are not entitled to *qisās* and indemnity; but since a slave is a piece of property, his owner must be compensated with his full value.

The Muslim law on crime and punishment is quite complicated. Though the Qurān gives the broad outline, the *Hadīs* alone provides a living source and image.

QASĀMAH

The fourteenth book is the "Book of Oaths" *(al-qasāmah). Qasāmah* literally means "taking an oath," but in the terminology of the *sharī'ah,* it is an oath of a particular type and taken under particular conditions. For example, when a man is found slain, and the identity of his slayer is unknown, fifty persons from the nearest district take an oath that they neither killed the man nor knew who did it. This establishes their innocence.*

This was apparently the practice among the pre-Islamic Arabs, and Muhammad adopted it. Once a Muslim was found slain. His relatives accused the neighboring Jews. Muhammad told them: "Let fifty persons among you take oath for leveling the charge of murder against a person among them, and he would be surrendered to you." They declined to take the oath since they had not witnessed the murder. Then Muhammad told them that "the Jews will exonerate themselves by fifty of them taking this oath." They replied: "Allah's Messenger, how can we accept the oath of unbelieving people?" Then Muhammad paid the bloodwite of one hundred camels for the slain man out of his own funds (4119-4125).

Another *hadīs* specifically tells us that Allah's Messenger "retained the practice of *Qasāma* as it was in the pre-Islamic days" (4127).

*This injunction is based on the Old Testament. The Mosaic law prescribes that when a man is found slain in open country, and the identity of his killer is unknown, the elders of the town nearest to the slain man take a young heifer to a running brook, break its neck, wash their hands over the heifer, and testify: "Our hands did not shed this blood, neither did our eyes see it shed" (Deuteronomy 21:1-9).

Death Penalty for Apostasy and Rebellion

One can accept Islam freely, but one cannot give it up with the same freedom. The punishment for apostasy—for giving up Islam—is death, though not by burning. "Once a group of men apostatized from Islam. 'Ali burnt them to death. When Ibn 'Abbās heard about it, he said: If I had been in his place, I would have put them to sword for I have heard the apostle say, Kill an apostate but do not burn him for Fire is Allạh's agency for punishing the sinners" (Tirmizī, vol. I, 1357).*

Eight men of the tribe of 'Ukl became Muslims and emigrated to Medina. The climate of Medina did not suit them. Muhammad allowed them "to go to the camels of *sadaqa* and drink their milk and urine" (urine was considered curative). Away from the control of the Prophet, they killed the shepherds, took the camels and turned away from Islam. The Prophet sent twenty *ansārs* after them with an expert tracker who could follow their footprints. The apostates were brought back. "He [the Holy Prophet] got their hands cut off, and their feet, and put out their eyes, and threw them on the stony ground until they died" (4130). Another *hadīs* adds that while on the stony ground "they were asking for water, but they were not given water" (4132).

The translator gives us the verse from the Qurān according to which these men were punished: "The just recompense for those who wage war against Allah and His Messenger and strive to make mischief in the land is that they should be murdered, or crucified or their hands and their feet should be cut off on opposite sides, or they should be exiled" (Qurān 5:36).

Qisās

Qisās literally means "tracking the footsteps of an enemy"; but technically, in Muslim law, it is retaliatory punishment, an eye for an eye. It is the *lex talionis* of the Mosaic law.

*Abū Huraira tells us: "The Apostle sent us on a raiding mission. He commanded us to burn two men of the Quraish if we encountered them. He gave us their names. But when we went to him to take his leave, he said, 'Don't burn them in fire but put them to sword, for to torture by fire is Allah's prerogative' " (Sahīh Bukhārī Sharīf, *sahīh*, 1219).

A Jew smashed the head of an *ansār* girl and she died. Muhammad commanded that his head be crushed between two stones (4138). But in another case, which involved the sister of one of the Companions, bloodwite was allowed. She had broken someone's teeth. When the case was brought to Muhammad, he told her that "*Qisās* [retaliation] was a command prescribed in the Book of Allah." She made urgent pleas and was allowed to go free after paying a money compensation to the victim's next of kin (4151).

A Muslim and the Death Penalty

A Muslim who "bears testimony to the fact that there is no God but Allah, and I [Muhammad] am the Messenger of Allah," can be punished with the death penalty only if he is a married adulterer, or if he has killed someone (i.e., someone who is a Muslim, according to many jurists), or if he is a deserter from Islam (4152-4155). The translator tells us that there is almost a consensus of opinion among the jurists that apostasy from Islam must be punished with death. Those who think such a punishment is barbarous should read the translator's justification and rationale for it (note 2132).

Diyat (Indemnity)

Muhammad retained the old Arab practice of bloodwite (4166-4174). Thus, when a woman struck her pregnant co-wife with a tent-pole, causing her to have a miscarriage, he fixed "a male or female slave of best quality" as the indemnity "for what was in her womb." An eloquent relative of the woman pleaded for the cancellation of the indemnity, arguing: "Should we pay indemnity for one who neither ate, nor made any noise, who was just like a nonentity?" Muhammad brushed aside his objection, saying that the man was merely talking "rhymed phrases like the rhymed phrases of desert Arabs" (4170).

HADŪD

Hadūd, the penal law of Islam, is dealt with in the fifteenth book. The *ahādīs* in this book relate to measures of punishment defined either in the Qurān or in the *Sunnah.* The punishments include the amputation of limbs for theft and simple robbery; stoning to death for adultery; a hundred stripes for fornication; eighty stripes for falsely accusing a married woman, and also for drinking wine; and death for apostasy, as we have already seen.

Punishment for Theft

'Āisha reports that "Allah's Messenger cut off the hands of a thief for a quarter of *dīnār* and upwards" (4175). Abū Huraira reports the Prophet as saying: "Let there be the curse of Allah upon the thief who steals an egg and his hand is cut off, and steals a rope and his hand is cut off" (4185).

The *Hadīs* merely confirms the Qurān, which also prescribes: "And as for the man who steals and the woman who steals, cut off their hand as a punishment for what they have done, an exemplary punishment from Allah, and Allah is Mighty and Wise" (5:38). The translator, in a long two-page note, tells us that "it is against the background of this social security scheme envisaged by Islam that the Qurān imposes the severe sentence of hand-cutting as deterrent punishment for theft" (note 2150).

'Āisha reports a similar case. At the time of the victorious expedition to Mecca, a woman committed some theft. Although Usāma b. Zaid, the beloved of Muhammad, interceded in her behalf, her hand was cut off. "Hers was a good repentance," 'Āisha adds (4188). The translator assures us that after the punishment "There was a wonderful change in her soul" (note 2152).

Adultery and Fornication

Adultery is severely punished. 'Ubāda reports the Prophet as saying: "Receive teaching from me, receive teaching from me. Allah has ordained. . . . When an unmarried male commits adultery with an unmarried female, they should receive one hundred lashes and banishment for one year. And in case of a married male committing adultery with a married female, they shall receive one hundred lashes and be stoned to death" (4191).

'Umar adds his own emphasis: "Verily Allah sent Muhammad

with truth and He sent down the Book upon him, and the verse of stoning was included in what was sent down to him." 'Umar is emphatic because in the Qurān there is no punishment for adultery as such, though there is one for the larger category of *zinā,* which means sexual intercourse between parties not married to each other. In this sense, the term includes adultery as well as fornication. And the punishment provided for both is one hundred stripes and not stoning to death as enjoined in the *Sunnah* for adultery. "The whore and the whoremonger. Flog each of them with a hundred stripes," preaches the Qurān (24:2).

'Umar was apprehensive that people might neglect the *Sunnah* and appeal to the Book as grounds for a lenient punishment for their adultery. Therefore, he said quite emphatically: "I am afraid that, with the lapse of time, the people may forget it and may say, 'We do not find the punishment of stoning in the Book of Allah,' and thus go astray by abandoning this duty prescribed by Allah. Stoning is a duty laid down in Allah's Book for married men and women who commit adultery" (4194).

SELF-CONFESSED ADULTERY

There are some gruesome cases. A fellow named Mā'iz came to Muhammad and told him that he had committed adultery. He repeated his confession four times. Confessing four times stands for the four witnesses who are required to testify in case of adultery. Upon finding that the man was married and also not mad, Muhammad ordered him to be stoned to death. "I was one of those who stoned him," says Jābir b. 'Abdullah, the narrator of this *hadīs* (4196).

After this incident Muhammad harangued his followers: "Behold, as we set out for *Jihād* in the cause of Allah, one of you lagged behind and shrieked like the bleating of a male goat, and gave a small quantity of milk. By Allah, in case I get hold of him, I shall certainly punish him" (4198). The translator explains that by the metaphor of goat and milk, the Prophet means sexual lust and semen.

Similarly, a woman of Ghāmid, a branch of Azd, came to

Muhammad and told him that she had become pregnant as a result of fornication. She was spared till she had given birth to her child. An *ansār* took the responsibility of suckling the infant and "she was then stoned to death" (4025). Another *hadīs* tells us how it was done. "She was put in a ditch up to her chest and he [Muhammad] commanded people and they stoned her" (4206). Other traditions tell us that the Prophet himself cast the first stone.

Fornication and Adultery Joined

In a case of *zinā* in which one party is married and the other party unmarried, the former is punished for adultery and the latter for fornication. Abū Huraira narrates one such case involving a man and woman belonging to desert tribes. A young bachelor found employment as a servant in a certain household and committed *zinā* with the master's wife. His father gave one hundred goats and a slave-girl in ransom, but when the case was brought before Muhammad, he judged it "according to the Book of Allah." He ordered the slave-girl and the goats to be returned and punished the young man for fornication "with one hundred lashes and exile for one year." The woman was punished for adultery. "Allah's Messenger made pronouncement about her and she was stoned to death" (4029).

Model Persecution

These cases provide a model for all future persecutions. When a woman is to be stoned, a chest-deep hole is dug for her, just as was done in the case of Ghamdīya (the woman of Ghāmid), so that her nakedness is not exposed and the modesty of the watching multitude is not offended. No such hole need be dug for a man, as no such hole was dug for Mā'iz, the self-confessed adulterer whose case we have just narrated.

The stoning is begun by the witnesses, followed by the *imām* or *qāzī*, and then by the participating believers. But in the case of a self-confessed criminal, the first stone is cast by the *imām* or *qāzī*, following the example of the Prophet in the case of Ghamdīya. And then the multitudes follow. The Qurān and the *Sunnah,* in fact, enjoin the believers to both watch and actively participate in the execution. "Do not let pity for them take hold of you in Allah's religion. . . . and let a party of the believers witness their torment," the Qurān urges while prescribing punishment for the fornicators.

A Mosaic Practice Revived

The punishment of stoning to death *(rajm)* is Mosaic. The Old Testament prescribes it for adultery and fornication (Deuteronomy 22:19-23), and also for those who "serve other gods" (Deuteronomy 13:10). Muhammad retained it for adultery but prescribed death by other means for crimes like apostasy.

Among the Jews themselves, by the time of Muhammad, stoning had fallen into disuse. According to one tradition, a Jew and a Jewess who had committed adultery were brought to Muhammad. He asked the Jews what their *Torah* prescribed for such offenses. The Jews replied: "We darken their [the culprits'] faces and make them ride on a donkey with their faces turned to the opposite direction." Muhammad said: "Bring the *Torah*." The prescribed punishment was found to be stoning to death. So "Allah's Messenger pronounced judgment about both of them and they were stoned," says 'Abdullah, the son of 'Umar. "I was one of those who stoned them, and I saw him [the Jew] protecting her [the Jewess] with his body," he adds (4211).

Another *hadīs* gives more details about the same incident. The Jews sent the two accused to Muhammad, telling their chiefs: "Go to Muhammad; if he commands you to blacken the face and award flogging as punishment, then accept it; but if he gives verdict for stoning, then avoid it." Muhammad was grieved at this softening of the Scriptures. But Allah comforted him: "O Messenger, the behaviour of those who vie with one another in denying the truth should not grieve you" (Qurān 5:41). Allah also told him that "they who do not judge in accordance with what Allah has revealed—they are indeed wrongdoers, they are the iniquitous" (5:45, 47). The man and woman were stoned to death at Muhammad's order, and he was happy and thanked Allah: "O Allah, I am the first to revive thy command when they had made it dead" (4214).

A Slave Adulteress

A more lenient view was taken in cases of adultery involving slave-women. A slave-woman, even if she was married, was not to be stoned to death, and if she was unmarried, she was liable to half the penalty (fifty strokes). If a slave-girl is unprotected (unmarried) and "commits adultery, then flog her and if she commits adultery again, then flog her and then sell her even for a rope of hair" (4221).

Flogging Could Be Postponed

If a woman has just delivered and there is an apprehension that flogging might kill her, she may be spared "until she is alright" (4225).

'Alī says: "O people, impose the prescribed punishment upon your slaves, those who are married and those not married, for a slave-woman belonging to Allah's Messenger had committed adultery, and he committed me to flog her. But she had recently given birth to a child and I was afraid that if I flogged her I might kill her. So I mentioned that to Allah's Messenger and he said 'You have done well' " (4224). The Prophet was a merciful man.

On the basis of this *hadīs,* Muslim jurists conclude that flogging can be spread over several days, depending on the physical condition of the offender; and if he is sick, the flogging can be postponed until he recovers.

Punishment for Drinking

The punishment for drinking is equally harsh. Muhammad prescribed "forty stripes with *two* lashes." So did Abū Bakr, but 'Umar came and prescribed eighty stripes (4226).

A man charged with drinking was brought before 'Usmān, the third Khalīfa, and 'Usmān ordered 'Alī to lash him. 'Alī in turn ordered Hasan and then 'Abdullah b. Ja'far to lash him. While 'Abdullah was flogging the victim, 'Alī counted the stripes. When the number forty was reached, 'Alī said: "Stop now. Allah's Messenger gave forty stripes, and Abū Bakr also gave forty stripes, and 'Umar gave eighty stripes, and all these fall under the category of the *Sunnah,* but this one [forty stripes] is dearer to me" (4231).

TA'ZĪR

Hadūd punishments are prescribed by the Qurān and the *Hadīs.* But there is another class of punishment, called *ta'zīr,* in which the judge can use his own discretion. In such cases, "none should be given more than ten lashes" (4234). But the majority of later Muslim jurists think differently. They hold that the number of stripes is to be determined on the basis of the enormity of the crime.

PUNISHMENT HAS ITS REWARD

At the end, Muhammad assures the believer that if he committed a crime, and upon him is "imposed the prescribed punishment and that is carried out, that is his expiation for that sin" (4237).

JUDICIAL DECISIONS

The sixteenth book deals with judicial decisions *(aqdiyya).* It is small in size and discusses such matters as the qualities of a good judge and a good witness. A judge "should not judge between two persons when he is angry" (4264). If he does his best and also gives the right judgment, he has two rewards. If he does his best but errs, he still has one reward (4261). The excellent witness is he "who produces his evidence before he is asked for it" (4268).

According to the Qurān, a woman's testimony *(shahadah)* has half the weight of a man's (2:282). In a dispute regarding property or debt, the evidence of two men or of one man and two women is required. In cases involving *hadūd,* the evidence of a woman is not considered at all. Nor is the testimony of Jews, Christians, and unbelievers considered in a strictly Islamic law court.

A few other matters that are not connected with judicial decisions, such as hospitality, are also discussed in this book. Muhammad says that one should show hospitality to guests but wisely adds that "hospitality extends for three days, and what is beyond that is *Sadaqa* [charity]" (4286).

Crime with Impunity

The Islamic laws on crime and punishment seem to be foolproof and ironclad, but apparently this is not really so. According to some, Maulana Mohammad Matin Hashmi's book *Islamic Hadūd,* recently published in Pakistan, is as good as a manual on how to steal without attracting extreme penalties under Islamic law. Hashmi says that the theft of many articles, such as books, birds, and bread, is not covered by Islamic law. Fresh vegetables, fruit and firewood, meat and chicken and musical instruments can be stolen with impunity. Also exempt are bricks, cement, marble, glass, mats, and carpets from mosques, and loaded camels and merchandise from trade centers (PTI, November 15, 1981).

9

Religious Wars (Jihād)

The seventeenth book is the "Book of Religious Wars and Expeditions" *(Kitāb al-Jihād Wa'l-Siyar).*

Jihād is a divinely ordained institution in Islam. By many authorities it is counted as one of the pillars of Islam. Theologically, it is an intolerant idea: a tribal god, Allah, trying to be universal through conquest. Historically, it was an imperialist urge masked in religious phraseology.

Three Options

Muhammad told those whom he made chiefs of his raiding parties: "Fight in the name of Allah and in the way of Allah. Fight against those who disbelieve in Allah. Make a holy war; do not embezzle the spoils." He also told them to offer their enemies three options or courses of action: "Invite them to accept Islam; if they respond to you, accept it from them. . . . Then invite them to migrate from their lands to the land of *Muhājirs* [i.e., Medina; in the early days of Muhammad's stay in Medina, living there was a sign of acceptance of Islam and loyalty to Muhammad], and inform them that, if they do so, they shall have all the privileges and obligations of the *Muhājirs.* If they refuse to migrate, tell them that they will have the status of Bedouin Muslims and will be subjected to the Commands of Allah like other Muslims, but they will not get any share from the spoils of war or *Fa'i.* . . . If they refuse to accept Islam, demand from them the *Jizyā.* . . . If they refuse to pay the tax, seek Allah's help and fight them" (4294). Allah, the spoils of war, the *jizyā*—all beautifully and profitably interwoven.

RAID WITHOUT WARNING

It is not always necessary to give warning or offer options in advance. If need be, this requirement can be waived. Religious conversion is likely to ensue from a military victory followed by pillage and plunder. "The Messenger of Allah made a raid upon Banū Mustaliq while they were unaware and their cattle were having a drink at the water. He killed those who fought and imprisoned others" (4292).

All is fair in love and war, particularly a war fought in the Way of Allah. As the Prophet says, "war is a stratagem" (4311), or, as some others have translated it, "cunning."

CHILDREN OF THE POLYTHEISTS

In *jihād,* all arms-bearing males of the enemy are killed, but Muhammad "disapproved of the killing of women and children" (4319). They are generally taken prisoners and then enslaved or sold or released after ransom is exacted. But if they are killed, no song need be made about it. Sa'b b. Jassāma said to Muhammad: "Messenger of Allah, we kill the children of polytheists during the night raids. He [Muhammad] said: They are from them" (4323).

JUSTIFICATION OF BURNING TREES

Muhammad surrounded a Jewish tribe called Banū Nazīr, residing in the vicinity of al-Madina, and ordered their date-palms "to be burnt and cut." Since destroying palm trees was something of a sacrilege in Arabia, this shocked the Arabs. So Allah hastened to speak through Muhammad: "Whatever trees you have cut down or left standing on their trunks, it is with the permission of Allah so that he may disgrace the evil-doers" (Qurān 59:5; *hadīs* 4324).

Fortified by this revelation, Muhammad cut down and burned the celebrated vineyards of the enemy at at-Tā'if in the eighth year of the Hijra. That was another contribution by Muhammad to the new ethics of war, unknown to the Arabs before.

SPOILS OF WAR

The plundering of infidels and polytheists is a central concept in the Muslim religion, and was the linchpin in the economy of the *ummah* for centuries. Allah made war booty lawful for the Muslims. "Eat ye the spoils of war, it is lawful and pure," says the Qurān (8:69).

One *hadīs* tells us that the spoils were made lawful especially for the *ummah*. "The spoils of war were not lawful for any people before us. This is because Allah saw our weakness and humility and made them lawful for us" (4327).

Division

Essentially, the spoils belong to Allah and His Apostle. "They ask thee concerning the spoils of war. Say: "The spoils of war are for Allah and the Apostle" (Qurān 8:1). But since the *mujāhid* does not live by Allah alone, and also as a favor and extra incentive, he is given a share in it.

The translator explains: "A *mujāhid* fights to uphold the cause of righteousness and for the supremacy of Islam, and if in this fight he gets a share in the spoils of war, it is an extra favour to him" (note 2229).

Abdullah Yusuf 'Alī, translator and commentator of the Qurān, in commenting on this verse puts the matter still more eloquently. He says that "booty taken in a lawful and just war does not belong to any individual. If he fought for such accessory rewards, he fought from wrong motives. It belongs to the Cause, in this case the cause of God, as administered by his Apostle. Any portion given out to individuals are accessory gifts, windfalls from the bounty of the Commander."*

*Abdullah Yusuf 'Alī, trans., *Glorious Qurān* (Cairo: Daral-Kitab al Masri, 1934).

A GREAT MOTIVATING FORCE

Despite the pious rhetoric, material incentives had to be provided. The lure of plunder was a great motivating force, all the more powerful because of the religious phraseology. In fact, Muhammad fully satisfied this motive and constantly appealed to it. He reminded the believers of how they "slew a part [of their enemies] and another part made captive"; and how Allah gave them "their [enemies'] land, and their dwellings, and their property for an inheritance" (Qurān 33:26–27).

Muhammad was as good as his word. Within a few months, he set out on an expedition against Khaibar, which he took by surprise. The booty was very large, but Muhammad distributed it only among those who had accompanied him on the previous occasion.

MUHAMMAD ACCUSED OF CONCEALING SPOILS

The spoils of war were most welcome, but the process of allocating the plunder was rarely easy sailing. The occasions when the spoils were distributed were, in fact, pretty rough. The atmosphere was charged with expectation and excitement, and was full of claims, grievances, recriminations, suspicion, and accusations. Even Muhammad was once accused of concealing spoils (Tirmizī, vol. II, *hadīs* 868), and supernal intervention had to take place in order to quiet the suspicion. "It is not for a prophet to cheat or be false to his trust. If any person is so false, he shall, on the Day of Judgment, restore what he misappropriated," said Allah (3:161). Commenting on this verse, the translator of the *Glorious Qurān*, Abdullah Yusuf 'Alī, assures us that "those low suspicions were never believed in by any sensible person, and they have no interest for us now" (note 472).

The distribution of the booty was always a passionate issue. Ibn Ishāq reports that on one such occasion, after the capture of Hunain, Muhammad was mobbed by the men. "Divide our spoil of camels and herds among us," the *mujāhids* demanded, surrounding Muhammad "until they forced him back against a tree and his mantle was torn from him." He cried: "Give me back my mantle. I swear by Allah that if I had as many sheep as the trees of Tilham I would distribute them among you. You have not found me niggardly or cowardly or false."*

Al-Ghanimah and Fai'

There are two forms of war gains: *al-ghanīmah* and *fai'*. The first includes spoils which fall to the lot of the Muslims after an armed conflict; the other accrues when the non-Muslims surrender without offering resistance. "If you come to a township which has surrendered without a formal war and you stay therein, you have a share [in the form of an award] in [the properties obtained from] it. If a town disobeys Allah and the Messenger [and fights against the Muslims] one-fifth of the booty seized therefrom is for Allah and His Apostle and the rest is for you" (4346).

The Qurānic sanction for this principle of the division of the booty is contained in the following verse: "Know that of that which you seize as spoils [*ghanīmah*], a fifth-part [*khums*] belongs to Allah, to His Apostle, his family, the orphans, the poor, the traveller . . . " (8:41).

The *fai'*, gains from a war not actively fought, on the other hand,

**Sīrat Rasūl Allah*, p. 594.

belongs wholly to the Prophet. Along with the *khums,* it is entirely at his disposal. The very word and the principle of its disposal derive from the Qurān: "What Allah gives [*afā'a*] to His Apostle of the people of the cities belongs to Allah, His Apostle, his family, orphans, the poor, and the traveller" (59:7). This is based on the divine principle that all the possessions of the unbelievers must revert to Muhammad and his family and, when they are no more, to the Muslims in general.

In due course, the rules relating to the distribution of booty and the disposal of *fai'* were codified by the various *fiqh* schools. According to this code, it was unlawful for a Muslim conqueror to leave anything in the hands of the infidels. Such property must be carried away and four-fifths of it distributed among the soldiers. During a retreat, any such property that cannot be carried away, including the cattle, should be destroyed.

From the beginning of Muhammad's sojourn in Medina, all prisoners, whether men, women, or children, were regarded as legitimate items of plunder. They were either distributed among the believers as slaves or sold into slavery or held against payment of ransom by their relatives. Thus prisoners were a rich source of revenue. When seventy men were captured in the Battle of Badr, Muhammad consulted Abū Bakr and 'Umar about their treatment. Abū Bakr took a view that was more economic and also more humane. "They are our kith and kin. I think you should release them after getting from them ransom. This will be a source of strength to us against the infidels," he advised. But 'Umar took a view that was more theological and also more cruel. He advised that they should be put to death, for they were "leaders of the disbelievers and veterans amongst them" (4360). The economic view prevailed, at least in this case.*

*Most male prisoners were released on the payment of ransom money, except for a few who were killed. One of these was Nassar b. Alhāris. A Muslim combatant, Muqdād, tried to save him by claiming him as his prisoner, but Muhammad exclaimed: "O Allah, deprive by Thy bounty Muqdād of the reward of his worship. O 'Alī, arise and strike off his [Nassar's] head," which 'Alī readily did. Another unfortunate fellow was Utbah, who had "uttered two distichs" (couplets) when Muhammad fled Mecca. Utbah pleaded with Muhammad: "O Muhammad, if thou slayest me who will take care of my children and little ones?" "The fire of hell!" Muhammad replied. And

A Muslim chief who conquered a territory was at liberty to leave the land in the possession of the conquered, provided that they paid tribute and became tenants on their own land. This provision was supported by Muhammad's own example. When the Jews of Khaibar were defeated, they were allowed for some time to continue cultivating their land on the payment of half the harvest (3762). The chief was also at liberty to distribute the land among his soldiers, but more often this was not done. The land was considered *fai'* and declared to be part of the public domain. It was used in the interest of the whole Muslim community (for the payment of troops and officers, and for the building of bridges, forts, and mosques), and kept as a permanent source of income for future generations.

Another imposition, called *jizyā,* also belongs to the *fai'*. It was a poll tax levied on all unbelievers of certain categories and on payment of this tax they were allowed freedom in the exercise of their faith. At first this benefit was limited to the Jews and Christians, but later on, as the Muslim empire grew, it was extended to other subject peoples. These peoples were called *zimmīs,* "responsibility" of the Muslims. Imperialism has the same language in every age.

The institution of *jizyā* derives from the Qurān: "Fight those who believe not in God and in the last day, and . . . those to whom the Book has been brought, until they pay the tribute [*jizyā*] in abasement" (9:29). "In abasement" is an active clause and includes many humiliating provisions. The *zimmīs* are to carry no weapons; they are not to ride on horseback; they are to wear a special kind of girdle (*zunnār*) and are to fasten a piece of colored cloth (*ghiyār*)—Jews a yellow one and Christians a blue one—on their clothes to make it easy to distinguish them from Muslims. They are not to build new churches and temples, though they can repair old ones; they cannot engage in public worship; they are not to give offense to the Muslims by ringing church or temple bells; in short, they are not to do anything that would display their infidelity in the face of the tokens of Islam, such as their public prayers and festivals. There are many other disabilities of the same kind.

at his command, as the victim's head was struck off, the Apostle exclaimed: "I thank Allah that He has caused thee to be slain, and has thereby gladdened my eyes" (Mirkhond, vol. I, part II, pp. 338-339).

THE MAIN SOURCE OF LIVELIHOOD

After Muhammad established himself in Medina, the main source of livelihood for his Companions for quite some time was loot from raids on non-Muslim tribes. Tirmizī tells us that a goatherd belonging to the Banū Salīm once passed by a group of the Companions of the Apostle. When he greeted them in the Muslim fashion, they said among themselves: "This man has saluted us in this way with a view to protect himself." "Then they got up and killed him and took away his goats" (vol. II, p. 889). Muhammad sent out his men to waylay non-Muslim tribes and to make raids on them. He gave the belongings of anyone who was killed to the Muslim who killed him as "a sort of encouragement to the Muslims to participate in *jihād,*" as the translator puts it (note 2230).

Abū Qatāda reports that while accompanying the Prophet on an expedition in the year of the Battle of Hunain, he killed a polytheist enemy and was awarded his belongings. "I sold the armour (which was a part of my share of the booty) and brought with the sale proceeds a garden in the street of Banū Salam. This was the first property I acquired after embracing Islam," he says (4340). 'Umar tells us: "The prophet sent an expedition to Najd and I was among the troop. They got a large number of camels as booty. Eleven or twelve camels came to the lot of every fighter and each one of them also got one extra camel" (4330). He also tells us that he acquired land in Khaibar that had belonged to the defeated Jews, a property more valuable than anything he had ever possessed (4006). Khaibar was a populous valley inhabited by the Jews. They were raided and captured and their property confiscated.

As the amount of war booty increased, Muhammad and the other Emigrants became rich enough to pay the *ansārs* for their help and gifts. Anas reports that after Muhammad's migration to Medina, "a person placed at his [Muhammad's] disposal some date-palms . . . until the lands of Quraiz and Nazīr were conquered. Then he began to return to him whatever he had received" (4376). So did the others. "When the Messenger of Allah had finished the war with the people . . . the *Muhājirs* [Emigrants] returned to the *Ansārs* [Helpers] all the gifts they had given them" (4375).

Muhammad's Share

In the distribution of the booty, the Prophet received a fifth of all the spoils taken from the enemy. As a chief, he also had the first choice in everything, whether slaves or women or property. Spoils obtained without a battle went entirely to him. The properties of the exiled Banū Nazīr, a Jewish tribe of Medina, were confiscated by Muhammad. He distributed some of them among his Quraish followers, to the exclusion of the *ansārs,* but kept a large part for himself. "As 'Umar says: 'The properties abandoned by Banū Nazīr were the ones which Allah bestowed upon His Apostle for which no expedition was taken either with cavalry or camel. These properties were particularly meant for the Holy Prophet. He would meet the annual expenditure of his family from the income thereof, and would spend what remained for purchasing horses and weapons as preparation for *Jihād*' " (4347).

One plot of land from the confiscated properties Muhammad turned into what is known as the "summer garden of Mary," his Coptic slave-wife. He also had seven other gardens in Medina, which according to some were bestowed on him by a Jew named Mukhayrīq, but according to others were a portion of the confiscated estates of the Banū Nazīr. Similarly, he had properties at Khaibar, part of the spoils that accrued to him when the Jewish community there was defeated.

The Quarrel over Muhammad's Properties

After Muhammad died, there was a quarrel over the inheritance of his property. 'Āisha tells us that Muhammad's other wives sent 'Usmān, the son-in-law of the Prophet and a future Khalīfa, "to Abū Bakr to demand from him their share from the legacy of the Holy Prophet." But, 'Āisha sided with her father's faction and not with her co-wives. She told them what Muhammad is supposed to have said: "We prophets do not have any heirs; what we leave behind is charity" (4351).

It was not much of charity, though, for as Abū Bakr says, "the household of the Messenger of Allah will [continue to] live on the income from these properties," but there was no formal transfer of ownership. Instead, the properties were placed under the joint management of 'Abbās, the Prophet's uncle, and 'Alī, the Prophet's son-in-law. The denial of this property so angered Fātimā, the Prophet's daughter, that she never spoke to Abū Bakr again for the rest of her life (4352).

In due course, 'Abbās and 'Alī themselves quarreled over the property which they jointly managed. They took their dispute to 'Umar, who had succeeded Abū Bakr as Khalīfa. "Commander of the Faithful, decide between me and this sinful, treacherous, dishonest liar ['Alī]," petitioned 'Abbās (4349).

RAIDS AND BATTLES

The book refers to many forays, raids, and battles of the Muslims. These are of two kinds, *ghazwāt* and *sariya.* A *ghazwāt* is a military expedition led by the *rasūl* or *imām* himself; a *sariya* is one led by his appointed lieutenant. The total number of expeditions was eighty-two, two every three months during Muhammad's stay in Medina. "Twenty-six are the *Ghazwāt* in which the Holy Prophet himself participated and fifty-six are the *Sariya*" (note 2283). Nine of the twenty-six *ghazwāt* expeditions were armed conflicts. So Muhammad's share of the booty must have been considerable.

There are other traditions too, more or less in confirmation of the above. According to Zaid b. Arqam, the Prophet personally led nineteen expeditions, in seventeen of which the narrator himself participated (4464, 4465). According to Jābir b. 'Abdullah, the number was twenty-one, and he himself participated in nineteen of them (4466). Another narrator participated in "seven military expeditions led by the Messenger and nine led by his lieutenants including Abū Bakr and Usāma b. Zaid (4469).

Many battles, not always in the order in which they were fought, are described by name; for example, the Battle of Hunain (4385-4392), the Battle of Tā'if (4393), the Battle of Badr (4394), the Battle of Ahzāb, or as it is popularly known, the Battle of the Ditch (4412), the Battle of Uhud (4413-4419), and the Battle of Khaibar

(4437-4441). The conquest of Mecca is also mentioned (4395-4396).

Miracles

In the accounts of these battles, several miracles are mentioned. On many an occasion, angels came and fought on the side of the Muslims. In most of the battles, Muhammad's own role was planning and praying. For example, at the Battle of Badr, Muhammad stretched out his hands and supplicated Allah in these words: "O Allah, accomplish for me what Thou hast promised to me. O Allah, if this small band of Muslims is destroyed, Thou will not be worshipped on this earth" (4360).

People who accompanied the Prophet on these expeditions report several miracles. Ibn Salama tells us that when they arrived at Hudaibiya "fourteen hundred in number," they found that the water in the local well was insufficient for such a large company. "The Messenger of Allah sat on the brink of the well. Either he prayed or spat into the well. The water welled up. We drank and watered the beasts as well" (4450). Another tradition in the same vein is quoted by Mirkhond, author of the Prophet's Persian biography. During the Battle of the Ditch, Jābir b. 'Abdullah slaughtered a young goat and placed its flesh in a pot, then ground one measure of barley into flour and leavened it, and invited Muhammad to a humble repast. To the consternation of Jābir and his family, Muhammad came with the whole army, numbering one thousand men. But Muhammad "approached in his holy person the pot and leaven, throwing into each of them some of the saliva of his *Kausar*-like mouth," and the meat and the loaves sufficed for the whole assembly (*Rauzat-us-Safa,* vol. II, part II, p. 467).

On another occasion, when people failed to respond to Muhammad's call to become Muslims, the angel in charge of the mountains greeted the Prophet and said: "I am the Angel in charge of the mountains, and thy Lord has sent me to thee. . . . If thou wishest that I should bring together the two mountains that stand opposite to each other at the extremities of Mecca to crush them in between, I would do that." This was told to 'Āisha by the Prophet himself (4425).

EXPULSION OF THE JEWS AND CHRISTIANS

"I will expel the Jews and Christians from the Arabian Peninsula and will not leave any but Muslims," Muhammad declared to 'Umar (4366).

Abū Huraira reports: "We were sitting in the mosque when the Messenger of Allah came and said: Let us go to the Jews. We went out. . . . The Messenger of Allah called out to them: O ye assembly of Jews, accept Islam and you will be safe." When the answer was unsatisfactory, he told them: "You should know that the earth belongs to Allah and His Apostle, and I wish that I should expel you from this land" (4363).

Muhammad's expulsion plan began with the Jews of Medina and was implemented with great cruelty. He played on their hopes and fears and took them one by one. He first "expelled Banū Nazīr, and allowed Quraiza to stay on, and granted favour to them until they too fought against him. Then he killed their men, and distributed their women, children and properties among the Muslims. . . . The Messenger of Allah turned out all the Jews of Medina, Banu Qainuqā, and the Jews of Banū Hārisa and every other Jew who was in Medina," we are told by 'Abdullah, the son of 'Umar (4364).

THE BANŪ QURAIZA

The fate of the Banū Quraiza was rather gruesome. Muhammad said that Allah had commanded him to destroy the Quraiza. According to 'Āisha, the Prophet had hardly laid down his arms after returning from the Battle of the Ditch when Gabriel appeared and told him: "You have laid down arms. By God, we haven't laid down ours. So march against them." "Where?" Muhammad asked. Then Gabriel "pointed to the Banū Quraiza. So the Messenger of Allah fought against them . . . they surrendered . . . those of them who can fight [were] killed, their women and children taken prisoners and their properties distributed among Muslims" (4370).

A Qurānic verse put Allah's seal on the fate of this tribe of the People of the Book: "God did take them down from their strongholds, and cast terror into their hearts; [so that] some ye slew, and some ye made prisoners. And He made you heirs of their lands, their houses, and their goods" (Qurān 33:26-27).

Commanded by Allah through Gabriel, Muhammad approached the fort of the Quraiza, where they had gathered for shelter. He told them: "O ye brothers of monkeys and swines, we have arrived, Allah has disgraced you and brought His vengeance upon you." The Apostle "besieged them for twenty-five nights until they were sore pressed and God cast terror into their hearts." They surrendered unconditionally and were taken captive. Traditions and the pious biographies of the Prophet tell gleefully and in detail about the fate of the prisoners. We give the story as summarized by W. Muir in his *Life of Mahomet,* vol. III, pp. 276–279:

> The men and women were penned up for the night in separate yards. . . . [they] spent the night in prayer, repeating passages from their scriptures, and exhorting one another in constancy. During the night graves or trenches . . . were dug in the market-place. . . . when these were ready in the morning, Mahomet, himself a spectator of the tragedy, gave command that the captives should be brought forth in companies of five and six at a time. Each company was made to sit down by the brink of the trench destined for its grave, and there beheaded.* Party after party they were thus led out, and butchered in cold blood, till the whole were slain. . . . For Zoheir, an aged Jew, who had saved some of his allies of the Bani Aus . . . Sābit intervened and procured a pardon. . . . "But what hath become of all our chiefs—of Kāb, of Huwey, of Ozzāl, the son of Samuel?" asked the old man. . . . He received

*The victims remained in the dark about their fate till the end. Ibn Ishāq tells a touching story. When the men were being taken out in batches to the Apostle, they asked Ka'b what he thought would be done with them. He replied, "Will you never understand? Don't you see the summoner never stops and those who are taken away never return? By Allah it is death." "This went on until the Apostle made an end of them," Ibn Ishāq adds.

Ka'b was one of the chiefs of the Quraiza. His people loved him and said that his "face was like a Chinese mirror in which the virgins of the tribe could see themselves."

> to each inquiry the same reply;—they had all been slain already—"Then of what use is life to me any longer? Leave me not to that bloodthirsty man who has killed that are dear to me in cold blood—But slay me also, I entreat thee. Here take my sword, it is sharp; strike high and hard." Sābit refused, and gave him over to another, who under Alī's orders beheaded the aged man.
>
> Having sated his revenge, and drenched the market-place with the blood of eight hundred victims, and having given command for the earth to be smoothed over their remains, Mahomet returned from the horrid spectacle to solace himself with the charms of Rīhāna, whose husband and all whose male relatives had just perished in the massacre. He invited her to be his wife, but she declined, and chose to remain (as, indeed, having refused marriage, she had no alternative) his slave or concubine. She also declined the summons to conversion and continued in the Jewish faith.

The booty was divided into four classes—land, chattels, cattle, and slaves; and Muhammad took a fifth of each. There were (besides little children, who were counted with their mothers) a thousand captives; from his share of these, "Mahomet made certain presents to his friends, of female slaves and servants; and then sent the rest of the women and children to be sold among the Bedouin tribes of Najd, in exchange for horses and arms; for he kept steadily in view the advantage of raising around him a body of efficient horses."

The whole story in all its gruesomeness is narrated by Ibn Ishāq, Tabarī, and Mirkhond, Muhammad's biographers. Tabarī quotes Wāqidī, an earlier biographer, to the effect that Muhammad himself had "deep trenches dug up, took his seat there, and Alī and Zubair did the killing in his presence."* Ibn Hishām, another biographer, provides some material omitted in the other accounts. One of his stories shows how Muhammad utilized local conflicts to his own advantage. The two most important non-Jewish tribes of Medina were the Aus and the Banū Khazraj. The Quraiza were allied to the Aus, and therefore were not well liked by the Banū Khazraj. Thus, when Muhammad ordered the Jews beheaded, the "Khazraj began to cut

**Tārīkh Tabarī,* vol. I, pp. 303-304.

off their heads with great satisfaction. The Apostle saw that the faces of Khazraj showed pleasure, but there was no such indication on the part of the Aus, and he suspected that that was because of the alliance that had existed between them and Banū Quraiza. When there were only twelve of them left he gave them over to Aus, assigning one Jew to every two of Aus, saying, 'Let so-and-so strike him and so-and-so finish him off.' "*

Those who follow the Prophet must become new men with a new conscience and new loyalties. They must be hardened in the difficult school of Islam. They must become participants in its blood-rites. They must become parties to an act which is effective in the measure that it is compromising. A man who still has some integrity is unsafely independent. In any case the followers should not be allowed to feel superior and to refrain from an act simply because they regard it as iniquitous or cruel. They must learn to have a conscience equal to their prescribed part and acts and to be worthy of their new role.

Besides the aged Zoheir, Ibn Ishāq and Mirkhond mention another case touching in its bravery. Huyayy b. Akhatab, a Jewish leader, was known affectionately among his people as "the grandee of the town," "the friend of the destitute and the poor," and "the prince of the desert and the sown." He too was brought before Muhammad, with his hands bound to his neck with a rope. Muhammad exultantly told him: "O enemy of Allah, at last the Most High and Glorious has given thee into my power, and has made me thy judge." Huyayy replied: "I do not blame myself for having borne enmity to thee . . . but God the most High has given thee victory, and there is no remedy. . . . He who forsakes God will be forsaken . . . God's command is right. A book and a decree, and massacre have been written against the Sons of Israel." Then he sat down, and at a signal from Muhammad, his head was struck off. He had come in a shirt so torn and tattered that it was not worth taking as a spoil.† In fact, before dying, he told 'Alī, his executioner: "I beseech thee not to take off my robe from my body."**

Sīrat Rasūl Allah, p. 752.

†*Sīrat Rasūl Allah*, p. 464.

**Mirkhond, *Rauzat-us-Safa*, vol. II, part II, p. 476.

There is a similar tale about a woman who was beheaded in the same fashion. 'Āisha says of her, "I shall never forget my wonder at her good spirits and loud laughter when all the time she knew that she would be killed."*

Muhammad's court poets duly celebrated his victory. Hassān sang:

Quraiza met their misfortune
And in humiliation found no helper.
A calamity worse than that which fell Banū al-Nazir befell them
The day that God's Apostle came to them like a brilliant moon,
With fresh horses bearing horsemen like hawks,
We left them with the blood upon them like a pool
They having accomplished nothing.
They lay prostrate with vultures circling round them.†

THE CONQUEST OF MECCA

Though Muhammad and the Meccans had entered into a ten-year truce, he made secret preparations to invade Mecca. "O God, take eyes and ears from Quraish so that we may take them by surprise," he prayed to Allah, and stealthily advanced on Mecca with ten thousand men. Ibn Ishāq tells us that when the Apostle reached Marr al-Zaharān, the Quraish were completely ignorant of the fact and did not even know what he was doing. He took Mecca by surprise.**

Muhammad knew how to use men and utilize their psychology. In fighting the Meccans, he gave the pride of place to the *ansārs,* who were from Medina, and not to the Emigrants, who were themselves Meccans and therefore might be somewhat inhibited. He called the *ansārs* and said to them: "O ye Assembly of *Ansārs,* do you see the ruffians of the Quraish? . . . When you meet them tomorrow, wipe them out." Abū Huraira adds: "Whoever was seen

*Sīrat Rasūl Allah, p. 465.
†Ibid., p. 480.
***Sīrat Rasūl Allah,* pp. 544, 546.

by them that day was put to death." But on representation by Abū Sufyān, Muhammad dealt with them leniently, so much so that the *ansārs* murmured: "After all the man has been swayed by tenderness towards his family and love for his city" (4396).

Eventually Muhammad entered the city and destroyed the idols around the Ka'ba,* declaring: "Truth has come and falsehood has vanished" (4397). Wonderful! To say the least, the sentiment was merely optimistic and lacked true spiritual insight. It takes more than an invading army of crusaders or a demolition squad with sledgehammers to establish the domain of Truth. Truth cannot be ushered in by replacing one godling with another, say Al-lāt with Al-lāh. To win something of the spiritual light requires self-work, self-churning, self-shedding, self-discovery. The enemy on the path is not the multiplicity of god-symbols but the unregenerate heart and the wanderings of a diffused mind, or what the Yogas call the *mūdha* and the *vikshipta* consciousness.

*'Alī was chosen to destroy the idols (which he did by mounting the shoulders of Muhammad) and 'Umar the pictures on the walls of the Ka'ba. Other men were sent to the neighboring areas for the same purpose and for looting the temple treasuries. Khālid b. Walīd was sent to Nakhl to destroy the idol of Al-'Uzzā, the tutelary goddess of Banū Kinān and the Quraish; Umro b. Al'as to destroy the idol of Suwā'; and Sa'd b. Zaid al-Ashahalī to destroy Al-Manāt, the deity of the tribes of Aus and Khazraj (*Tabaqāt*, vol. I, pp. 484–486).

A little later, in A.H. 9, Muhammad sent 'Urwa, a chief of the tribe of Saqīf, and a convert to Islam, to his people to persuade them to become Muslims. His people killed him. Then they took counsel among themselves and concluded that they could not fight the Arabs around them, and, therefore, they submitted to the authority of Muhammad. Muhammad sent Abū Sufyān along with Al-Mughīra b. Shu'ba, one of their kin, to demolish the idol of Allāt, their goddess. As Al-Mughīra, protected by his soldiers on all sides, struck the idol with his pickaxe, the women of Saqīf came out with their heads uncovered mourning and saying:

> We weep for our Protector,
> Deserted by Her servants,
> Who did not show enough manliness in defending Her.
>
> (Tārīkh Tabarī, vol. I, pp. 434–435)

This destruction and pillage of other people's temples and images set the tone for the Muslims of the future.

Similarly, it is not that easy to get over "falsehood" according to Hinduism, a more psychological and mystical religion. Spiritual darkness, or falsehood, has a source deep in our being; it is rooted in the dualities of the mind (*dvandva*), in egoistic life (*aham, asmitā*), and in a deeper nescience (*avidyā*). It is easy to demolish stone or copper gods on the altars, but more difficult to demolish false gods enshrined in one's own heart. True, spiritual demolition involves the demolition of the desire-gods and the ego-gods, the demolition of the false gods that reside in conceited theologies, in pretentious revelations and fond beliefs. According to the Yogas, the real difference is not between "one god" and "many gods" but between an ordinary mind and an awakened mind. A fixed and fanatic idea of God is worse than a plurality of god-forms. A gentle god-form which exists in harmony with other god-forms is to be preferred to a Leviathan-God, whether Jehovah or Allah.

After the conquest of Mecca, Muhammad declared: "No Quraishite will be killed bound hand and foot from this day until the Day of Judgment" (4399). But this did not save the Meccans from other forms of killing as sure and disgraceful as this one, and that too at the hands of their fellow Muslims.

ASSASSINATION

Assassination, like *jihād,* is an extension of a fanatic creed and psychology. Muhammad had at his disposal a band of hatchet men ready to do his bidding. Through them, he got inconvenient elements eliminated, particularly those who questioned his apostolic inspiration and had the ability to put their opposition into poetry and satire. "Who will kill Ka'b. b. Ashraf? He has maligned Allah, the Exalted, and His Messenger," said Muhammad. Volunteered one Muhammad b. Maslama: "Messenger of Allah, do you wish that I should kill him?" The Prophet replied: "Yes." Then the assassin sought Muhammad's permission to talk to the intended victim as he thought best—even to talk ill of the Prophet in order to win his confidence. The permission was given. Then the assassin, accompanied by some accomplices, went to Ka'b's house at night. Posing as a disgruntled follower of the Prophet, he lured his intended victim outside. Ka'b's wife warned: "I hear a voice which sounds like the voice of murder." But Ka'b replied: "It is only Muhammad b. Maslama and his foster brother, Abū Mā'ila. When a gentleman is called at night even if to be pierced with a spear, he should respond to the call." He went down and was killed (4436). Very soon, Ka'b's head was flung at the feet of the Prophet.

Further details are available in various other accounts, such as the *Sahīh Bukhāri,* and the biographies of Muhammad by Ibn Ishāq and Tabarī. Ibn Ishāq also quotes from the poems written by Muhammad's court poets to celebrate the event. Another Ka'b, a poet, sang:

> *Of them Ka'b was left prostrate there;*
> *Sword in hand we cut him down*
> *By Muhammad's order when he sent secretly by night*
> *Ka'b's brother to go to Ka'b;*
> *He beguiled him and brought him down with guile.**

Hassān b. Sabit, another poet, describes the assassins "bold as lions, travelling by night with their light swords," who made the victim taste his death "with their deadly swords, seeking victory for the religion of their prophet."† Another tradition quoted by Ibn Ishāq says that "our attack upon God's enemy cast terror among the Jews, and there was no Jew in Medina who did not fear his life."**

Jihād Takes Precedence over Prayer

Returning from the Battle of Ahzāb, Muhammad announced that nobody would say his *zuhr* prayer (the afternoon prayer, recited when the sun has begun to decline) but in the quarters of the Banū Quraiza, the unlucky victims of his aggression, as we have seen. Some, fearing that the time for the prayer might be over, said the prayer before

**Sīrat Rasūl Allah,* p. 368.
†Ibid., p. 369.
** Ibid., pp. 368-369.

reaching the street of the Banū Quraiza. Others did not say it at all for fear of losing time and not reaching the spot in time. On learning this, Muhammad "did not blame anyone from the two groups" (4374).

HELP FROM A POLYTHEIST IN JIHĀD

The last *hadīs* of this book is about a man who approached Muhammad and said: "I have come so that I may follow you and get a share from the booty." Muhammad asked him if he believed in Allah and His Messenger. When the man said he did not, Muhammad declined his offer till he corrected his theology. (4472).

The translator makes an interesting comment on this *hadīs*. He says that it apparently contradicts some other *ahādīs* from which we learn that the Holy Prophet accepted help offered by non-Muslims in his military campaigns. For example, Safwān b. Umaya fought on his side at the Battle of Hunain, and Quzmān was present on the day of Uhud, and both were polytheists. According to the translator, "these two instances go to prove that the help of a non-Muslim can be accepted when it is essential" (note 2285).

10
Government (Al-Imāra)

The eighteenth book is the "Book on Government" (*al-imāra*). It is not a treatise on the theory and practice of government as understood today. The spirit and informing principles are very different.

An Islamic state is necessarily a theocracy. The function of a truly Islamic government is not merely to maintain law and order but to enforce the law of *sharī'ah*, with which we have been making acquaintance to some extent in these pages. *Sharī'ah* does not pertain merely to prayer, general morality, *zakāt,* and pilgrimage; rather, it enters intimately into every detail of the believer's life: his modes and manners, food, dress, marriage, and so on. It includes all his beliefs and affairs. God has given a prototype for imitation in Muhammad. "We [Allah] put thee [Muhammad] in the right way concerning affairs" (Qurān 14:17). The function of an Islamic state is to enforce this model as best it can. Has not Allah sent "His apostle with guidance and the religion of Truth, to make it prevail over every other religion"? (Qurān 9:33).

An Islamic state is totalitarian in the philosophic sense. A closed politics or civics is a necessary corollary of a closed theology. In Islam, the concept of *ummah* dominates over the concept of man or mankind. So in a Muslim polity, only Muslims have full political rights in any sense of the term; non-Muslims, if they are allowed to exist at all as a result of various exigencies, are *zimmīs,* second-class citizens.

THE SUPREMACY OF THE QURAISH

At the very beginning, in thirteen *ahādīs* (4473-4484), the "Book on *al-Imāra*" establishes the supremacy of the Quraish, the tribe to which Muhammad belonged, in all matters, political and intellectual. "People are subservient to the Quraish: the Muslims among them being subservient to the Muslims among them, and the disbelievers among them, being subservient to the unbelievers among them," says Muhammad (4473-4474). In another version, "people are the followers of Quraish in good as well as evil" (4475).

ONLY A QURAISH MAY BE KHALĪFA

"The Caliphate will remain among the Quraish even if only two persons are left on the earth," Muhammad says (4476). This principle has been held very high in the Muslim world, though the Shias limit the office still further to the descendants of Muhammad, and specifically to the branch descended from 'Alī, the Prophet's cousin and son-in-law, and his wife Fātima, the Prophet's daughter.

As a result, for six hundred years, though the center of power of Islam shifted from Mecca to Damascus to Baghdad, the Caliphate remained with the Quraish till Halāku, the grandson of Genghis Khan, put to death the last Khalīfa at Baghdad. Later, a shadowy Caliphate, shorn of temporal power yet still Quraish, emerged in Egypt. Then it passed on to the Turkish Sultān Usmān (A.D. 1299-1326), who added to his many titles three others: Protector of the Two Lands (al-Hijāz and Syria, the holy lands of Islam), Successor of the Apostle of God, and Ruler of the Faithful.

But the sentiment that the Khalīfa should be a Quraish or at least an Arab was so strong that the Sultān of Turkey was never given universal recognition by Muslim theologians. The present-day Sauds, helped by petro-dollars, may one day revive this idea. At present they are busy laying the first, necessary foundations, strengthening fundamentalism and pan-Islamism, and buying up political support in Muslim countries and among Muslim populations. There can be no Arab Caliphate (a euphemism for Arab imperialism) without Muslim fundamentalism. Muslim fundamentalism feeds pan-Islamism under the Arab aegis.

Thanks to Muhammad, the Arabian Quraish became a most durable caste with not many parallels in history. They were warriors, rulers, financial tycoons, and scholars. A branch of them, the Saiyids, who are supposed to be descendants of the Prophet, are held in very high esteem and their persons are considered sacred.

Rulers

Islamic rulers should be just to the *ummah* and follow Muhammad's *sharī'ah* faithfully. "O God, who happens to acquire some kind of control over the affairs of my people and is hard upon them—be Thou hard upon him, and he who acquires control over the affairs of my people and is kind to them—be Thou kind to him," Muhammad prays to Allah (4494).

There are other conventional exhortations. A man should not seek a "position of authority" (4487-4492). An official should not accept "gifts" (4509-4516), for as we know, gifts are given to the office, not to the officer. A man in charge of *sadaqa* comes to Muhammad and says: "This wealth is for you, and this is a gift presented to me." Muhammad told him: "Why didn't you remain in the house of your father and mother to see whether gifts were presented to you or not?" (4510).

War booty is sacred; it is a religious obligation, but misappropriation of booty is a serious offense. "I shouldn't find that any of you should come on the Day of Judgment. . . . and should appeal to me for help," Muhammad warns misappropriators of booty (4505-4507).

Obedience to Rulers

Closed theologies claiming a perfected revelation and denying a place to man's ever-living reason, and to his moral and spiritual sense, have to invoke God at every step; but they end by establishing the tyranny of men. Muhammad establishes the following chain of command: "Whoso obeys the commander [appointed by me] obeys me, and whoso disobeys the commander disobeys me" (4518). Allah Himself enjoins this chain. "O you who believe, obey Allah, His

Apostle, and those in authority from amongst you" (4517; Qurān 4:59).

Some exceptions are mentioned. "It is obligatory upon a Muslim that he should listen to the ruler appointed over him and obey him whether he likes it or not, except that he is ordered to do a sinful thing" (4533). This is a big loophole which was fully used. But other *ahādīs* try to fill this gap.

WARNING AGAINST SCHISM

Muhammad tells his followers that after him there will be no prophet but many Khalīfas. Somebody asks him what to do when there are more Khalīfas than one. Muhammad says: "The one to whom allegiance is sworn first has a supremacy over the others" (4543). In fact, "When oath of allegiance has been taken for two Khalīfas, kill the one for whom the oath was taken later" (4568). Very thorough.

This injunction was followed to the letter by 'Umar. As he lay dying, he appointed a board of six electors to choose the new Khalīfa after him. Some of the guiding principles he laid down for the council were:

1. If the electors choose someone unanimously, then that person is designated as the Khalīfa.
2. If any five of them agree on one man and the sixth disagrees, then the dissenter should immediately be killed.
3. If any four of them agree on one person and two disagree, then those two should be killed.
4. If there is an equal division, then the deciding vote would be that of 'Abdullah b. 'Umar, his own son and one of the electors.*

SOLIDARITY AND SINGLE LEADERSHIP

"Anyone who tries to disrupt the affairs of this *Ummah* while they are united you should strike him with the sword" (4565). "Kill him," enjoins the next *hadīs*. Hold on to a single leader in order

*All four points are taken from S. Ghaffari, *Shiaism,* p. 68.

to ensure solidarity. "When you are holding to one single man as your leader, you should kill him who seeks to undermine your solidarity or disrupt your unity" (4567).

Warning against Bad Times

Muhammad warns against the coming bad days when people will arise "who will adopt ways other than mine and seek guidance other than mine" and yet "they will be a people having the same complexion as ours and speaking our language." What should a believer do if he lives in those times? He "should stick to the main body of the Muslims and their leader" (4553).

In those days "there will be leaders who will not be led by my guidance and will not adopt my ways. There will be among them men who will have the hearts of devils in the bodies of human beings." Under the circumstances, answering a follower, Muhammad says: "You will listen to the *Amīr* [ruler] and carry out his orders; even if your back is flogged and your wealth is snatched, you should listen and obey" (4554).

A crisis psychology indispensable for any dictatorship. A theology which teaches unceasing war against the peoples of the *Daru'l Harb* (territories not held by Muslims) makes a complete somersault and now teaches patient submission to the authorities of *Daru'l Islam* (territories under Islam) and to all its *Ulu'l-amr,* men of authority. These include not only its administrators but its divines.

There is also a warning not only against schismatics and innovators but also against false prophets. Is not Muhammad the final prophet? But "before the Day of Judgment, there will appear a number of impostors. You are to guard against them" (4483).

Horses and Archery

There are sixteen *ahadīs* on horses, among them two on horse racing (4610-4611). Muhammad used to have a horse race between two particular points six miles apart. The translator assures us that it was not a horse race used for betting as in modern times. "There is almost a consensus of opinion amongst the jurists that it is an act of great piety to break the horses for *Jihād* and for other useful purposes and there is no harm if there is a competition of race in them'' (note 2335).

There are also some *ahādīs* on archery (4711-4714). ''Beware, strength consists in archery,'' Muhammad repeated thrice in a sermon from the pulpit (4711). Again, ''Lands shall be thrown open to you and Allah would suffice you, but none of you should give up playing with his arrows'' (4712). Yet again, ''Who learnt archery and then gave it up is not from us or he has been guilty of disobedience to Allah's Apostle'' (4714).

THE AGE OF MAJORITY

Let us take up one or two more small items before we turn to *jihād,* which is also an important subject of this book.

The son of 'Umar went to fight in the Battle of Uhud when he was fourteen, but the Prophet did not accept him. The next year, when he was fifteen, he went to fight in the Battle of Khandaq, and this time he was accepted. That decided the issue. One of fifteen years is considered an adult, and one below fifteen is a minor (4605).

But the translator tells us that in Islamic law the age of majority differs with different conditions and circumstances. For example, for purposes of marriage, the puberty of a boy is established by other criteria, such as nocturnal emission and his capacity for impregnation. Similarly, the puberty of a girl is established by menstruation, nocturnal emission, or pregnancy (note 2331).

JIHĀD

Jihād appears again. In a book on government containing 358 *ahādīs,* 92 are on *jihād* and *mujāhids* (crusaders) and martyrs. This is understandable, for *jihād* is central to Islam and *mujāhids* are its Army of Liberation. Without *jihād,* there is no Islam. *Jihād* is a religious duty of a Muslim state. All lands not belonging to the territory of Islam *(dār al-islām)* must be conquered by the Muslims, and are therefore called the ''territory of war'' *(dār al-harb).* But it is left to the discretion of the *imām* to decide when the attack should begin. According to some *fiqh* schools, one campaign at least must be undertaken against the unbelievers every year, but since this is not always practical, it is enough if he keeps his army in preparedness and trains it for *jihād*.

Jihād as Proof of True Conversion

After Muhammad migrated to Medina from Mecca, prospective converts to Islam used to come to Medina to swear fidelity to him and as a proof of their sincerity would leave their hometowns and settle in Medina. Having no home and no livelihood, and being uprooted from their old loyalties, they became desperate, and motivated soldiers of Islam. After the conquest of Mecca, when the power of Muhammad was fully vindicated, there must have been a rush of people wanting to become Muslims. So the rules were changed. The proof of a sincere conversion was no longer migration but *jihād*. Muhammad told someone who intended to settle in Medina: "There is no *Hijra* now, but only *Jihād* and sincerity of purpose; when you are asked to set out [on an expedition undertaken for the cause of Islam] you should [readily] do so" (4597).

The Merits of Jihād

"Allah has undertaken to look after the affairs of one who goes out to fight in His way believing in Him and affirming the truth of His Apostles. He is committed to His care and He will either admit him to Paradise or bring him back to his home with a reward or booty" (4626). If he dies in the Way of Allah, his body will not decay. "Every wound received by a Muslim in the Way of Allah will appear on the Day of Judgment in the same condition as it was when it was inflicted. . . . and the colour [of its discharge] will be the colour of blood, but its smell would be smell of musk" (4630).

Jihād for the spread of Islam is most meritorious and the easiest gateway to Paradise. "Paradise is under the shadows of the swords," Muhammad tells his followers (4314).

"Think not of those who are slain in Allah's way as dead." In fact, " the souls of the martyrs live in the bodies of green birds who have their nests in chandeliers hung from the throne of the Almighty. They eat the fruits of Paradise from wherever they like." They have no other desire except to be reborn so that they can be "slain in Thy [Allah's] way once again" (4651). Muhammad had the same desire for himself. "I love to fight in the way of Allah and be killed, to fight and again be killed and to fight and again be killed" (4626).

THE SUPERIORITY OF JIHĀD TO OTHER ACTS

The spiritual merits that accrue to the believer for participating in *jihād* are equal to the merits he can obtain by performing all the other religious duties required by Islam, such as fasting, praying, and going on pilgrimage. "One who goes out for *jihād* is like a person who keeps fasts, stands in prayer constantly and obeys Allah's verses in the *Qurān*" (4636).

Some people disputed the excellence of different virtues. One said: "I do not care, if after embracing Islam, I do not do any good except distributing drinking water among the pilgrims." Another thought that maintainers of service to the mosque were superior. Yet a third wanted only to be a *mujāhid*. Muhammad was consulted. Allah sent him a verse: "Do ye make the givers of drink to pilgrims, or the maintainers of the Sacred Mosque equal to the believers in Allah and the Last Day [*yaum'l-ākhirat*], and the crusaders [*jāhid*] in the cause of God? They are not comparable in the sight of God. And God guides not those who do wrong" (Qurān 9:19, *hadīs* 4638).

There is more reward in *jihād* than in anything this world has to offer. "Leaving for *jihād* in the way of Allah in the morning or in the evening will merit a reward better than the world and all that is in it" (4639).

THE HIGHEST GRADE OF HEAVEN IS RESERVED FOR THE MUJĀHID

The rewards of being a Muslim are great, but the rewards of being a *mujāhid* are immensely greater. The Prophet said: "Whoever cheerfully accepts Allah as his Lord, Islam as his religion and Muhammad as his Apostle is necessarily entitled to enter Paradise . . . [yet] there is another act which elevates the position of a man in Paradise to a grade one hundred [higher], and the elevation between one grade and the other is equal to the height of the heaven from the earth. . . . What is that act? . . . *Jihād* in the way of Allah! *Jihād* in the way of Allah" (4645). But even the delights of this grade of paradise are no attraction to a martyr (*Shahīd)*. Therefore, the martyr "will desire to return to this world and be killed ten times for the sake of the great honour that has been bestowed upon him" (4635).

The Story of a Martyr

The promise of heaven was tempting. On the way to the Battle of Uhud, one believer asked Muhammad: "Messenger of Allah, where shall I be if I am killed? He [Muhammad] replied: In paradise. The man threw away the dates he had in his hand and fought until he was killed" (4678).

Brain-teasers

Muslim theology is not without its brain-teasers. Two men, one the slayer and the other the slain, both go to Paradise. The Companions ask Muhammad: "How?" He replied: "One is slain in the Way of Allah [in *jihād*] and dies a martyr. Then Allah turns in mercy to the murderer who embraces Islam; he too fights in the Way of Allah and dies a martyr" (4658-4659).

Another puzzle seeking solution. Two men, again one of them a slayer and the other the slain, go to hell but never "gathered together." "Who are they?" the Companions ask Muhammad. He answers: "A disbeliever and a believer" (4661-4662). But how? The translator clarifies: A believer goes to hell for some great sin, and a disbeliever goes there as a matter of course. But there is still a great difference between the two. A sinful believer and a disbeliever are not the same in the eyes of Allah. So a believer "would not be kept there [in hell] for ever as is the case with the disbeliever; . . . [and also] a disbeliever would be made to occupy the most terrible place in Hell, whereas the sinful believer would be in a comparatively less tormenting situation and thus they would not be together in Hell" (note 2348).

We may give here another paradox, taken from tradition quoted by Ibn Ishāq. A man goes to the Muslim Paradise without ever having offered a single Muslim prayer! He was Al-Aswad, a shepherd who was called to participate in *jihād* as soon as he became a Muslim, without having had the time to say a single prayer. In the engagement, a stone struck him and he died a martyr. Muhammad visited his corpse and delicately averted his face. Asked to explain why, he said: "He has with him now his two wives from the dark-eyed houris."*

AN EARTHLY NOTE

After all this Paradise-mongering, the book ends on a more down-to-earth note. Jābir reports: "We accompanied the Messenger of Allah on an expedition. When we came back to Medina and were going to enter our houses, he said: 'Wait and enter your houses in the later part of the evening so that a woman with dishevelled hair may have used the comb, and a woman whose husband has been away may have removed the hair from her private parts' " (4727).

Another tradition forbids a *mujāhid* to "come to his family like an unexpected night visitor doubting their fidelity and spying into their lapses" (4730). One interpretation is that the *mujāhids* have been away so long that their return is not expected, and thus their wives may be with their paramours. In such instances, let them not be taken by surprise, and let there be no avoidable breaking of homes. Give them time to separate. Homely wisdom.

Two men did not heed this command. And the result: "they both found their wives with other men," according to Ibn 'Abbas (Tirmizī, vol. II, *hadīs* 571).

***Sīrat Rasūl Allah*, p. 519.

11
Hunting, Food and Drink

The nineteenth book is the "Book of Game and the Animals Which May Be Slaughtered and the Animals That Are to Be Eaten."

Muhammad did not set much store by the many Jewish restrictions on the subject of food (*ta'ām*), and softened them a good deal. "O ye who believe! eat of the good things wherewith we have provided you," says the Qurān (2:172), repeating the sentiment in another verse (5:87). Yet some ritualistic restrictions were still there from the very beginning. Some animals were considered *halūl* (lawful), some *mubāh* (permitted), some *makrūh* (disapproved but not penalized), and some were altogether *harām* (forbidden).

Animals that are "clean" must be hunted and slaughtered in a particular way, with the help of a particular incantation, for their flesh to be lawful food. When slaughtering an animal, one should draw the knife across its throat, cutting the windpipe, and at the same time repeat the words *Bi'smillahi, Allāhu akbar* ("In the name of Allah, Allah is great"). However, if an animal is slaughtered in this way by an idolater or an apostate from Islam, its flesh is not lawful.

Game

There are similar restrictions on game. It is not enough to recite the formula *Bi'smillāh-i-Allāh-o-Akbar* over game caught and killed by one's trained dog before eating it. One must also recite Allah's name over the dog that one sets off to catch a game animal (4732-4734). "When you set off your trained dogs having recited the name of Allah, then eat what these hounds have caught for you, even if the game is killed, provided the hunting dog has not eaten any part of the game" (4733). When someone asks: What "if I find along with my dog another dog, and do not know which of them caught [the game]?" Muhammad answers: "Then don't eat it" (4734).

What applies to the hunting dog applies to any animal used for hunting—a falcon, a cheetah. The test of a trained dog is that it catches a game animal three times without eating it. The test of a trained hawk is that it returns to its master in response to his call.

The same holds true for game animals shot with an arrow. "When you shoot your arrow, recite the name of Allah, and if the arrow killed [the game] then eat, except when you find it [the prey] fallen into water, for in that case you do not know whether it is water that caused its death or your arrow" (4742).

DOS AND DON'TS

"If you are in the land of the People of the Book [Jews and Christians], do not eat from their utensils. But if it cannot be avoided, then wash them before using them" (4743).

FLESH LAWFUL AND UNLAWFUL

The eating of all fanged beasts of prey and of all birds having talons is prohibited (4748-4755), but it is permissible to eat water animals even if they die of natural causes. There is a story behind this particular permission. Jābir gives us an eyewitness account. "Allah's Messenger sent us on an expedition so that we might intercept a caravan of the Quraish," he says. During the journey, supplies ran short and they were on starvation rations when they saw rising before them on the coast of the sea "something like a big mound." It was a whale called *al-'Anbar*. The beast was dead. But as they were "sent by the Messenger of Allah in the path of Allah," and as they were hard pressed, they ate even the dead animal. It fed them, "three hundred of them," for a month till they grew bulky. "I saw how we extracted pitcher after pitcher full of fat from the cavity of its eye, and sliced from its compact piece of meat equal to a bull. . . . Abū 'Ubaid [the chief] called forth thirteen men from us and he made them sit in the cavity of its eye," Jābir tells us. When they came back and mentioned this to Muhammad, he said that it "was a special provision which Allah had brought forth" for them. "Is there any piece of meat left with you?" Muhammad inquired. They gave him one "and he ate it" (4756).

Asses

It is unlawful to eat the flesh of domestic asses (4763-4778), for they "are loathsome or impure" (4778), and their flesh "is a loathsome evil of Satan's doing" (4777).

The prohibition came on the day of Khaibar, when the earthen pots of the Companions were boiling with the flesh of domestic asses. "Throw away your pots," came the order. Some thought at first that the prohibition was temporary, "since one-fifth of the booty has not been given to the treasury, as is legally required" (4768). The point is that no personal use can be made of any spoils of war unless the booty has been properly distributed and one-fifth made over to the treasury. To illustrate, we give another tradition, narrated by Rāfi b. Khadīj: "We got hold of goats and camels. Some persons amongst us made haste and boiled the flesh of goats and camels in their earthen pots. He [the Prophet] then commanded and these were turned over" (4847). The translator tells us that "it is permissible to make use of these spoils in *Dar-ul-Harb* [in the territory of the enemy], but it is not allowed in *Dāru-ul-Islām*" (note 2388).

Horses

The flesh of a horse is lawful (4779-4782).

Lizards, Locusts, Hares

The flesh of lizards is not forbidden, but to eat it is "against the high standard of piety" (4783-4800). A roasted lizard was sent to the Prophet. He did not accept it, saying: "I neither eat it, nor do I prohibit it." His reason for not eating it: "It is not found in the land of my people, and I feel that I have no liking for it" (4790).

The eating of locusts is permissible. "We went on seven expeditions with Allah's Messenger and ate locusts," report Ibn Abū Aufā and Abū Bakr (4801-4803).

Similarly, the flesh of hares is lawful. Anas reports that he and his companions chased a hare, caught and slaughtered it, and "sent its haunch and two hind legs to Allah's Messenger. . . . and he accepted them" (4801).

KILL WITH A GOOD ATTITUDE

The Prophet was not without compassion. Shaddād b. Aus reports: "Two are the things which I remember Allah's Messenger having said: Verily Allah has enjoined goodness to everything; so when you kill, kill in a good way and when you slaughter, slaughter in a good way. So every one of you should sharpen his knife, and let the slaughtered animal die comfortably" (4810).

SACRIFICES

Intimately connected with the above is the next book, the "Book of Sacrifices" *(Kitāb al-Azāhi)*.

The Qurān uses many words for animal sacrifice. *Azāhi* itself derives from the root *zabh,* which means "to split or pierce." Another word used is *nahr,* which means "to injure the jugular vein"; the word stands for stabbing the breast of a camel as in a sacrifice, and hence derivatively for the sacrifice itself.

In many religious traditions, compassion for all living beings is a strong element, which itself has its basis in a deeper vision of the unity of all life. But this feeling and this vision are rather conspicuous by their absence in Semitic religions. Some portions of the Old Testament read almost like a manual of animal slaughter. The menu of the early Christians also did not exclude flesh food, except for flesh of a particular kind and flesh obtained in a particular way. They were only required to "abstain from meats offered to idols, and from blood, and from things strangled." The Holy Ghost wanted to lay upon them no greater burden than was necessary (Acts 15:28-29).

In Islam, too, animal sacrifice is highly meritorious. Muhammad tells his Companions that "there is reward annexed to every hair of the animal sacrificed; verily its blood reacheth the acceptance of God, before it falleth upon the ground" (Tirmizī, vol. I, *hadīs* 1392). But in order to be meritorious, the sacrifice should be made to Allah, not to Al-lāt or Al-'Uzzā or Al-Manāt. Let only theology change but facts remain the same for this miracle to happen. Among the people whom "Allah cursed," Muhammad tells us, are those "who sacrificed for anyone besides Allah," and those "who accommodated an innovator in religion" (4876-4878).

Some people talk glibly about what the Holy Ghost wants or what Allah wills but are deaf to the voice of conscience and compassion within the human heart.

The Proper Time for Sacrifice

The proper time for sacrificing an animal on the day of *Īdu'l Azā* is after the morning prayer (4818-4835). In Muhammad's lifetime, many slaughtered their animals before Muhammad had said his prayer. They were asked to slaughter other ones in their stead. People "should not sacrifice an animal before Allah's Messenger had sacrificed [his animal]" (4837).

Proper Age

As there is a proper time for sacrificing, so there is also a proper age for the sacrificial animal. "Sacrifice only a grown-up animal, unless it is difficult for you, in which case sacrifice a ram [of less than a year, but more than six months' age]" (4836).

Proper Agency

It is meritorious to sacrifice the animal with one's own hand as

Muhammad did. Muhammad "commanded that a ram with black legs, black belly and black circles round the eyes should be brought to him." He then said to 'Āisha, "Give me the large knife," and told her to "sharpen it on a stone." When she did, he took the knife and the ram; "he placed it on the ground and then sacrificed it" (4845). Another *hadīs* adds that when Muhammad sacrificed rams, "he placed his foot on their sides" (4841).

While sacrificing, Muhammad recited: "In the name of Allah, O Allah, accept [this sacrifice] on behalf of Muhammad and the family of Muhamamd and the *Ummah* of Muhammad" (4845).

The proper instrument for slaughtering an animal is a sharp knife. Muhammad is informed by a Companion: "Allah's Messenger, we are going to encounter the enemy tomorrow, but we have no knives with us." (The knives were not required for use against the enemy but for slaughtering the animals which might fall to their lot as spoils of war, the translator explains.) The Prophet answered: "Make haste or be careful [in making arrangements for procuring knives] which would let the blood flow, [and along with it] the name of Allah is also to be recited" (4846).

The same *hadīs* tells us that no nail or bone should be used in slaughtering an animal. "As for the nail, it is bone, and the bone is the knife of the Abyssinians."

SACRIFICE IS COMPULSORY

The translator in a note quotes a *hadīs* to show that animal sacrifice on the day of *Īdu'l Azā* is compulsory for every Muslim adult. According to Abū Huraira, Muhammad said: "He who can afford sacrifice but does not offer it, he should not come near our place of worship" (note 2378).

This is understandable, for is not animal sacrifice Allah's own command? Allah ordains: "The sacrificial camels, we have made for you as among the symbols from God . . . then pronounce the name of Allah over them as they line up for sacrifice, and when they are down on their sides eat of them. . . . We made animals subject to you, that you may be grateful" (Qurān 22:36).

POT AND PIETY

On the ordinary level of consciousness on which religions operate, there is nothing exceptionable in the Muslim institution of sacrifice. We offer to our gods what we ourselves eat. In animal sacrifice, the flesh comes to us, and we like to believe that the piety of the act (whatever it may be) goes to God. "It is not their meat nor their blood, that reaches Allah, it is your piety" (Qurān 22:37).

Let it be so if you like. But when a deeper consciousness dawns, all this changes. We realize that this unregenerate piety is not good enough. We experience a new togetherness, a new reverence for all living beings. We realize that an animal sacrifice can never be a fitting and acceptable offering to any god worthy of man.

DRINKS

The twenty-first book is the "Book of Drinks" *(Ashriba).* Muhammad forbade all intoxicating liquors, all liquors in the various stages of fermentation.

It seems that the habit of drinking was quite popular with the Companions of Muhammad. Many *ahādīs* in this book show Abū Talha, Abū Ayyūb, Abū Dujāna, Mu'āz b. Jabal, Sahil b. Baiadā, Abū Ubaida, and Ubayy b. Ka'b drinking. The worst case is that of Hamza b. 'Abd al-Muttalib, the Prophet's uncle. 'Alī, the Prophet's son-in-law, narrates an interesting story. "There fell to my lot a she-camel out of the spoils of war on the day of Badr, and Allah's Messenger gave me another on that day out of the *khums* [the fifth reserved for Allah and His Messenger]." Some business took 'Alī to the house of an *ansār,* and he brought his camels along. He tied them up outside, but when he returned, he found their "humps were chopped off and their haunches had been cut off and their livers had been taken out." When 'Alī asked who had done this, people said, Hamza and "he is in this house dead drunk in the company of the *Ansārs* with a singing girl."

'Alī reported the matter to Muhammad, who put on his mantle, went to where Hamza was, and began to reprimand him. "Hamza's eyes were red. He cast a glance at Allah's Messenger and then looked towards his knees, and then lifted his eyes and cast a glance at his waist and then lifted his eyes and saw his face. And then Hamza said: 'Are you anything but the slaves of my father?' Allah's Messenger came to know that he was intoxicated, and he thus turned upon his heels, and came out" (4881).

Liquor was forbidden.

NABĪZ

Also forbidden was *nabīz,* a kind of wine made by mixing fresh dates and unripe dates together (4896-4912). Muhammad also forbade its preparation in varnished jars, gourds, green pitchers, or hollow stumps (4913-4995).

MUHAMMAD AND DRINKING

There are many *ahādīs* to show that the Prophet himself drank *nabīz* (4971-4982). 'Āisha reports: "We prepared *nabīz* for him [Muhammad] in a waterskin. . . . We prepared *nabīz* in the morning and he drank it in the evening and we prepared the *nabīz* in the night, and he would drink it in the morning" (4977). Ibn 'Abbās, the Prophet's cousin, reports: "*Nabīz* was prepared for Allah's Messenger in the beginning of the night and he would drink it in the morning and the following night and the following day and the night after that up to the afternoon. If anything was left out of that he gave it to his servant, or gave orders for it to be poured out" (4971).

How to reconcile the Prophet's prohibition with his indulgence? The theologians are not at a loss. They say: "This prohibition is not a complete prohibition but it implies disapproval. So long as *nabīz* does not turn into liquor, it is not forbidden." For Imām Abū Hanīfa and Qāzi Abū Yūsuf, there is not even a disapproval, but the prohibition "was valid only in the early period of Islam when the people had to be trained for the prohibition of liquor" (note 2409).

Milk

Muhammad approved of drinking milk. "I milked for him [the Prophet] a small quantity of milk and brought it to him and he drank it," reports Abū Bakr (4983).

Table Manners

Etiquette relating to eating and drinking is also given. Muhammad says: "None of you should eat with his left hand and drink with the left hand, for Satan eats with the left hand and drinks with that hand" (5010).

In another tradition, he tells 'Umar, the son of his wife Umm Salama by her first husband: "Boy, mention the name of Allah, and eat with your right hand and eat from what is near you" (5012).

One should not drink water while standing (5017-5022), but one could do so with water from Zamzam (the well-known well within the precincts of the mosque at Mecca) as Muhammad himself did (5023-5027). In ordinary course, if one drinks water standing, one "must vomit" (5022).

It is also meritorious to lick one's fingers after taking one's food. 'Abdullah b. Ka'b reports that "the Messenger of Allah used to eat food with three fingers, and he licked his hand before wiping it" (5040). The injunction is: "When anyone of you eats food he should not wipe his hand until he had licked it or got it licked by someone else" (5038).

Pumpkins and Cucumbers

It is meritorious to eat pumpkin (5067-5069) and also cucumber with dates, because Muhammad did so (5072). Anas reports: "I saw Allah's Messenger going after the pumpkin round the dish, so I have always liked the pumpkin since that day" (5067).

Garlic

Muhammad himself did not eat garlic because of its odor (5097), but it is permissible for other Muslims. Still, it should be avoided when one has to talk to eminent persons. Abū Ayyūb Ansārī tells us that the "holy prophet did not take garlic as he was visited by angels who brought him the message of Allah" (5099).

MIRACULOUS FEEDING

Miraculous feeding after the fashion of Jesus is repeated in Islam too. The roasted liver of one sheep and two cups containing soup and meat suffice, with the blessing of the Prophet, for feeding 130 persons (5105).

DO NOT FIND FAULT

Do not find fault with the food served to you. It is said about the Prophet that "if he liked anything, he ate it and if he did not like it, he left it" (5121). A laudable practice. In fact, a man should eat with thankfulness in his heart—thanks for the gods that reside in his food, thanks for the elements that have gone into making it, thanks for the farmer who produced it, and thanks for the mothers, sisters and wives, and cooks who lovingly cooked it and served it.

However, it is not enough to thank "our Father who art in heaven" for giving "us this day our daily bread." Let us pray that this bread is also honest. What Lord Buddha calls Right Livelihood (*samyak ājiviikā*) is a great spiritual truth. Food derived from the spoils of war and tribute is a negation of this insight. Though we may placate Him with soulful praises and pious thanks, no God can legitimize it.

Similarly, it is self-deception to believe that we adore or glorify God by reciting *Allah-o-Akbar* ("Allah is Great") while killing an animal. That way we really profane Him, negate Him. Be a meat-eater if you like, but one ought not to feel so pious about it.

12

Clothing, Decorations, General Behavior, Greetings, Magic, Poetry, Visions, Dreams

The twenty-second book pertains to clothing and decorations (*Kitāb al-Libās wa'l-Zīnah*). The book begins with *ahādīs* which forbid the use of gold and silver vessels (5126-5140). "He who drinks in the vessel of silver in fact drinks down in his belly the fire of Hell" (5126).

Silk

Silk is also forbidden. "Do not wear silk, for one who wears it in the world will not wear it in the Hereafter" (5150).

It is also not permissible for a man to wear clothes of yellow color (5173-5178), for "these are the clothes usually worn by the non-believers" (5173). A man was wearing clothes dyed in saffron; finding that the Prophet disapproved of them, he promised to wash them. But Muhammad said: "Burn them" (5175).

The mantles of Yemen, on the other hand, were considered excellent (5179-5180). These were striped and made of coarse cloth.

It is permissible to use carpets (5188-5189).

Sandals

Sandals are recommended. Jābir reports that "during an expedition in which we all participated," the Prophet said: "Make a general practice of wearing sandals, for a man is riding as it were when he wears sandals" (5230).

HAIR

Not only clothes, but the hair too should not be dyed in saffron (5241).

On the day of the conquest of Mecca, Abū Quhāfā, the father of Abū Bakr, a veteran old man of one hundred years, met the Prophet to pledge his loyalty to him. His head and his beard were white like hyssop. The Prophet said: "Change it with something but avoid black" (5244).

But why this change or dyeing at all? The Prophet gives the reason: "The Jews and Christians do not dye their hair, so oppose them" (5245).

DOGS

Many *ahādīs* tell us that "angels do not enter a house in which there is a dog" (5246-5251). In fact, Gabriel himself told this to the Prophet. The angel had promised a rendezvous with Muhammad but did not turn up because meanwhile a puppy had gotten into his house and was sitting under a cot. "Then on that very morning, he [Muhammad] commanded the killing of the dogs until he announced that the dog kept for the orchards should also be killed, but he spared the dog meant for the protection of extensive fields [or big gardens]," reports Maimūna, one of the wives of the Prophet (5248).

PICTURES AND STATUES

The same is true of statues and pictures in any form, whether of birds or animals or men. They effectively keep out the angels. 'Āisha tells us: "We had a curtain which had portraits of birds upon it. . . . The Messenger of Allah said to me: Change them, [they bring] to my mind [the pleasures of] the worldly life" (5255).

On seeing portraits on a curtain, he told 'Āisha: "The most

grievous torment from the Hand of Allah on the Day of Resurrection would be for those who imitate Allah in the act of His creation" (5261). On that day Allah would ask these imitators: "Breathe soul into what you have created" (5268).

False Hair and Facial Culture

Some of Muhammad's prohibitions relate to practices which are surprisingly modern. He forbade women to add false hair to their head, or to pluck their eyebrows (5295-5309). The Prophet "cursed the woman who adds false hair and the woman who asks for it" (5298).

We are also told that "Allah has cursed those women who tattooed and who have themselves been tattooed, those who pluck hair from their faces and those who make spaces between their teeth for beautification changing what God has created" (5301). 'Abdullah, the son of 'Umar, tells us that if he found any of these things in his wife, he "would have never slept with her in the bed."

Muhammad tells us also of women wearing see-through dresses: "women who would be dressed but appear to be naked will not enter paradise" (5310).

Muhammad also disapproved of *qaza,* i.e., having a part of a boy's head shaved and leaving a part unshaven. This may have been an old ritualistic practice or a thoughtless current fashion (5289-5292).

GENERAL BEHAVIOR AND SALUTATIONS

The twenty-third and twenty-fourth books are the "Book of General Behavior" *(al-Ādāb)* and the "Book on Salutations and Greetings" (*as-Salām*).

Personal Names

Curiously, the book on *ādāb* starts with personal names. Muhammad took great interest in this matter. He said that ugly personal names should be replaced with good ones (5332-5334). He changed the name of 'Umar's daughter 'Āsiya ("disobedient") to Jamīla ("good and handsome") (5332). But he also changed the name of one of his wives from Barra to Juwairīya (5334). Barra means "pious," and it is a perfectly good name.

Muhammad said that the dearest names to Allah are Subhān Allah ("Hallowed be Allah"), and al-Hamidulillah ("praise be to Allah") (5329). But he forbade giving the following four names to servants: Aflah ("successful"), Rabāh ("profit"), Yasār ("wealth"), and Nāfi ("beneficial") (5327).

"The vilest name in Allah's sight is Malik al-Amlāk (king of kings)." So is the appellation Shahinshāh, having the same meaning (5338).

NAMING INFANTS AFTER MUHAMMAD

People who wanted to name their sons after Muhammad were only allowed to use his personal name (Muhammad), but not his *kunya* (a name descriptive of some quality or attribute), *Qāsim*. Jābir narrates that a man named his newborn babe Muhammad. When other Muslims objected, he went to Muhammad for clarification. Muhammad said: "Give him my name but do not give him my *kunya,* for I am *Qāsim* in the sense that I distribute [the spoils of war] and the dues of *Zakāt* amongst you" (5316).

TAHNĪK

Tahnīk is the practice of blessing a newborn infant with religious piety. *Azān* and *Iqāma* are recited in its right and left ears, and some chewed dates are rubbed over its palate. Asmā, the daughter of Abū Bakr, gave birth to a baby. The baby was taken to Muhammad. Muhammad called for some dates, "chewed them and then put his saliva in his [the infant's] mouth. The first thing that entered his stomach was the saliva of Allah's Messenger. . . . He then rubbed him and blessed him and gave him the name of *'Abdullah.* He ['Abdullah] went to him [the Holy Prophet] when he had attained the age of seven or eight years in order to pledge allegiance to Allah's Messenger" (5344).

Asking Permission before Entering a House

One should not enter anybody's house without his permission. When a man seeks permission three times, and it is not granted, "he should come back" (5354).

Don't Peep into Another Man's House

It is forbidden to peep into the house of another person. A man peeped through a hole in the door at Allah's Messenger, who was using a pointed object of some kind to arrange the hair on his head. Allah's Messenger said to him: "If I were to know that you had been peeping, I would have thrust it into your eyes" (5367). Then Muhammad pronounced: "He who peeped into the house of people without their consent, it is permissible for them to put out his eyes" (5370).

SALUTATIONS AND GREETINGS

"Six are the rights of a Muslim over another Muslim . . . When you meet him, offer him greetings; when he invites you to a feast accept it; when he seeks your counsel give him; and when he sneezes and says: 'All praise to Allah,' you say, 'May Allah show mercy to you'; and when he falls ill visit him; and when he dies follow his bier" (5379).

When the People of the Book (Jews and Christians) offer you salutations, you should say: "The same to you" (5380). Some Jews once made a pun and greeted Muslims by saying *as-sām-u-'alaikum* ("death be upon you") instead of the usual *as-salām-u-alaikum* ("peace be upon you"). Muhammad teaches his followers to respond by saying: "Let it be upon you" (5380-5388). The Prophet himself followed this practice.

First Greetings

"The rider should first greet the pedestrian, and the pedestrian the one who is seated" (5374). And all should greet the children (5391-5392). Muhammad also taught his followers to "avoid sitting on the paths"; or if that cannot be helped, then "give the path its due right" (5375-5377).

But it is different with the People of the Book. "Do not greet the Jews and the Christians before they greet you and when you meet any one of them on the roads force him to go to the narrowest part of it" (5389).

VEIL

'Umar wanted Muhammad to ask his women to wear the veil, but Muhammad did not respond. One day, when the Prophet's wife Saudā, who was tall in stature, went out to the fields in the dark to ease herself, 'Umar called out: "Saudā, we recognize you." He did so "with the hope that the verses pertaining to veil would be revealed." His hope was fulfilled. "Allah, the Exalted and Glorious, then revealed the verses pertaining to veil," says 'Āisha (5397).

Also, "beware of getting into the houses and meeting women." "But what about the husband's brother," an *ansār* asked. "Husband's brother is like death," the Prophet replied (5400).

MAGIC AND SPELLS

With rather slovenly classification, the "Book of Salutations and Greetings" also contains many *ahādīs* on magic, spells, medicine, poisons, and incantations.

The Prophet believed that "the influence of an evil eye is a fact." A bath is prescribed as its remedy. "When you are asked to take a bath from the influence of an evil eye, you should take a bath" (5427).

Muhammad also believed in witchcraft. In fact, he believed that he himself had once been put under a spell by a Jew and his daughters. During this period, he lost his appetite and even became impotent; or, in the language of Ibn Ishāq, "could not come at his wives." And under the influence of the charm, he also felt "that he had been doing something whereas in fact he had not been doing that." But two angels came and revealed everything: the nature of the sickness, those who had brought it about, and the way they did it. The angels told Muhammad that "the spell has affected him," and that "it was Labīd b. A'sam [who cast the spell]." The angels explained that hairs combed from the head of the Prophet had been stolen, tied in eleven knots around a palm branch, and deposited at the bottom of a well. The effect of the charm was transmitted "by the comb and by the hair stuck to the comb and the spathe of the date-palm—[and that it was] in the well of Zi Arwān." Muhammad sent his men there and they found it at the very spot revealed by the angels. Muhammad told 'Āisha: " 'Āisha, by Allah, its [the well's] water was yellow like henna and its trees [i.e., the trees around the well] were like heads of the devils" (5428).

As the knots were untied, the Prophet got well. He sought "refuge with the Lord of the Dawn from the mischief of women who blow on knots [i.e., practice the secret art of casting spells]" (Qurān *Sūra* 113).

In the same *Sūra*, the Prophet also seeks refuge "from the mischief of darkness as it overspreads." Has this prayer to do with his fear of darkness? His biographers say he was afraid of the dark and would not sit in a dark room unless a lamp was brought for him.*

On another occasion, a Jewish woman gave Muhammad poisoned mutton, but, of course, it had no power over him (5430). The Jewish woman was none other than the unfortunate victim who had seen her father and husband killed in the Prophet's raid on Khaibar and whom he was now contemplating to marry. She poisoned the mutton she was asked to cook for Muhammad. He had just taken a morsel and finding the taste unusual spat it out. This saved him for the time being, but the poison had a delayed effect, and according to some traditions, it caused his last illness.

Cures by Incantation

Muhammad used to "cure" people with the help of incantations (5442-5457). Among others, he treated cases of "evil eye" and

**Tabaqāt*, vol. I, p. 156.

snakebite. He even granted the sanction of treating snakebite with incantation to a family of *ansārs* (5443).*

'Āisha reports: "When any person fell ill with a disease or he had any ailment or he had any injury, the Apostle of Allah placed his forefinger upon the ground and then lifted it by reciting the name of Allah and said: 'The dust of our ground with the saliva of any one of us would serve as a means whereby our illness would be cured with the sanction of Allah' " (5444).

The translator extends the area from the Prophet's four walls and household to the whole of Medina. He says that according to some Muslim scholars, the word "dust" in the *hadīs* "refers to the sacred dust of Medina on which had fallen the saliva of the pious Muslims" (note 2579).

On another occasion, a Companion of the Prophet cured a man bitten by a poisonous scorpion with the help of *Sūra al-Fātiha,* reinforced by the application of his saliva (5459).†

No Evil Omen, No Hāma, No Infection

Muhammad said that there are "no ill omens, no ghouls," and "no star promising rain." There is also no *hāma (*5507-5516). According to the Arab belief of that time, the soul of a slain man took the form of a bird known as *hāma,* which kept crying for the blood of the slayer until the slayer was killed.

Muhammad also taught that there is no infection, no epidemic disease. About the plague he said: "When you hear that it has broken out in a land, don't go to it, and when it has broken out in the land where you are, don't run out of it" (5493). The fever is due to "the intense heat of the Hell. Cool it down with water," Muhammad says (5484).

*He saw "no harm in the incantation which does not smack of polytheism" (5457), i.e., which invoked the name of Al-lah but not of Al-lāt.

†Saliva exists in many modes and performs many functions. It has a sexual potential, as several *ahādīs* show; it is a wonder drug; and it also has the power to confer great spiritual merit.

LEPROSY

Don't mix with lepers. A delegation that included a leper once came to pay homage to Muhammad. The Prophet would not meet the leper but sent him a message: "We have accepted your allegiance, so you may go" (5541).

LUCK

Though Muhammad did not believe in divination, he believed in good omens and luck. "There is no transitive [i.e., epidemic] disease, no divination, but good omens please me," he says (5519).

About luck he says: "If a bad luck is a fact, then it is in a horse, the woman and the house" (5526). According to the translator, "the unluckiness of a horse is that the horse is used not for *Jihād* but for evil designs" (note 2602).

KĀHINS

Muhammad was against *kāhins,* i.e., augurs, soothsayers, and fortune-tellers. The reason for this opposition was personal as well as ideological; personal because he himself was accused of being no better than a *kāhin* but wanted to be known as a prophet. Allah had assured him that "by the favour of the Lord, thou art neither a soothsayer [*kāhin*], nor one possessed or mad [*majnūn*]" (Qurān 52:29).

His other ground of opposition was of a more general nature. Muhammad believed that Gabriel was the true source of the knowledge of the unseen world now contained in the Qurān and the *Sunnah*. But the source of the knowledge of a *kāhin* is the *jinn,* a knowledge which he steals from heaven but mixes up with lies. 'Āisha puts it to Muhammad: "Messenger of Allah! they [*kāhins*] at times tell us things which we find true." Muhammad replies: "That is a word pertaining to truth which a *jinn* snatches away and then cackles into the ear of his friend [the *kāhin*] as the hen does. And then they [the *jinns*] mix in it more than one hundred lies" (5536). For pure and unadulterated knowledge of the occult world, the Qurān and the *Sunnah* are the source. "All other avenues of knowledge of the unseen world are limited and thus not fully authentic and reliable," the translator assures us (note 2603).

METEORS

Muhammad did not believe in a star promising rain, but that does not make him a rationalist as we understand the word today. The two worlds—the world of Muhammad and that of the modern rationalist—are very different. There is an interesting *hadīs* on shooting stars which tells us what Muhammad believed about the world, nature, and the law of causality, and incidentally about how the *jinns* steal their knowledge of the heavens.

The pre-Muslim Arabs believed that meteors symbolized the death or birth of a great man, a belief found in the lore of many countries, including India. Muhammad corrected this belief and provided another explanation. His view is a little complicated but worth quoting. It seems that Muhammad believed in the hierarchy of angels. First in rank are the "supporters of the Throne"; next come the "dwellers of the heaven"; the third group lives in the "heaven of the world." When these different orders communicate with each other, the *jinn* has his chance. Muhammad explains: "Allah, the Exalted and the Glorious, issues Command when He decides to do a thing. Then the angels supporting the Throne sing His glory, then sing dwellers of the heaven who are near to them until this glory of God reaches them who are in this heaven of the world. Then those who are near the supporters of the Throne ask those supporters of the Throne: What has your Lord said? And they accordingly inform them what He says. Then the dwellers of heaven of the world seek information from them until this information reaches the heaven of the world. In this process of transmission the *jinn* snatches what he manages to overhear and he carries it to his friends. And when the angels see the *jinn* they attack them with meteors. If they narrate which they manage to snatch that is correct, but they alloy it with lies and make additions to it" (5538).

The snatching of the heavenly news by the *jinn* is referred to in several places in the Qurān. The interested reader may look up the *Sūras Hijr* (15:16-18), *Sāffāt* (37:7-10), *Mulk* (67:5), and *Jinn* (72:8-10).

Winds and Clouds

The fact is that the world of Muhammad is as weird and full of imps and *jinns* as the world of the *kāhins* and has little in common with the world as moderns understand it. As we have already seen in the chapter on *salāt* (see page 31) Muhammad's approach even to phenomena so close to home as clouds and rain and wind was neither scientific nor even poetic but magical and superstitious. Their sight filled him with fear. 'Āisha tells us that when he "saw dark clouds or wind, the signs of fear were depicted on his face." She asked him: "I find people being happy when they see the dark cloud in the hope that it would bring rain, but I find that when you see that [the cloud] there is an anxiety on your face." He replied: " 'Āisha, I am afraid that there may be a calamity in it, for it may be like the people of 'Ād who saw a cloud formation and thought 'It is a cloud which would give us rain,' but were destroyed by it" (Qurān 46:24; *hadīs* 1963).

Snakes, Ants, Cats

'Āisha reports that the Prophet "commanded the killing of a snake having stripes over it, for it affects eyesight and miscarries pregnancy" (5542). Like snakes, dogs too "cause miscarriage and affect the eyesight adversely." So they too should be killed (5545).

Ants fared better, but this was due to the intervention of Allah Himself. "An ant had bitten a prophet . . . he ordered that the colony of the ants should be burnt. And Allah revealed to him: Because of an ant's bite you have burnt a community from amongst the communities which sing My praise" (5567).

The book ends on a compassionate note. It is forbidden to kill a cat (5570-5576). It is also meritorious to supply water to thirsty animals (5577-5579).

CORRECT WORDS, POETRY, VISIONS

The next three books are very small. One relates to the use of correct words; another is on poetry (*kitāb al-shi'r*); and the third is on visions *(kitāb al-rūyā*).

At a place known as 'Arj, Muhammad once saw a poet reciting a poem. "Catch the Satan," Muhammad commanded. "Filling the belly of a person with pus is better than stuffing his brain with poetry," the Messenger of Allah added (5611).

This is only a part of the story and does not represent the positive side of the Prophet's attitude toward poets. True, he did not think highly of them. He himself was described by some as a poet but declined the honor because it detracted from the dignity of apostleship, the only status he cared to claim. "This is the speech of an honoured Apostle; it is not the speech of a poet nor of a soothsayer," he vehemently insisted (Qurān 69:40-42).

Muhammad took a utilitarian view of poets. The more inconvenient ones he had eliminated, even by the method of assassination, as in the cases of 'Asmā, the daughter of Marwān, the centenarian poet Abū 'Afak, and Ka'b ibn Ashraf. This taught many of the others to behave better. Muhammad also employed and honored some of the more pliable poets, among them Ka'b ibn Mālik, Hassān ibn Sābit, and Ka'b ibn Zuhair. The last-mentioned was the son of a famous poet of his times. At first Ka'b ibn Zuhair put himself under the ban by writing poems unfavorable to the Muslims. When Mecca was conquered, his brother, who was already a convert, warned him of the fate suffered by many other opponents of Islam and advised him to either submit or seek asylum somewhere else. He wrote Ka'b that the Apostle had killed some of the men in Mecca who had satirized him and that the Quraish poets who were left, like Ibn al-Ziba'rā and Hubayra b. Abū Wahb, had already fled in all directions. "If you have any use for your life then come quickly to the Apostle, for he does not kill anyone who comes to him in repentance. If you do not do that, then get to some safe place," he advised, according to Ibn Ishāq.*

**Sīrat Rasūl Allah,* p. 597.

Ka'b took his brother's advice and one day appeared before Muhammad without revealing his identity. "O Apostle, Ka'b b. Zuhair has come to ask security from you as a repentant Muslim. Would you accept him as such if he came to you?" Ka'b inquired of the Prophet. Receiving an affirmative answer, he said, "I am Ka'b, the son of Zuhair." Some of the people around Muhammad wanted his permission to kill him, but he was spared.

Then Ka'b sought the Prophet's permission to recite a *qasīda* in his praise. The permission was readily given. He began reciting: "He surpassed all the prophets in constitution and disposition, / Nor did any approach him either in knowledge or nobleness." But when he came to the lines, "Indeed, the Prophet is a Light providing guidance to the world / And a drawn sword from the armoury of Allah [*suyūf Allah*]," the Prophet was so delighted that he took off his mantle and bestowed it on Ka'b. The poem came to be known in the Muslim world as the "Poem of the Mantle" (*Qasīdat-ul-Burda*). The mantle became a precious heirloom of the poet's family and was bought from one of his descendants by a future Khalīfa, Mu'awiyah, for 40,000 dirhams. The *khirqai-sharīf* (holy mantle) became successively the property of the Ummayads and then of the Abbasides. Some say it was burned when Baghdad was sacked by the Tartars; others believe that it passed into the hands of the Ottoman caliphate. Whether real or fake, the Ottoman mantle is taken out as a national standard in times of great emergency.

Chess

Playing chess is also forbidden. "He who played chess is like one who dyed his hand with the flesh and blood of a swine," says Muhammad (5612).

VISIONS

The next book, again very small, is on visions and dreams. A bad dream is called *hulm,* an ordinary one *manām* and *al-rūyā* is a heavenly vision.

Muhammad says that good dreams come from Allah and bad

ones from Satan (5613). If one has a bad dream (*hulm*), he should do two things: "he should spit thrice on his left side" (5615-5616) and "not disclose it to any one" (5618). But a good dream one may reveal to his beloved friends (5618-5619).

Muhammad says that "the vision of a believer is the forty-sixth part of prophecy" (5622-5630); in other *ahādīs* it becomes "the seventieth part" (5632-5634). The difference between the forty-sixth and the seventieth parts "depends upon the difference in the standard of piety" of the dreamer, as the translator explains (note 2618).

Here too is some bad news for professional psychoanalysts. "Do not narrate to the people the vain sporting of Satan with you in your sleep," Muhammad advises his followers (5641).

Muhammad also makes a very self-satisifed statement: "He who saw me in a dream in fact saw me, for the satan does not appear in my form" (5635).

MUHAMMAD'S DREAMS

Muhammad also narrates some of his own dreams and gives their interpretations. Once in a dream, he was made to wear "two bangles" on his hands. At this he felt "a sort of burden" upon him (for a "bangle is the ornament of women," the translator explains); Muhammad then was made to blow upon them and they both disappeared. "I interpreted the two bangles as the two great liars who would appear after me and the one amongst them was 'Anasī the inhabitant of San'a and the other one was Musailima the inhabitant of Yamāma," Muhammad says (5650).

Both of these men lived at the time of the Prophet. Both claimed prophethood; Musailima al-Kazzāb ("the greater liar" as he is called by Muslim theologians) even claimed a joint share in the prophethood of Muhammad. 'Anasī and Musailima both led revolts and were killed.

13

Muhammad on Muhammad

The twenty-eighth book pertains to the "Excellent Qualities of the Prophet" (*Kitāb al-Fazā'il*).

Self-estimation

The book opens with the Prophet's own self-estimation. "Verily Allah granted eminence to Kinān from amongst the descendants of Ismā'il and He granted eminence to the Quraish amongst Kināns and He granted eminence to Banū Hāshim amongst the Quraish and He granted me eminence from the tribe of Banū Hāshim" (5653).

"I recognize the stone in Mecca which used to pay me salutations before my advent as a Prophet and I recognize that even now" (5654). So it seems that a stone can pay but not receive salutations. Idolatry in reverse.

"I shall be preeminent among the descendants of Adam on the Day of Resurrection and I will be the first intercessor and the first whose intercession will be accepted" (5655).

Muhammad uses an effective simile to show the difference between himself and the five or six Apostles that he recognized as having preceded him. The religion of the other apostles is like a building "imposing and beautiful" but for one brick. "I am that final brick," he says (5673-5676). With his coming, the edifice of religion becomes perfect, and there is no room or use left for any future prophet. "I have come to finalize the chain of Apostles," he says (5677). With him the old religions are abrogated and the possibility of any new one is exhausted. So any new religion or revelation must be a mischievous innovation.

Muhammad uses another simile to characterize three types of people who receive his message, which itself is like "rain falling upon the earth." The first are like "a good piece of land which receives the rainfall eagerly" and produces "herbage and grass abundantly." These people absorb the message of the Prophet and develop understanding about it and become a source of benefit to others. The second ones are like a "land hard and barren," which itself grows nothing but retains water for the benefit of others. These people have no deep understanding of the message but "acquire knowledge of religion and impart it to others." The third type is like a barren land which neither absorbs nor retains the rainwater. These people do not "accept the guidance of Allah with which I [Muhammad] have been sent" (5668).

In yet another simile, Muhammad tells the believers that while he is trying to save them from the hellfire, they are rushing headlong into it. "My example and your example is that of a person who lit the fire and insects and moths begin to fall in it and he would be making efforts to take them out, and I am going to hold you back from fire, but you are slipping from my hand" (5672).

THE NAMES OF MUHAMMAD

A little further in the book, Muhammad says: "I am Muhammad and I am Ahmad, and I am al-Māhī [the obliterator] by whom unbelief would be obliterated and I am Hāshir [the gatherer] at whose feet mankind will be gathered, and I am 'Āqib [the last to come] after whom there will be no prophet." He is also Muqaffī (the last in succession), and also the Prophet of Repentance as well as the Prophet of Mercy (5810-5813).

The statement will have Vedantic echoes for some ears; and many Hindus, predisposed to find "synthesis" and not caring whether it is a false one, may seize on this *hadīs* to "prove" that Vedantism and Prophetism are the same. But in fact the two approaches are widely apart in spirit.

Muhammad at the Heavenly Cistern

We learn from thirty-three *ahādīs* (5680-5712), on Muhammad's own assurance, that he will be at the Cistern in heaven waiting to receive his followers. "I shall be there ahead of you at the *Hauz Kausar*," he tells them (5712). The Hauz Kausar, or Cistern, is a great water reservoir in Paradise, requiring "a month's journey to go around it" (5684).

All the followers of Muhammad will be presented to him here except those who disobeyed the Prophet and made "innovations" in his religion. According to some authorities quoted by the translator, these are the people "who turned apostates after the death of the Holy Prophet and were killed by the army of Hazrat Abū Bakr" (note 2630).

A Prophet's Double Role

When an *ummah* is safe from the wrath of God, He calls back his Messenger as "a harbinger and recompense in the world to come." But when God intends to cause destruction to an *ummah,* He punishes it through His living Apostle. Allah "destroys it [the *Ummah*] as the Apostle witnesses it and he cools his eyes by destruction as they had belied him and disobeyed his command" (5679).

Adulation

The book also tells us what Muhammad's followers thought of him. It gives many *ahādīs* on this subject, many of them by Anas, who was the Prophet's servant for nine or ten years. He found Muhammad most valorous, most courageous, "sublimest among people and the most generous amongst them and he was the bravest of men" (5715-5717).

'Āisha, however, tells us that whenever the Prophet "had to choose between two things he adopted the easier one, provided it was no sin" (5752).

MUHAMMAD'S GENEROSITY

Muhammad gave freely from his war booty not only to his followers but also to other important chiefs to "incline" them to Islam. This was called his charitable disposition. Anas says that the Prophet never failed to give when "asked for anything in the name of Islam." A person came and Muhammad gave him a large flock of sheep and goats. "He went back to his people and said: My people, embrace Islam, for Muhammad gives so much charity as if he has no fear of want" (5728). Anas adds that this man "embraced Islam for the sake of the world but later he became Muslim until Islam became dearer to him than the world" (5729).

Another *hadīs* tells us that after he was granted a victory at Hunain by Allah, the Prophet gave one hundred camels to Safwān b. Ummaya. He then gave him another hundred and yet another hundred. The man was overwhelmed. "He [Muhammad] was the most detested person amongst people in my eyes. But he continued giving to me until now he is the dearest of people to me," the recipient said (5730).

Muhammad's promises of booty were fulfilled even posthumously. He promised someone: "In case we get wealth from Bahrain, I would give you so much." The Prophet died before the wealth arrived from Bahrain, but when it did, Abū Bakr gave the man a handful of coins. "He asked me to count them. I counted them as five hundred dinars and he [Abū Bakr] said: Here is double of this for you," the beneficiary tells us (5731).

Even prophets are not above using material inducements to win converts. "Do not be angry, for I give property to the *Mūlfat Qulūb*," Muhammad tells his faithful followers, according to a tradition quoted in Mirkhond's Persian biography of the Prophet. This is done in order "to rivet their hearts to faith" more securely. The *mūlfat qulūb* are nominal Muslims, or what Mahatma Gandhi calls in another context "rice Christians"; they are convinced by more palpable economic and political advantages. In their new mission work in India and other countries of Asia and Africa, the oil-rich sheikhs are following a holy and hoary tradition.

Rob Peter to pay Paul. In the prophetic theology both acts are meritorious. One is called *jihād,* the other *sadaqa,* or charity.

THE PROPHET'S BODILY CHARACTERISTICS: FRAGRANCE

There are many *ahādīs* about the Prophet's bodily characteristics: his face, appearance, complexion, hair, eyes, and even heels.

The Prophet's body was soft. Anas "never touched brocade or silk and found it as soft as the body of Allah's Messenger" (5759). His perspiration "shone like pearls." His body was also fragrant. Anas "never smelt musk or ambergris and found its fragrance as sweet as the fragrance of Allah's Messenger" (5760). His mother collected the Prophet's sweat in a bottle. She told Muhammad: "That is your sweat which we mix in our perfume and it becomes the most fragrant perfume" (5761).

THE PROPHET'S APPEARANCE

Al-Barā says that Muhammad was "neither very tall nor short-statured" (5771). He also found his face very handsome. "He put on a red mantle over him, and never have I seen anyone more handsome than Allah's Apostle" (5770).

THE PROPHET'S HAIR

There are many *ahādīs* on the Prophet's hair. The hair grew in the lobes of his ears. He used to part his hair. Ibn 'Abbās says the following on the subject: "The People of the Book [Jews and Christians] used to let their hair fall on their forehead and the polytheists used to part it on their heads, and Allah's Messenger liked to conform his behaviour to the People of the Book in matters in which he received no command from God; so Allah's Messenger let fall his hair upon his forehead, and then he began to part it after this" (5768).

That the Prophet reverted to the ways of the polytheists after following the Jewish practice shows, according to the translator, that a revelation was involved in the matter. Furthermore, to him the *hadīs* is a "clear proof of the fact that Allah's Messenger received *wahy* [revelation] from the Lord, in addition to what is contained in the *Qurān,* and he acted according to it" (note 2639).

Muhammad had some white hair but he did not dye it; Abū Bakr and 'Umar, younger than he, dyed their hair "with pure henna" (5779-5789).

His hair was collected. Anas reports that when the Prophet "got his hair cut by the barber, his Companions came round him and they eagerly wanted that no hair should fall but in the hand of a person" (5750).

THE SEAL OF PROPHETHOOD

His followers believed that Muhammad carried the "seal of prophethood" even physically as a protuberance on his back. 'Abdullah b. Sarjis says that he "saw the seal of Prophethood between his shoulders on the left side of his shoulder having spots on it like moles" (5793). Another man, Jābir, also saw it "on his back as if it were a pigeon's egg" (5790).

PHYSICAL CHANGES UNDER THE INFLUENCE OF WAHY

According to 'Āisha, when a revelation descended upon Muhammad, "his forehead perspired" (5764). According to Ubāda, under its influence, the "colour of his face underwent a change" (5766), and his head was lowered (5767). Muhammad himself says that at times *wahy* "comes to me like the ringing of a bell and that is most severe for me. . . . and at times an Angel in the form of a human being comes to me and speaks. . . ." (5765). The reference is to Dihya Kalbī, a young follower of his of striking beauty. In fact, Umm Salama, Muhammad's wife, once saw Gabriel talking to Muhammad and mistook the angel for Dihya Kalbī (6006).

Muhammad was commissioned as a prophet by Allah when he

was forty years old; and he died at the age of sixty-three (5794-5798). He stayed in Medina for ten years (5799-5809).

The Prophet Had the Best Knowledge

The Prophet had the best knowledge, and therefore it was obligatory for the believers to follow him obediently. Sometimes, Muhammad did or said something that some of the Companions did not approve. When this reaction was conveyed to the Prophet, he stood up and delivered an address: "What has happened to the people to whom there was conveyed on my behalf a matter for which I granted permission and they disapproved it and avoided it? By Allah, I have the best knowledge amongst them" (5814).

The test of true faith in Allah is for the believer to submit willingly to every decision made by His Apostle. Once there was a dispute between Zubair and an *ansār*. Muhammad gave his decision, but the *ansār* openly said that it favored Zubair, who was the Prophet's cousin—his father's sister's son. The Prophet's color changed and Allah sent him this verse: "Nay, by the Lord, they will not really believe until they make thee a judge of what is in dispute among them, and find in this no dislike of what thou decidest and submit with full submission" (Qurān 4:65; *hadīs* 5817).

But there is one *hadīs,* rather unusual, in which the Prophet strikes a more modest note. Muhammad once passed by as some people were grafting date-palm trees, i.e., combining the male with the female tree for a larger yield. Muhammad said: "I do not find it of any use." As a result, people no longer grafted their trees and the yield declined. When Muhammad, a practical man, learned this, he said: "If there is any use of it, then they should do it, for it was just a personal opinion of mine, and do not go after my personal opinion; but when I say to you anything on behalf of Allah, then do accept it, for I do not attribute lie to Allah, the Exalted and Glorious" (5830).

This is the only instance of its kind but a godsend for Muslim reformers who seek the emancipation of secular thought from the clutches of the *ulemas.* I do not think this approach can go very far, but Muslim reformers and "innovators" have to make the best of it.

MIRACLES

The book also reports many miracles, mostly patterned after those of Jesus. A small quantity of water was brought to Muhammad, but when he placed his hand in the vessel, everyone was enabled to perform ablution. "I saw water spouting from his fingers and the people performing ablution until the last amongst them performed it," the irrepressible Anas tells us (5657). But he has two options to offer about the number of people seeking ablution. In one place, he tells us that their number was "between fifty and eighty" (5656), in another three hundred (5658).

On another occasion, the Prophet gives someone half a *wasq* of barley. It sufficed him and his family and his guests till the curious one weighed it. "Had you not weighed it, you would be eating out of it and it would have remained intact for you," Jābir heard Muhammad telling him (5661).

On the battlefield, on the day of Uhud, Sa'd saw Gabriel and Michael on the right and left sides of the Prophet "in white clothes" (5713-5714).

OTHER APOSTLES

At the end of the book, there are *ahādīs* on the "merits" of other apostles like Jesus, Abraham, and Moses.

Muhammad's world was not very large. He knew his own people, the tribes allied with them, the Arab Bedouins, the neighboring Jews and Christians. To the Jews and Christians, he offered his leadership, and in making that bid adopted some of their beliefs and practices and also gave recognition to their apostles. But when he failed in his bid, he made another use of these apostles—he used them against their own followers. What he spoke was not merely the voice of Allah but also the voice of all the apostles that had come before him. Therefore, those who did not believe in him did not in fact believe in their own apostles; and therefore they were as good as apostates.

Recognizing the other prophets, though on his own terms, served a still greater purpose. It provided him with an apostolic lineage.

Speaking of himself and Jesus, Muhammad says: "Prophets are brothers in faith, having different mothers. Their religion is, however, one and there is no apostle between us [between Jesus and himself]" (5836). Muhammad comes as the last of the apostles and abrogates all previous revelations.

AL-ZIMMA' *(People of the Covenant or Obligation)*

Some *ahādīs* on the "merits" of Moses reveal an interesting fact: the *zimmīs* did not originate with 'Umar but were already there in the time of the Prophet. The Jews were already second-class citizens and were treated roughly by the believer-hoodlums in Muhammad's own day. For example, a Jew was selling goods; when an *ansār* offered a price that was not acceptable to him, a dispute rose. During the dispute, the Jew said: "By Allah, Who chose Moses amongst mankind." The *ansār* gave him a blow on the face, chiding him for invoking Moses when "Allah's Messenger is living with us." The Jew went to Muhammad, narrated the whole story, and supplicated him, saying: "Abu'l-Qāsim, I am a *Zimmi* [thus need your protection] by a covenant." Muhammad chided the *ansār* and told him: "Don't make distinction amongst the Prophets of Allah" (5853-5854).

This is the liberalism we have found from Muhammad at his rare best. But he could not arrive at the still larger truth which declares: Don't make a distinction between different *ummahs,* for they are all part of one human brotherhood; don't make a distinction between different gods, for they all express the same Truth; don't make a distinction between Allah and Allāt, for one is also the other. An exclusive concept of God leads to an exclusive concept of *ummah.* This is so with other religions of Semitic origin too, an attitude of either/or, seldom both.

14

The Prophet's Companions

The twenty-ninth book is on the "Merits of the Companions" (*Kitāb Fazā'il Al-Sahābah*) of the Prophet. It praises Muhammad's "Companions," his lieutenants and relatives like Abū Bakr, 'Umar, and 'Usmān; members of his family like Fātima, 'Alī, Hasan, and Husain; his wives like Khadīja, 'Āisha, Salama, and Zainab; and some loyal *ansārs* and other men associated with events and occasions important in the eyes of the Muslims of the days of the Prophet, like the Battle of Badr and the "Oath of Allegiance under the Tree" (*Bay'at al-Rizwān*) at Hodeibia in March A.D. 628 (those who took this oath were promised by Muhammad that they would never enter the fire of hell).

All of these people are praised not because they had a larger vision or a deeper humanity or a wider sense of justice than others but solely on one basis: their loyalty and utility to Muhammad's person and cause. In totalitarian ideologies and creeds, faith and loyalty to the leader are the supreme virtues. The followers need have no other. To be saved, it is enough to be subservient.

The Merits of Abū Bakr Siddīq

The original name of Abū Bakr Siddīq was 'Abdu'l Ka'bah. Muhammad changed his name to 'Abdu'llah Ibn Abī Quhāfa, but he soon came to be known by another name, Abū Bakr, "the father of the maiden," the maiden being 'Āisha, whom Muhammad betrothed when she was six and married when she was nine. Abū Bakr became Islam's first Khalīfa after Muhammad.

Muhammad had a high regard for Abū Bakr's services. "If I were to choose as my bosom friend I would have chosen the son of Abū Quhāfa as my bosom friend," Muhammad said (5873). When Muhammad was asked whom he loved best, he answered: " 'Āisha, 'Āisha's father, Abū Bakr, and 'Umar in that order" (5876).

There are *ahādīs* justifying the succession of Abū Bakr that may have been manufactured by their authors, even half-believingly, during the conflict around the question of succession that arose after Muhammad's death. A woman came to Muhammad during his last sickness and asked him whom she should go to when he was no longer there. "To Abū Bakr," Muhammad answered (5878). 'Āisha's report is even more to the point: "Allah's Messenger in his last illness asked me to call Abū Bakr, her father, and her brother too, so that he might write a document, for he feared that someone else might be desirous of succeeding him" (5879).

Abū Bakr came to power through a coup d'état. As soon as Muhammad died, the struggle for power began in earnest. 'Alī and 'Abbās, the Prophet's cousin and uncle, respectively, made the most of his dead body; they kept it to themselves and allowed no one else to take a hand in preparing it for burial. They locked the room from inside and secretly buried the body during the night in the very room in which he had died. Even 'Āisha, his favorite wife, was kept in the dark about it—she was sleeping in another hut at this time.

Outside, the struggle raged between the *ansārs* and the Emigrants. The *ansārs* met in the hall of Banu Sā'ida to choose Sa'd b. 'Ubāda, one of their own tribesmen, as the chief. When Abū Bakr and 'Umar got wind of this, they hurried to the spot with their own supporters. Abū Bakr told the Medinans that the Quraish were the "best of the Arabs in blood and country," and that the "Arabs will recognize authority only in this clan of Quraish." He told them: "We are the *Ameers*; and you are our *Wazeers*." When this drew a protest from the *ansārs*, it was proposed that each party should choose its own separate *Ameer*. But this was not acceptable to the Meccan party, and Abū Bakr was "chosen" as the *Ameer* of Islam. "In doing this, we jumped on Sa'd b. 'Ubāda and someone said that we killed him.

I said, 'God kill him,' " 'Umar reports according to Ibn Ishāq.* The story is repeated by Tabarī.†

The next day, Abū Bakr declared himself the Khalīfa of Islam.

The Excellent Qualities of 'Umar b. Khattāb

'Umar b. Khattāb and Abū Bakr were an inseparable pair. "I came and there came too Abū Bakr and 'Umar; I entered and there entered too Abū Bakr and 'Umar; I went out and there went out too Abū Bakr and 'Umar," Muhammad observed (5885).

'Umar was loyal to Muhammad. Once, while asleep, Muhammad found himself "in Paradise and a woman performing ablution by the side of a palace." When he inquired, he was told that it (it is not clear whether *it* stands for the woman or the palace or both) was for 'Umar. So Muhammad thought of 'Umar's feelings and turned back and went away. 'Umar wept when he was told about it. "Could I at all feel any jealousy about you?" he said to Muhammad (5898).

'Umar was fanatical, narrow-minded, and strong in his hatred. Once Muhammad was persuaded to offer a funeral prayer for someone whom the Muslims called a hypocrite. 'Umar "caught hold of the clothes of Allah's Messenger and said: Allah's Messenger, are you going to offer prayer, whereas Allah has forbidden to offer prayer for him?" (5904). But Muhammad persisted. And lo, as he prayed, Allah revealed the following verse: "Nor do thou ever pray for one of them that dies, nor stand at his grave; for they rejected God and His Apostle, and died in a state of perverse rebellion"

**Sīrat Rasūl Allah,* p. 279.

†'Umar with his party also went to the house of 'Alī, where Hāshimites had forgathered. "Either take the vow of obedience to Abū Bakr, or I shall put this house to fire and burn you all," 'Umar threatened them. Zubair, with a sword in his hand, walked toward him but his foot got entangled in the carpet. 'Umar's men jumped on him and brought him under control (Tārikh Tabarī, vol. I, p. 529). Eventually, when 'Alī submitted to Abū Bakr's Caliphate, Abū Sufyān taunted him that "only two ignoble things would bear their beatings and injustice so patiently: A tent nail and a village donkey" (Ibid., pp. 527–528).

(Qurān 9:84). Islam carried its hatred of its enemies even beyond the grave.

In fact Allah vindicated 'Umar more than once. The Muslim doctors mention fifty cases in which 'Umar's ideas became Qurānic revelations. 'Umar, however, modestly mentions only three. "My Lord concorded with my Judgments on three occasions. In case of the Station of Ibrāhīm, in case of the observance of the veil, and in case of the prisoners of Bardr" (5903).

The first instance refers to the fact that Muhammad and his followers prayed facing Jerusalem, the place of the Jewish Temple, during the first fifteen months of their stay in Medina. Later on, by a divine injunction, the direction was changed to Mecca, a course which 'Umar had advocated even earlier.

We have already recounted the incident about the veil in our discussion of the "Book of Salutations and Greetings," and shown how the divine injunction merely corroborated what 'Umar already stood for.

The third incident refers to the Quraish prisoners, one of whom was the Prophet's uncle, 'Abbās. Bakr had advised that they be freed for ransom, and 'Umar that they be killed. Muhammad accepted Bakr's advice in this particular case, but Allah concorded with the general approach of 'Umar. In fact, Allah chided the Prophet and told him that greed for gain in the shape of ransom should have no part in his calculations, and that his first duty as a Prophet was to engage in slaughter in the land: "It is not for a Prophet to have captives until he has made slaughter in the land. . . . Had it not been for a previous ordainment from Allah, a severe penalty would have reached you for the ransom you took" (Qurān 8:67–68).

'Umar is highly honored in Islamic history for his role in the spread of Arab imperialism. True, its real founder was Muhammad himself, a founder par excellence, who provided it with a theory, an ideology, a continuing motive, and the necessary religious rhetoric, successfully working out a grand model for his successors to imitate. But after him, 'Umar's contribution too was considerable. He forged new instrumentalities, provided a new taste for booty, a new incentive. He put every Arab, even including newborn babes, on the state's payroll. An Arab, he made it clear, had no other function except to be a colonizer and a soldier of Islamic imperialism.

This role of 'Umar's is brought out in several *ahādīs*. In a dream Muhammad saw himself drawing water from a tank. Then Abū Bakr took hold of the leather bucket, but he drew only "two buckets"; there was also "weakness in his drawing." Then 'Umar took over with real strength. "I did not see a person stronger than he drawing water," said Muhammad (5890–5896). These *ahādīs*, we are told, refer to 'Umar's future role in the spread of Muslim hegemony.

In the Muslim annals, we find that 'Umar needed no great provocation to flourish his sword but was no great warrior on the battlefield. In the lists of the slayers of the polytheists in the Battles of Badr and Uhud, his name appears only once. But if a man was a captive or was otherwise in his power, then 'Umar was quite brave with his sword. He met Mabad ibn Wahb, a Meccan who was captured in the Battle of Badr, and said to him tauntingly, "Well, you are beaten now." The man said, "Nay, by Lāt and Uzza." "Is that the manner of speech for a captive infidel towards a Believer?" asked 'Umar as he cut off his head with his sword.*

On another occasion, as we have already seen, 'Umar advised similar treatment for seventy other prisoners. "Hand them over to us so that we may cut off their heads," he told Muhammad. "Give 'Aqil [Alī's brother] to 'Alī that he may cut off his head, and hand over such and such relative to me that I may cut off his head," he said (4360).

Killing captives in cold blood was cruel enough. But why should a man be made to slay his own kith and kin so pointedly? This agreed with the requirements of the new creed, which weakened a man's old ties and strengthened his new ones as a means of increasing his "*ummah* consciousness." This was also the most effective way of proving one's loyalty to the new creed and the new leader. If one killed a parent or a brother or a cousin for the sake of Allah, it was something to be proud of. It was a feather in one's ideological cap. The same psychology was at work when 'Umar, on another occasion, tried to persuade Abū Jandal, the son of Soheil, to kill his own father because the father was merely one of the "idolators

*Wāqidī, quoted in Muir, *Life of Mahomet,* vol. III, p. 110.

whose blood is equivalent to that of dogs." The story is quoted in full in Mirkhond's biography of the Prophet.*

'Umar was fortunate in this respect. The only man he was able to slay in the Battles of Badr and Uhud was his maternal uncle. "You are under the impression that I killed your father," 'Umar said to Sa'īd b. al-'Ās. "As a matter of fact I killed my maternal uncle al-'Ās b. Hashām b. al-Mughīra," he said, trying to correct Sa'īd's mistaken impression.†

It is difficult to accept this attitude, so contrary to human nature and custom. But there is nothing unusual about it. The same things have taken place in our own time under Communism. Only a few decades ago, in Russia and even in China, members of the Party were encouraged to denounce their parents and close relatives and inform on them. It was supposed to strengthen their "class consciousness." Those who indulged in such unfilial behavior were honored as heroes. Similar ideologies and attitudes lead to similar values and usages.

The ethics of this practice was valid for the followers but not necessarily for the Prophet. And though he sent his parents and uncle to hellfire, he was more considerate toward his living kinsmen. He was kind to Abu'l 'Ās b. al-Rabī, his son-in-law, who was taken prisoner in the Battle of Badr, releasing him without any ransom. In the same battle, Muhammad also ordered his followers not to kill any member of the Banū Hāshim, the family to which he belonged, and also to spare his uncle, al-'Abbās. But one Muslim, Abū Huzayfa, who had participated in the slaying of his own father, did not like this. "Are we to kill our fathers and sons and our brothers and our families and leave al-'Abbās? By Allah, if I meet him I will flash my sword in him," he said aloud.

When this reached the ears of Muhammad, he was much troubled. "O Abū Hafs, ought the face of the apostle's uncle to be marked with the sword?" he said to 'Umar, who replied, "Let me off with his head! By Allah, the man is a false Muslim." Abū

*Mirkhond, *Rauzat-us-Safa,* vol. II, part II, p. 507.
†*Sīrat Rasūl Allah,* p. 739.

Huzayfa used to say, "I never felt safe after my words that day. I was always afraid unless martyrdom atoned for them." He was killed as a martyr in the Battle of al-Yamāma. This story is narrated by Ibn Ishāq.*

'Usmān b. 'Affān

'Usmān b. 'Affān converted to Islam because of his love for Ruqayya, one of the daughters of Muhammad, whom he married. After she died, Muhammad gave him another of his daughters, Umm Kulsūm.

According to Muslim tradition, 'Usmān was somewhat of a dandy. When the Emigrants went to Medina and built their mosque with voluntary labor, it was complained that he shirked manual work while one 'Ammār, a convert from the proletarian strata, was burdened with work that was too heavy. 'Usmān became the third Khalīfa of Islam and died, in the tradition of many other Muslim Khalīfas, at the hands of his brethren in faith.

'Āisha reports that the Prophet would receive Bakr and 'Umar while lying in bed with his thigh or his shank uncovered. But when 'Usmān came, he arranged his clothes and covered his thigh and shank, saying, "Should I not show modesty to one whom even the Angels show modesty" (5906).

From this *hadīs*, some Muslim doctors have derived a rule of decorum that when one is receiving a visitor, "the thigh of a person is not that part of the body which should be necessarily covered." Other doctors of theology and law, with great ingenuity, did not agree with this conclusion. From the arguments advanced on both sides, one can get the feel of Islamic scholarship at work, the order of truth it deals with, and its way of arriving at truth. It can be subtle about nothing, and its concerns are mostly with trifles.

There is another interesting *hadīs* given under this head. "Allah's Messenger was in one of the gardens of Medina [he had seven], reclining against a pillow—a person came asking for the gate to be

**Sīrat Rasūl Allah*, p. 301.

opened, whereupon he said: Open it for him and give him glad tidings of Paradise and lo, it was Abū Bakr." 'Umar and 'Usmān also visited the Prophet under the same circumstances and received the same tidings (5909). Here we have in one *hadīs* the trinity of successive Khalīfas with the promise of Paradise in store for each.

'ALĪ B. ABĪ TALIB

'Alī b. Abī Talib was the cousin and son-in-law of Muhammad. There were several *ahādīs* to support the claim that the supreme position in Islam rightfully belonged to him and his family by inheritance. Muhammad had once told 'Alī: "You are in the same position with relation to me as Aaron [Harun] was in relation to Moses but with this explicit difference that there is no prophet after me" (5913).

Another *hadīs* tells us whom Muhammad regarded as his family and, therefore, as the rightful heirs of at least his secular powers. In a *mubahala* (trial by prayer and curses) with the Christians, Muhammad had said: "Let us summon our children and your children." For his part the Prophet called 'Alī, Fātima, Hasan, and Husain. "O Allah, they are my family," he said (5915).

According to another *hadīs*, almost on his deathbed Muhammad told the believers: "I am leaving behind you two weighty things: . . . the Book of Allah . . . [and] the members of my household. I remind you of your duties to the members of my family." The definition of "the members of my family," or "people of the house" (*ahlul-bait*), is such that it excluded the Prophet's wives but included those for whom *zakāt* was forbidden; i.e., 'Alī, 'Aqil, Ja'far, and 'Abbās and their offspring (5920).

Another *hadīs* also "proves" 'Alī's claim. On the day of Khaibar, Muhammad said he would give the standard to a person who "loves Allah and His Messenger and Allah and His Messenger love him too." Then he called 'Alī, whose eyes were inflamed, and applied his own saliva as a cure. Then the Prophet told him: "Fight with them until they bear testimony to the fact that there is no god but Allah and Muhammad is his prophet." 'Alī accepted the responsibility and told the Prophet: "I will fight them until they are like us" (5915, 5918).

Now in granting 'Alī the banner of victory, to the exclusion of Bakr and 'Umar, was not the Prophet symbolically granting him the future leadership of Islam,* a leadership which 'Umar coveted in his heart? "Never did I cherish for leadership but on that day [the day of Khaibar]," 'Umar says (5917).

Allah is partial. The fact that He and His Messenger loved 'Alī made many things different for him. Acts of omission and commission which were punished in others were overlooked in 'Alī. After a battle fought under his general command, he took a slave-girl for himself even before the holy one-fifth had been made over to the Apostle's exchequer, a serious lapse inviting secular as well as divine punishment. Khālid b. Walīd, the second-in-command, complained to Muhammad. The Prophet was furious, "his face becoming red with anger," at the complaint. He would not even entertain such an accusation against 'Alī, for " 'Alī loves Allah and His Messenger, and Allah and His Messenger love 'Alī" (Tirmizī, vol. II, *hadīs* 1582).† What would you say of the state of justice when the authorities refuse even to record the first report?

In a battle, 'Alī was both brave and cunning. During the Battle of the Ditch, 'Amr b. 'Abdu Wudd, a man of ninety years, and 'Alī agreed to meet in single combat. At one point in the contest, 'Alī said to 'Amr: "Have we not agreed that no one should come to my or to thy aid." 'Amr asked: "Then what has happened?" 'Alī replied: "See, thy brother is coming behind thee." As 'Amr looked to his rear, 'Alī "snatched an opportunity to strike that accursed man." 'Amr exclaimed: "Boy, thou hast deceived me." But the "lord and receptacle of victory exclaimed: War is a deception."

*After Muhammad's death, 'Alītes are sure that he meant to bestow the Caliphate on 'Alī, but 'Alī himself was not so sure while the Prophet lived. When Muhammad was dying, 'Abbās, his uncle, took 'Alī aside and told him: "In three nights you will come under the sway of their rod. I know how the faces of the sons of 'Abdul-Muttalib look when they are on the verge of death; it appears to me that the Prophet will not survive. Let us, therefore, go to him and ask him who should inherit the Caliphate." But 'Alī declined, saying: "I shall never do it, for if he says 'no' to us now, people will never give us the Caliphate again." *(Tabaqāt*, vol. II, pp. 292–293; Tārīkh Tabarī, vol. I, p. 521).

†On another occasion, involving a complaint of a similar nature, Muhammad said in anger: "Indeed, 'Alī is from me, and I am from 'Alī" (Tirmizī, vol. II, *hadīs* 1569).

The story is given by Mirkhond.*

'Alī was not only Muhammad's best general, he was also his executioner. While Muhammad awarded the punishments, 'Alī was often chosen to execute them. He was asked to flog people found guilty of drinking (4231) or of fornication (4225); he also beheaded people on the orders of the Apostle (6676). But the most gruesome case was that of the captives of the Banū Quraiza, eight hundred strong, who were all beheaded in a single day in the market of Medina by 'Alī and Zubair (see above p. 112). "The apostle of God ordered a trench to be dug in a suitable place, and as they [the prisoners] were brought out in squads . . . 'Alī and Zubair set about striking off their heads, by order of his lordship the apostle. . . . On that day 'Alī and Zubair were till the evening engaged in slaying the Banī Quraiz, and when the night set in, the lamp of life of those who yet remained [to be executed] was extinguished by torchlight," Mirkhond records in his Persian biography of the Prophet.†

SA'D B. ABĪ WAQQĀS

Sa'd b. Abī Waqqās joined Muhammad when he was only thirteen and accompanied him on almost all his campaigns. He was one of those ten men who had been promised Paradise during their own lifetime by Muhammad. He worked as a doorman or sentinel for Muhammad during the night. After he was appointed to this responsibility, 'Āisha tells us, "Allah's Messenger slept such a sound sleep that I heard the noise of his snoring" (5925).

Sa'd was also the impetus for several Qurānic verses. We give one example. His mother took an oath that "she would never talk with him until he abandoned his faith, and she neither ate nor drank and said: Allah has commanded you to treat well your parents and I am your mother and I command you to do this." This, however, was the old polytheistic morality. But Allah now taught a new code and revealed the following verse of the Qurān: "We have enjoined on man kindness to parents: but if they strive to force thee to join

Rauzat-us-Safa, vol. II, part II, p. 456.

†Ibid., pp. 477–478.

with Me anything of which thou hast no knowledge, obey them not" (29:8; *hadīs* 5933).

The Merits of Zaid b. Haris

Zaid b. Haris was the adopted son of Muhammad and participated in most of his expeditions. Muhammad saw Zaid's wife half-uncovered and felt a great attraction for her. Though the whole matter caused a great scandal, he got Zaid to divorce her and married her. This was facilitated by the descent of a revelation from the High Heaven (Qurān 33:36–40). Until now, following the old Arab custom, Zaid was socially known as the son of Muhammad; but after this marriage, he again began to be called by the name of his natural father. This too was dictated by a revelation from Allah: "Call them by the name of their fathers. This is more equitable with Allah" (Qurān 33:5; *hadīs* 5956).

The Merits of Khadīja

In the list of merits, only four wives of the Prophet are mentioned: Khadīja, 'Āisha, Salama, and Zainab.* Khadīja was

*Muhammad married many women. Mirkhond gives us an account of eleven wives and four concubines. At-Tabarī mentions twenty-three names besides five more to whom proposals were made but without success. With some women, the marriage was not consummated. For example, one Asma'bint Alna'man was found leprous and, therefore, dispatched home. Another woman, Shanba' bint 'Umar alghafaria, probably a Quraiza or a Kināna, newly married, developed doubts about the apostleship of Muhammad when his infant son, Ibrāhīm, died. She was turned out. Muhammad also married a sister of Dihyā Kalbī whose youthful beauty had made such an impression on the Prophet that even Gabriel used to come to him in his likeness.

'Aisha tells us that the Prophet loved three things foremost: women, perfumes, and food. Muhammad himself says that "women, and the perfumes are the only delights of the world that I care about." Another tradition makes him prefer women to everything else. Muhammad says: "Jibrīl came to me with a pot; I ate from it, and I was granted the strength of forty men for coition." (*Tabaqāt*, vol. II, pp. 147, 164).

Muhammad's first employer and, though senior to him in age by fifteen years, his first wife; she was also the first to encourage him in his apostolic mission. According to Muhammad, Khadīja was the best of the women of her time, just as Mary, the daughter of Imran, was the best of the women of her time (5965).

'Āisha says: "Never did I feel jealous of any woman as I was jealous of Khadīja. She had died three years before he [Muhammad] married me. I often heard him praise her, and his Lord . . . had commanded him to give her the glad tidings of a palace of Jewels in Paradise, and whenever he slaughtered a sheep he presented its meat to her female companions" (5971). Once, in a fit of jealousy, 'Āisha told Muhammad: "Why do you remember one of those old women of the Quraish with gums red and who is so long dead—while Allah has given you a better one in her stead?" (5976).

Another *hadīs* throws some more light on Muhammad's conjugal life and also on the life of the women around him. 'Āisha reports that "when Allah's Messenger set out on a journey, he used to cast lots amongst his wives" to determine which of them would accompany him. Once, as luck would have it, Hafsa and 'Āisha were selected. "When it was night Allah's Messenger used to travel on camel with 'Āisha." But Hafsa asked 'Āisha if she would agree to change seats with her, for then "you would see what you do not generally see and I would see what I do not generally see." 'Āisha generously agreed, but when she saw Hafsa and the Prophet together she fell into a tantrum (5991). The translator explains that though 'Āisha's position was eminent and exalted, she was yet a woman and "thus could not be absolutely free from envy." About Muhammad's own behavior, he says that "in journey it is not compulsory to observe perfect equity amongst women in all respects" (note 2734). A rule within a rule, but all very convenient.

Even during his last illness, Muhammad was thinking of 'Āisha. "Where I would be tomorrow, where I would be tomorrow?" he inquired, thinking that the turn of 'Āisha was not near. "And when it was my turn, Allah called him to his heavenly home and his head was between my neck and chest," 'Āisha tells us (5985).*

Once Muhammad told her: " 'Āisha, here is Gabriel offering you greetings." She replied: "Let there be peace and blessing of Allah upon him," and added: "He sees what I do not see" (5997). One may wonder whether she always believed in Muhammad's angels, but certainly she enjoyed her role as the Prophet's favorite wife.

In fact, 'Āisha knew her Prophet a little too well. There is an interesting story narrated by Ibn Ishāq. During his last illness, just a few days before his death, Muhammad found 'Āisha crying with headache. Muhammad said to her: "Would it distress you if you were to die before me so that I might wrap you in your shroud and pray over you and bury you?" 'Āisha replied: "Methink I see you if you had done that returning to my house and spending a bridal night therein with one of your wives." The Apostle smiled and then his pain overcame him as he was going the round of his wives, until he was overpowered in the house of Maimūna. He then "called his wives and asked their permission to be nursed in my house, and they agreed," 'Āisha adds.† And there Muhammad died in her bosom.

THE MERITS OF FATĪMA

Fatīma was Muhammad's daughter by his first wife, Khadīja.

*Just before Muhammad died, 'Āisha's brother came in the room holding a green twig in his hand. Muhammad looked at it intently. 'Āisha took the hint, took the twig from her brother's hand, put it in her mouth, chewed it to make it soft and gave it to the Prophet. He cleansed his teeth and then he died. "The Prophet died in my room, on my day, and in my bosom, and even, in the last moment of his death, our salivas mingled," says 'Āisha counting these things as "gifts and blessings from Allah" (*Sahīh Bukhārī Sharīf, hadīs* 1650; *Tabaqāt*, vol. I, p. 282).

†*Sīrat Rasūl Allah*, pp. 678–679.

She was married to 'Alī, his cousin. She had two surviving sons, Hasan and Husain, from whom are descended the posterity of Muhammad, known as the *Saiyids*, meaning "masters."

Stating the position of Muslim theology, the translator assures us that Fatīma "is undoubtedly the chief of the ladies of Paradise and her two sons Imām Hasan and Husain are the chiefs of the young people of Paradise" (note 2751). Muhammad himself called her *al-batūl*, "the virgin."

The *ahādīs* on Fatīma tell us an interesting story. After Mecca was conquered, 'Alī sent a proposal of marriage to the daughter of the late Abū Jahl, an adversary of Muhammad and important chief of the Banū Makhzūm. Fatīma, his wife, complained about it to Muhammad. Muhammad put his foot down on the proposal and declared from the pulpit: "I would not allow them; I would not allow them; the only alternative is that 'Alī should divorce my daughter [and then marry their daughter], for my daughter is part of me. He who disturbs her disturbs me and he who offends her offends me" (5999).

So it seems that if the father of a woman had sufficiently strong influence, her husband could not marry another woman in spite of the custom of polygamy. In the case of Khadīja, she had the influence in her own right and as an employer held all the strings in her hands. Therefore, even though she was very much older than Muhammad, she was his only wife while she lived. It was only after her death that Muhammad started on his practice of polygamy.

The Merits of Zubair and Talha

Zubair embraced Islam when he was fifteen or sixteen. He was Muhammad's cousin and Abū Bakr's son-in-law. Thanks to his political connections, he later became the richest person in Arabia. He was the proud owner of a thousand slaves—a number unknown in pre-Muslim Arabia. Slavery in earnest and on such a large scale began with the advent of Islam.

About Zubair Muhammad said: "For every prophet there is a helper and my helper is Zubair" (5938). In the battle over the succession that raged later on, Zubair fought against 'Alī with the help of 'Āisha and was killed at the age of sixty-four by one of the partisans of 'Āli.

During the Battle of Uhud, Talha saved the life of Muhammad, and subsequently he took part in all the campaigns led by Muhammad. On the day of the Battle of Camel (in which 'Āisha, sitting on a camel, led rebel forces against 'Alī), Talha was murdered by one Marwān b. Hakam in revenge; for it was alleged that he had a hand in the murder of 'Usmān, the third Khalīfa.

THE MERITS OF SA'D B. MU'AZ

When Sa'd b. Mu'az died as a result of wounds received at the Battle of Badr, Muhammad said that "the Throne of the most Gracious shook at his death" (6033–6035). Most Muslim traditionalists take this literally, but some regard it as a metaphor denoting Allah's joy at receiving a beloved friend in His heavenly home.

There are other traditions about him, some of them recorded by Ibn Ishāq. Sa'd was a fat man, but his bier was very light to carry. Muhammad said that unseen angels were giving him their shoulder. On the same occasion he also said: "Every wailing woman lies except the one who wept Sa'd b. Mu'az."* Sa'd was a chief of the Banū Aus, who embraced Islam at Medina after the first pledge at Al-'Aqaba. Seen through less-believing eyes, he was treacherous and a fanatical sadist. On the day of the Battle of Badr, he was guarding Muhammad's hut along with some other *ansārs*. He watched with displeasure as the Muslim soldiers laid their hands on the prisoners. "You seem to dislike what the people are doing," Muhammad said to him. "Yes," he replied. "By God, it is the first defeat that God brought on the infidel and I would rather see them slaughtered than left alive," he added, according to a tradition quoted by Ibn Ishāq.†

***Sīrat Rasūl Allah*, p. 469.
†Ibid., p. 301.

The conspiracy to murder Ka'b ibn Ashraf, the poet, was worked out in consultation with Sa'd b. Mu'az. He also played a prominent part in causing the slaughter of eight hundred men of the Banū Quraiza, the erstwhile allies of his own tribe, the Aus.

Bilāl

One night Muhammad heard the sound of Bilāl's steps before him in Paradise. The next day, he asked him to narrate the act by which he hoped to receive such a good reward. Bilāl replied that he had done nothing so deserving except that "I perform complete ablution during the night or day I observe prayer with that purification what Allah ordained for me to pray" (6015).

Consistent with his lowly position, this is all the notice Bilāl receives in the "Book of the Companions" (in fact it is the shortest notice in the whole book). We would have skipped over him altogether but for the fact that he exemplifies a certain moral. He was an Abyssinian slave who was persecuted by his master, Umayya b. Khalaf, in Mecca. Since the Arab custom allowed manumission, he was ransomed by Abū Bakr and then converted to Islam.

We are glad that Bilāl escaped his alleged persecution, but what does this "conversion to Islam" mean? Did he become a better man? Did he became more forgiving, more kind and compassionate, less of a persecutor in his own turn? The brief references we have to him in the annals of early Islam hardly give us that impression.

'Abdul-Rahmān, an important Companion, tells us a story which is narrated by Ibn Ishāq and repeated by Tabarī. On the day of the Battle of Badr, 'Abdul-Rahmān "was carrying coats of mail" which, he said, he "had looted." Just at that time he encountered his old friend Umayya b. Khalaf and his son. Umayya, who belonged to the routed army of the Quraish, saw that he might have a chance of saving his life if he fell into the hands of 'Abdul-Rahmān as a prisoner, a state which would give him protection and from which he could be redeemed by paying an appropriate ransom. "O 'Abdul-Rahmān," he said, "won't you take me a prisoner, for I am more valuable than the coats of mail which you have." 'Abdul-Rahmān in turn replied, "By God, I will." Then he threw away the coats of mail and took his friend and his friend's son, now his prisoners, by their hands.

Just then, Bilāl saw his old persecutor and began to shout: "The arch-infidel, Umayya b. Khalaf! May I not live if he lives." The Muslims gathered. In vain did 'Abdul-Rahmān claim immunity for his prisoners. Bilāl kept shouting, and the Muslims "hewed them to pieces with their swords until they were dead." In later days, 'Abdul-Rahmān used to say, "God have mercy on Bilāl. I lost my coats of mail and he deprived me of my prisoners."*

There is another instance of the same kind denoting a sadistic pleasure in cruelty for its own sake. At the Battle of Khaibar, after the great carnage of the day, Muhammad ordered Bilāl to bring to him Safīyya, the young wife of the chief of the vanquished tribe, whose husband, father, and brother had just been murdered. Bilāl brought her and her cousin across the battlefield, which was littered with the corpses of their kith and kin. They cried in pain and horror. Bilāl explained that he did it on purpose; he "wished to see their grief and anger stirred up."†

Most conversions carried out by the soldiers and priests of proselytizing religions are of this nature. They bring no change in the individual.** In fact, often they make him worse. But organized conversions are now, as they have always been, part of an aggressive politics.

THE MERITS OF ABŪ DUJĀNA

Anas reports: "Allah's Messenger took hold of his sword on the Day of Uhud and said: Who would take it from me? Everyone

Sīrat Rasūl Allah, pp. 302-303.

†W. Muir, *Life of Mahomet*, vol. IV, p. 68.

**Most conversions are of this kind. There is a telling example. When Mecca was conquered, 'Akrama, the son of Abū Jahl, a strong opponent of Islam, decided to become a Muslim. He promised Muhammad: "I swear by God that for every dirham I spent during the time of ignorance to obstruct the religion of God the Most High, I shall disburse two for the promotion thereof, and that for every one of the friends of God the Most High whom I have murdered during the time of my infidelity, I shall slay two of His foes" (Mirkhond, vol, II, pp. 611-612). Muhammad found nothing exceptionable in this.

present stretched his hand saying: I would do it. He [Allah's Apostle] said: Who would take it in order to fulfil its rights? Then the people withdrew their hands. Simāk b. Kharasha Abū Dujāna said: I am here to take it and fulfil its rights. He took it and struck the heads of the polytheists" (6040).

THE TWO 'ABDULLAHS

The names of two 'Abdullahs also appear on the merit list. One of them was the son of 'Umar; the other was the son of Zubair by Asma, the daughter of Bakr. Both were killed by the Umayyad general Hajjāj. The general even led the funeral prayer for 'Abdullah b. 'Umar after contriving to murder him. The body of 'Abdullah ibn Zubair was found hanging outside Medina on the road to Mecca (6176). He died when he was seventy-two after having been a Khalīfa of a sort for nine years.

THE MERITS OF ANAS AND HURAIRA

On the list of merits also appear the names of Anas, Muhammad's servant and bodyguard for ten years, and Huraira, to whom we owe a disproportionately large number of traditions. Huraira in his own lifetime was known as Huraira the liar. He explains: "You are under the impression that Abū Huraira transmits so many *ahādīs* from Allah's Messenger. . . . I was a poor man and I served Allah's Messenger . . . whereas the immigrants remained busy with transactions in the bazaar. . . . I never forgot anything that I heard from him [Muhammad]" (6083).

THE MERITS OF HASSĀN B. SĀBIT

An interesting person on the merit list is Hassān b. Sābit, a poet whom Muhammed employed for replying to the lampoons against him by unbeliever poets. Muhammad said to him: "Write satire against the unbelievers; Gabriel is with you" (6074). On another occasion, Muhammad told him: "Hassān, give a reply on behalf of the Messenger of Allah." And to Allah Himself, he petitioned: "O

Allah, help him with *Rūh-ul-Qudus* [the holy spirit]" (6073).

'Āisha gives us a fuller version of the story. According to her, Muhammad had said: "Satirise against the Quraish, for the satire is more grievous to them than the hurt from an arrow." With that end in view, Muhammad sent for two poets, Ibn Rawāha and Ka'b b. Mālik, and commissioned them to write satires. Unsatisfied with their compositions, the Prophet next sent for Hassān b. Sabit, who told him: "Now you have called for this lion who strikes the enemies with his tail. . . . I shall tear them with my tongue as the leather is torn." He then declared his intention to satirize Abū Sufyān. "Permit me to write satire against Abū Sufyān," he said to Muhammad. But there was a difficulty: how could it be done successfully without involving the Prophet, for Muhammad and Abū Sufyān shared the same lineage? Abū Bakr was appointed to help Hassān with the lineage of the Quraish, which he knew very well. Understanding the intricacies, Hassān then went to Muhammad and assured him: "By Him Who has sent you with Truth, I shall draw out from them your name as hair is drawn out from the flour."

Hassān gave Muhammad complete satisfaction. "I heard Allah's Messenger saying: Hassān satirised against them and gave satisfaction to the Muslims and disquieted the non-Muslims," says 'Āisha (6079, 6081).

Muhammad was grateful to Hassān, who was not altogether cut when he later took an active part in the scandal against 'Āisha, though all the participants were flogged. 'Āisha was the first to excuse Hassān. "Leave him for he defended Allah's Messenger," she said (6075).

Muhammad was opposed to poets and poetry, but when they were in his service, it was a different matter.

MUHAMMAD AT THE CENTER

Muhammad is at the center of everything. He tells his followers: "I am a source of safety and security to my Companions. . . . and my Companions are a source of security for the *Ummah*" (6147).

As things converge toward Muhammad, they become better, but as they proceed further away from him, they decline in status as well as in quality and authenticity. "The best of my *Ummah* would be those of the generation nearest to mine. Then those nearest to them, then those nearest to them" (6150). In this ranking and ordering, the Prophet comes first; then come his Companions; then come the successors of the Companions (*tābi'ūn*). Muslim divines have not been idle, and they have worked out the exact period of each era. According to one important opinion, the first period is coextensive with the life of the Companions (i.e., 120 years, as the last Companion died in A.H. 110); the second period extends till the life of the successors of the Companions (up to A.H. 170); and the third is coextensive with the life of those who followed the successors (till A.H. 220).

At the end of the book, the Prophet warns the coming generations of Muslims: "Do not revile my Companions, do not revile my Companions" (6167).

15

Virtue, Destiny, Knowledge, Remembrance of God

The thirtieth book is on "Virtue, Good Manners, and the Joining of the Ties of Relationship."

Many of the principles enunciated in this book are good except that they have a sectarian orientation. While the Muslim has a permanent quarrel with polytheists, he must not feel enmity toward a fellow Muslim. "It is not lawful for a Muslim that he should keep his relations estranged with his brother beyond three days" (6205).

"A Muslim is the brother of a Muslim. He neither oppresses him nor humiliates him nor looks down upon him. . . . All things of a Muslim are inviolable for his brother in faith: his blood, his wealth and his honour" (6219).

A Muslim should visit his sick brother. "When a Muslim visits his brother in Islam he is supposed to remain in the fruit garden of Paradise until he returns" (6229). And, of course, the sickness of a Muslim is no sickness; it is a reward. "When a Muslim falls ill, his compensation is that his minor sins are obliterated" (6235). If he suffers pain, even to the extent of stepping on a thorn, "Allah elevates him in rank or effaces his sins because of that" (6238). This idea runs through many *ahādīs* (6233–6245)

Believers should not nurse mutual rancor. "The gates of Paradise are not opened but on two days, Monday and Thursday, and then every servant of Allah is granted pardon who does not associate anything with Allah except the person in whose heart there is rancour against his brother" (6222).

In short, all Muslims should help each other, stand by each other, and feel for each other. "A believer is like a brick for another believer, the one supporting the other" (6257). All Muslims are one body. "The believers are like one person; if his head aches, the whole body aches with fever and sleeplessness" (6260).

OTHER VIRTUES

Charity and forgiveness are recommended (6264). Abuse and backbiting and tale-carrying are censured (6263, 6265, and 6306). It is meritorious to speak the truth, for "truth leads one to Paradise" (6307). But lying is permissible in three cases: "In battle, for bringing reconciliation amongst persons and the narration of the words of the husband to his wife, and the narration of the words of a wife to her husband" (6303).

NONVIOLENCE

Nonviolence of a sort is also preached. "When any one of you fights with his brother, he should spare his face" (6325).* The face should be avoided because, as the Prophet himself explains, "Allah created Adam in His own image" (2872).

Similarly, if a man goes to a bazaar or a mosque with arrows, he should take care of their "pointed heads so that these might not do any harm to a Muslim" (6332).

RETRIBUTION

If we could forget Allah's partiality for Muslims, the following could be considered an eloquent rendering of the law of retribution: "The claimants would get their claims on the Day of Resurrection so much so that the hornless sheep would get its claim from the horned sheep" (6252). Therefore a Muslim should not oppress another Muslim and, in fact, should help him. "A Muslim is the brother of a fellow-Muslim. He should neither commit oppression

*This is the nearest we have from Muhammad to Jesus' teaching: "Whosoever shall smite thee on thy right cheek, turn to him the other also" (Matthew 5:39).

upon him nor ruin him, and he who meets the need of a brother, Allah would meet his needs, and he who relieves a Muslim from hardship, Allah would relieve him from hardships to which he would be put on the Day of Resurrection, and he who did not expose the follies of a Muslim, Allah would conceal his follies on the Day of Resurrection'' (6250).

Subject People

Such benevolence as is compatible with *jizyā*, spoils, and holy war was allowed by some believers toward the nonbelievers too. When Hishām saw ''the farmers of Syria, who had been made to stand in the sun . . . [and] detained for *Jizyā*,'' he was reminded of the Prophet's words: ''Allah would torment those who torment people in the world'' (6328). Obviously, Hishām extended the definition of ''people'' to include men other than Muslims.

The Prophet's Covenant with Allah

Muhammad was somewhat more indulgent toward his own lapses. If he ill-treated his followers, that brought him no blame, secular or divine, and, in fact, turned into a blessing for the sufferers. ''O Allah, I make a covenant with Thee against which Thou wouldst never go. I am a human being and thus for a Muslim whom I give any harm or whom I scold or upon whom I invoke curse or whom I beat, make this a source of blessing, purification and nearness to Thee on the Day of Resurrection'' (6290). One would think that to err is human, not apostolic; at least, not in such grave matters.

THE ''BOOK OF PIETY AND SOFTENING OF HEARTS''

The subject of virtue is also discussed in the fortieth book, pertaining to ''Piety and Softening of Hearts'' (*al-zuhd wa al-raqā'iq*).

Here are mentioned certain acts which are considered pious and meritorious. Widows, orphans, and the poor should be treated benevolently (7107–7108). Charity should be given to the poor and the wayfarer (7112–7113). The merit of building mosques is stressed.

"He who builds a mosque for Allah, Allah would build for him a house in Paradise" (7110).

Any ostentatious display of one's deeds is deplored. "If anyone makes a hypocritical display, Allah will make a display of him" (7115). Therefore, one should not publicize one's lapses and omissions. "All the people of my *Ummah* would get pardon for their sins except those who publicize them" (7124).

The great theological sin of polytheism does not go unmentioned. Allah the Most High and Exalted states: "I am the One, One who does not stand in need of a partner. If anyone does anything in which he associates anyone else with Me, I shall abandon him with one with whom he associates Allah" (7114). This is the first time that Allah lets a man off so lightly and does not seize him and roast him in hellfire for the great sin of polytheism.

Muhammad also disapproved of sneezing and yawning. "The yawning is from the devil," he said (7129).

THE VANITY OF WORLDLY RICHES

Several *ahādīs* at the very beginning of the book show the "vanity of worldly possessions," and how worldly wealth perishes and only good deeds remain.

Muhammad sent Abū 'Ubaida to collect *jizyā* from the tribes of Bahrain. As soon as the news of his return came, the *ansārs* gathered round Muhammad. Muhammad smiled and said: "I think you have heard about the arrival of Abū 'Ubaida with goods from Bahrain." They said: "Yes." Muhammad now did some thinking out loud and said that the new riches might corrupt them. "By Allah, it is not the poverty about which I fear in regard to you but I am afraid in your case that the worldly riches may be given to you as were given to those who had gone before you and you begin to vie with one another for them as they vied for them, and these may destroy you as these destroyed them" (7065).

This sentiment was duplicated by 'Umar while distributing the "holy one-fifth" amongst the Medinans, part of a booty valued at thirty million dirhams (besides many maidens and a vast number of fine Persian horses, nine falling to the lot of every combatant) won at the Battle of Jalola under the generalship of Sa'd, from an outlying province of Persia. The sentiment sounded pious and it still does. It has come down the corridor of history "proving" the great "piety" of 'Umar. But the basic question about the whole business of holy war, burning, pillage, booty, *jizyā*, and how these can become legitimate and moral has really never bothered Muslim theologians and scholars or even the Sufis. They can strain at a gnat but are ready to swallow a camel.

Several *ahādīs* show that the holy war against the infidels was not only a pious act but a profitable business. Utba b. Ghazwān tells us: "I was the seventh amongst seven* who had been with Allah's Messenger and we had nothing to eat but the leaves of the tree. . . . We found a sheet which we tore in two and divided between myself and Sa'd b. Malik. I made the lower garment with half of it and so did Sa'd. . . . and today there is none amongst us who has not become the governor of a city" (7075).

Theology Dominates Morality

The Prophet's moral teaching is dominated by theology. For example, the "Book of Virtue and Good Manners" opens with *ahādīs* which enjoin the believers to accord benevolent treatment to their parents and to obey them. Who among the people is most deserving of good treatment? "Your mother, again your mother, again

*The phrase "seventh amongst seven" refers to a party of seven men sent by Muhammad under the leadership of 'Abdullah ibn Jahsh to waylay a caravan of the Quraish during the second year of his stay in Medina. In order to disarm the apprehensions of the men in charge of the caravan, one of the raiders shaved his head so that they would be taken for pilgrims. When the caravan-men were off guard and cooking their food, the raiders rushed upon them, killing one man, taking two prisoners, and securing spoils. This killing took place during the sacred month of the Arabs when, according to their tradition, no blood could be spilled. That was, however, only the old polytheistic morality. But Utba was hardly "the seventh of the seven," though he was one of the raiding party, for when the action was taking place, he had fallen behind to search for his camel, which he later said had wandered away.

your mother, then your father, then your nearest relatives according to the order of nearness," replies Muhammad (6181).

But if morality conflicts with Muslim theology, the latter prevails. We have already seen how Allah Himself ordered Sa'd b. Abī Waqqās not to obey his parents if they stood for polytheism (Qurān 29:8, 31:15).

Not merely to disobey them, but if necessary to oppose them in more active ways. The son of 'Abdullah ibn Ubayy, an *ansār*, tells Muhammad: "If you really want him [his father] killed, command me to do it and I will bring you his head . . . [but] if you order another to kill him, I shall not afterwards be able to bear the sight of his murderer. . . . I shall kill him—and then I shall have killed one of the faithful for an infidel, and I shall go to hell." What a combination of piety and filial duty!*

Similarly, there are several traditions which boast how Abū Hozayfa, an Emigrant, helped Hamza to kill his own father by giving him a cut with his sword at the Battle of Badr.

Muhammad is praised in Islamic lore for "joining of the ties of relationship." But the fact is that the believers were encouraged to rebel against these very ties in order to disorient them altogether from the old life and to strengthen their exclusive loyalty to the new leader and the new *ummah*. For the assassination of a poetess of Medina, 'Asma bint Marwān, one 'Umayr ibn 'Adi, a man of her own clan, was chosen. That helped him to prove his zeal and loyalty to the cause of Islam. After driving his sword through the sleeping woman with one of her children still at her breast, he came to Muhammad to inform him. "You have done a service to Allah and His Messenger," the Prophet told him gratefully.

MUHAMMAD'S MOTHER IN HELL

For the same theological reason, Muhammad was ready to consign his father, his noble-hearted uncle Abū Tālib, and even his mother to the flames of hellfire.

*The story is given in Ibn Ishāq and repeated in Tabarī. The version here is from *Sīrat Rasūl Allah*, pp. 491–492.

In this respect, the polytheists, who were not theological, were better than the Muslims. After the conquest of Mecca, when Muhammad became supreme in Arabia, and the smaller tribes had to pay homage to his power and prophethood, two brothers, chiefs of a tribe inhabiting Yemen, came to Muhammad and showed their willingness to embrace Islam. They were converted. They hated to eat the heart of an animal but were made to do so in order to prove that their break with their old polytheism was genuine. Later on, during a conversation with Muhammad, their late mother came in for a mention, and Muhammad told them that she was in hell. Both turned away from him in anger. "Come back, my own mother too is there with yours," Muhammad cried in an unsuccessful effort to entice them back. As they departed the two brothers said: "This man has not only made us eat the heart of the animals, but said that our mother is in hell: who would follow him?"*

Lack of Universality

Another feature of the Prophet's teaching on morals, inevitably flowing from its predominantly theological nature, is its lack of universality. Faith, equity, justice are only for the Muslims in their mutual relationships. To the infidels and unbelievers another code, another set of rules, is applied.† The lives of their males are forfeit; their women are legitimate objects of concubinage and bondage; their children are meant for slavery; and their wealth and property for pillage and booty.

A sectarian attitude informs all matters large or small. When two Muslims meet, they are to greet each other. "The better of the two is one who is the first to give a greeting" (6210). But Muhammad advises his followers not to greet Jews and Christians first (5389).

**Tabaqāt*, vol. II, p. 100; also W. Muir, *Life of Mahomet*, vol. IV, pp. 228-229.

†The Qurān frankly teaches this discriminatory ethic. "Muhammad is Allah's apostle. Those who follow him are ruthless to the unbelievers but merciful to one another," it says (48:29).

Similarly, if you meet a Muslim on the road, you are to be courteous and step aside to give him the way (5376), but if you meet a Jew or a Christian, you are to push him aside (5389).

When a Muslim dies, fellow Muslims should "follow his bier." In fact, this is one of the five or six "rights of a Muslim over another Muslim" (5379). And in the same vein, a Muslim should offer a prayer of mercy for a fellow Muslim. But Allah forbids this courtesy toward non-Muslims (Qurān 9:84). It is another matter that some Muslims do not live up to the Prophet's teachings. But Muhammad himself was very particular about keeping away from the funerals of non-Muslims. According to Muslim tradition, one Mukhayrīq, a learned Jewish priest, recognized Muhammad as the promised prophet and even bestowed seven gardens on him (according to some traditions, they were part of the war booty seized from the Jews of Medina). He also fought alongside Muhammad on the day of Uhud, though it was a Sabbath, and died in the battle. But though his corpse was allowed to be buried near the Muslims, Muhammad did not attend his funeral or pray for him. Mukhayrīq was "the best of the Jews," as Muhammad called him, but he was still not entitled to a Muslim funeral prayer.

LACK OF INWARDNESS

Muhammad's moral teaching also lacks inwardness. It does not seem to know that man's acts emanate from his thoughts and desires, which in turn are rooted in the separative ego and in nescience. True, Muhammad could not have heard of Indian Yoga, though the Buddhist influence had been penetrating the Middle East for many centuries; but this idea was not entirely unknown to Semitic traditions which he knew and in some ways had made his own. Jesus had preached that "out of the heart proceed evil thoughts, murders, adulteries, fornications, theft, false witness, blasphemies." But Muhammad failed to benefit from this source. The fact is that he founded a very outward religion.

Without inner purification, there can be no higher ethical life. Even piety is no substitute for purity and for inner self-understanding and inner self-culture and aspiration. An unpurified heart merely rationalizes man's lusts, violence, and prurience; garbing itself in pious clothing, it gives the theology of a Moloch-Allah demanding the blood of the infidels; it gives an ethics of *jihād*, war booty, and tribute.

The lack of a philosophy and praxis of inner culture fails to bring about any real sublimation; it imposes only an outer code, leading to a reluctant and even rebellious conformity. For example, Muhammad customarily visited his wives in rotation. But, as might be expected, he found it burdensome to observe this practice. "This I have power to do; but thou, O Lord, are the master over that of which I have no power [love for each]," he said.* So Allah had to intervene with more accommodating revelations.

DESTINY

The thirty-first book, the "Book of Destiny" (*Qadr*), contains only fifty-one *ahādīs* (6390–6441).

Muhammad believes that everything is predetermined. "Evil one is he who is evil in his mother's womb" (6393). Each person passes through a series of stages. "The constituents of one of you are collected for forty days in his mother's womb in the form of blood, after which it becomes a lump of flesh and forty days later Allah sends His angel to it with instructions concerning four things . . . his livelihood, his death, his deeds, his fortune and misfortune." As a result, it may even happen that a very good man who deserves Paradise and is only a cubit away from Paradise will suddenly be overcome by what destiny has written and begin to act like a denizen of hell. And, of course, the reverse may also happen (6390).

The Prophet assures us that "Allah has fixed the very portion of adultery which a man will indulge in" (6421).

This brings in the usual riddle: how to reconcile destiny with freedom of action. One day, Muhammad told his followers that "there is not one amongst you who has not been allotted his seat in Paradise or Hell." They logically asked: "Why then should we perform good deeds, why not depend upon our destiny?" Muham-

**Tabaqāt*, vol. II, p. 280.

mad replied: "No, do perform good deeds, for everyone is facilitated in that for which he is created" (6400).

Here is another theological riddle and another answer. If everything of men is decreed in advance, then "would it not be an injustice to punish them?" Muhammad replies: "Everything is created by Allah and lies in His power. He would not be questioned as to what He does, but they [His creatures] would be questioned" (6406).

KNOWLEDGE

The thirty-second book, even smaller than the previous one, is the "Book of Knowledge" (*'Ilm*).

The word "knowledge" here has a special connotation. It means the knowledge that we find in the Qurān. "Recite the *Qurān*," and do not dispute about it—that is knowledge. "Verily, the peoples before you were ruined because of their disputation in the Book," the Prophet warns the believers (6443).

Muhammad also warns against people who believe that certain portions of the Qurān are mere allegories and try to read their own meanings into them. Those who "have a yearning for error go after the allegorical verses seeking to cause dissension, by seeking to explain them." On the other hand, those "who are sound in knowledge say: We affirm our faith in everything which is from our Lord" (6442).

He also warns against "hair-splitting." "Ruined are those who indulged in hair-splitting," he says (6450).

But in spite of these warnings, Muhammad is still apprehensive about his followers and feels that they will take to the path of the Jews and the Christians. "You would tread the same path as was trodden by those before you inch by inch and step by step so much so that if they had entered into the hole of the lizard, you would follow them in this also," he remonstrates with the believers.

The book also includes a flattering reference to scholars. "Verily, Allah does not take away knowledge by snatching it from the people but he takes away the knowledge by taking away the scholars" (6462).

REMEMBRANCE OF ALLAH

The thirty-third book is on "Remembrance of Allah" (*Kitāb al-Zikr*).

The believers are exhorted to remember Allah. Though Muhammad rebelled against the idea that Allah had visible forms, he retained His audible names. "There are ninety-nine names of Allah; he who commits them to memory would get into Paradise," Muhammad tells us (6475).

Why ninety-nine? "God is odd [*witr*] and He loves odd number," Muhammad explains (6476).

Allah tells us that if a believer "draws near Me by the span of a palm, I draw near him by the cubit. . . . And if he walks towards Me, I rush towards him" (6471).

The statement is taken from the mystic lore, where it has a meaning very different from the one given to it in certain prophetic traditions. In the mystic tradition, "walking toward Me" means walking in truth, in conciliation, in compassion, in brotherliness, in purity, in wisdom; it means walking toward the Light within. In the prophetic tradition, the phrase means walking in enmity toward the polytheists, the infidels, in conformity to the commands conveyed by Allah through revelation to some favored fellow. Our own role is compliance and conformity and obedience to a revelation which is not ours. In this holy war which we are asked to wage with zeal, faith, and earnestness, our reward is booty, slaves, and empire if we succeed, and Paradise if we fall.

Muhammad's god, like his moral teaching, is sectarian and lacks both universality and true inwardness. Muhammad's Allah is a tribal god trying to be universal through *jihād*, conquest, and forced conversions. "There is no God but allah and Muhammad is the prophet of this godling" is the true import of the Muhammadan *kalimah* (creed).

Some theologians "exalt" God but denigrate man; they are tearful about God but are quite dry-eyed and even cruel-hearted toward their fellow mortals, whom they give all kinds of names: heathen, infidel, polytheist, and so on. We should be wary of such theologians and their theologies.

RECITING ALLAH'S NAME BEFORE GOING TO SLEEP

'Alī tells us that Fātima, his wife and the Prophet's daughter, "had a corn in her hand because of working at the hand-mill." They heard that "there had fallen to the lot of Allah's Apostle some prisoners of war." So Fātima came to the Holy Prophet in the expectation of acquiring a slave for herself. But Muhammad had none to spare at the time, so he told Fātima: "May I not direct you to something better than what you have asked for? When you go to your bed, you should recite *Takbīr* [*Allah-o-Akbar*] thirty-four times and *Tasbīh* [*Subhān Allah*] thirty-three times and *Tahmīd* [*al-Hamdu li-Allah*] thirty-three times and that is better than the servant for you" (6577).

Allah's name did not always suffice as a substitute for a servant. The Prophet was in the habit of giving prisoners of war to his favorite believers as slaves and concubines. For example, he gave 'Alī a captured girl named Rayta, the daughter of Hilāl, as a gift. She was part of the war booty won from the Banū Hawāzin, the tribe of Muhammad's foster mother. Two other girls from the same booty were given as gifts, one to 'Usmān, Muhammad's other son-in-law, and the second to 'Umar, who in turn gave her to his son 'Abdullah.*

SUPPLICATE ALLAH AND FLEE FROM SATAN IN THE MORNING

We may quote one more *hadīs* apropos: "When you listen to the crowing of the cock, ask Allah for His favour as it sees Angels and when you listen to the braying of the donkey, seek refuge in Allah from the Satan for it sees Satan," Muhammad tells the believers (6581). Demonology is the other side of theology.

*Sīrat Rasūl Allah, p. 593.

16

Paradise, Hell, Their Inmates, the Last Day

The next four books tell us something about Paradise and Hell and their respective inhabitants; they also tell us about the Day of Judgment, and the Turmoils and Portents of the Last Hour.

In book thirty-four, called the "Book of Heart-Melting Traditions" (*al-Riqāq*), Muhammad tells us that he "stood upon the door of Fire [Hell] and the majority amongst them who entered there was that of women" (6596). On the other hand, "amongst the inmates of Paradise," women will "form a minority" (6600).

Muhammad says that he has solved all the problems of the believers except the problems created by women. "I have not left after me turmoil for the people but the harm done to men by women" (6604). According to another tradition, he tells his *ummah*: "The world is sweet and green [alluring] and verily Allah is going to install you as Viceregent in it in order to see how you act. So avoid the allurement of women: verily, the first trial for the people of Israel was caused by women" (6606).

The Poor

The poor fare better at Muhammad's hand. "I had a chance to look into Paradise and I found that majority of the people was poor" (6597). If they so wish, the Communists can claim Muhammad as their own, though Paradise may be no more than an "opiate" of the poor.

THE DAY OF JUDGMENT

In book thirty-seven (*Al-Qiyāma wa'l Janna wa'n-Nār*), giving a description of the Day of Judgment, and of Paradise and Hell, Muhammad tells us that on the Last Day "Allah, the Exalted and Glorious, will take in His grip the earth . . . and roll up the sky in His right hand and would say: I am the Lord; where are the sovereigns of the world?" (6703).

THE CREATION

Muhammad tells us that Allah "created the clay on Saturday and He created the mountains on Sunday and He created the trees on Monday and created the things entailing labour on Tuesday and created light on Wednesday and He created the animals to spread on Thursday and created Adam after 'Asr [the afternoon prayer] on Friday; the last creation at the last hour of the hours of Friday, i.e., between afternoon and night" (6707).

THE DESTRUCTION

The Last Day—the day of the destruction of the world—is also described. On this day, Muhammad said, "the earth would turn to be one single bread . . . and the Almighty would turn it in His hand as one of you turns a loaf while on a journey. It would be a feast in honour of the people of Paradise." Then he laughed "until his molar teeth became visible"; then he asked his audience whether they would also like to be informed "about that with which they would season it [bread]." "With *bālām* and fish," he told them. *Bālām* is "ox and fish from whose excessive livers seventy thousand people would be able to eat" (6710).

NONBELIEVERS

On the Day of Resurrection, while the inmates of Paradise are feasting on the fare described above, "the nonbelievers would be made to assemble by crawling on their faces" (6737).

The believer will be doubly blessed. Allah "would confer upon him His blessings in this world and would give him reward in the Hereafter" (6739). But the next *hadīs* suggests a more balanced distribution of Allah's blessings. Allah rewards the nonbeliever in this world and the believer in the hereafter (6740). Thanks to his reward in this world, the nonbeliever "finds no virtue for which he should be rewarded in the Hereafter" (6739).

Either way, it is still not a fair deal. In fact, it is cheating. What is this world compared to the hereafter? Not even "a gnat" (6698). What are all the pleasures of the earth compared to even one distant feel of the hellfire? Nothing. But what can Allah do? The nonbeliever is a bad cost accountant, and heedless. On the Day of Resurrection, Allah will ask the nonbeliever, even the one least tormented, whether, if he possessed all the gold of the earth, he would like to secure his freedom from the awaiting fire by paying all that gold. The nonbeliever will answer yes, but "it would be said to him: You have told a lie; what had been demanded from you was quite easier than this [the belief in the Oneness of Allah] but you paid no heed to it" (6733-6736).

Allah's Patience

Allah is long-suffering. He shows "patience at listening to the most irksome things. . . . Partnership is associated to Him [polytheism], and fatherhood of a child is attributed to Him [Christianity], but in spite of this He protects them [people] and provides them sustenance" (6731).

Muhammad's Curses

Allah may be patient but not His Prophet. Muhammad simply could not stand the nonbelievers. "When Allah's Messenger saw people turning back from 'religion' he said: 'O Allah, afflict them with seven famines as was done in the case of Yusuf, so they were afflicted with famine by which they were forced to eat everything until they were obliged to eat the hides and the dead bodies because of hunger' " (6719).

THE SPLITTING OF THE MOON

Besides the power to curse, Muhammad had other miraculous powers at his command. For example, the "moon was split into two," one part of it behind the mountain and the other part on this side of the mountain. Muhammad told his companions: "Bear witness to this" (6725).

THE JEWISH SCHOLARS

While Muhammad had power over nature, this power failed him when it came to persuading the Jewish scholars. "If ten scholars of the Jews would follow me, no Jew would be left upon the surface of the earth who would not embrace Islam," Muhammad declared (6711).

SATAN AND THE PROPHET

Muhammad robbed Satan of his divinity but evidently not of his power for mischief, particularly in the matter of sowing dissension among the believers. "Verily, the Satan has lost all hopes that the worshippers would worship him in the peninsula of Arabia, but he is hopeful that he would sow the seed of dissension amongst them," Muhammad declared (6752).

EVERYONE HAS HIS OWN DEVIL: QARĪN

Muhammad did not believe that everyone has his own god but he did believe that everyone has his own devil. "There is none amongst you with whom is not an attache from amongst the *jinn* [devil]. The Companions said: Allah's Messenger, with you too? Thereupon he said: Yes, but Allah helps me against him and so I am safe from his hand and he does not command me but for good" (6757).

This concept is known as *qarīn* in Islamic theology. Literally, the word means "the one united" (pl. *quranā*), and it refers to the demon that is joined inseparably to every man. The concept is mentioned in the Qurān ("We assign unto him a devil who would be his mate," 43:36; also see 41:25), but it finds its full development in the *Sunnah*. In the Qurān, the demons are only attached to infidels; in the Sunnah, they are intimately joined to Muslims also.

A Gnostic theology sees a secret Godhead in man; a prophetic one, a devil. The former is pantheistic in approach and temper; the latter is *pandaimonic* or, more precisely, *pandemonic*.

Moderation in Giving Sermons

'Abdullah b. Mas'ūd tells us that "Allah's Messenger did not deliver us sermons on certain days fearing that it might prove to be boring for us" (6775). A practice worthy of emulation by most sermonizers.

PARADISE (*AL-JANNA*—"THE GARDEN")

The thirty-eighth book is called "The Book of Paradise; Its Description, Its Bounties, and Its Inmates"; but two-thirds of it really is on Hell and its inmates. In the Prophet's eschatology, Paradise and Hell go together. In the Qurān, the word "Paradise" (*jannat*) appears 64 times, less than the word "Hell" (*jahnam*), which appears 76 times. *An-Nār*, "the Fire," the Qurān's pet name for Hell, appears with still greater frequency—121 times.

"In Paradise, there is a tree under the shadow of which a rider of a fine and swift-footed horse would travel for a hundred years without covering the distance completely" (6784).

The inhabitants of Paradise show their happiness by telling Allah: "Why should we not be pleased, O Lord, when Thou hast given us what Thou hast not given to any of Thy creatures?" (6787). The pleasure of seeing others denied Paradise is in fact greater than the pleasure of seeing even one's own self rewarded.

Paradise has its own version of a beauty salon, a street to which the inhabitants "would come every Friday. The north wind will blow and would scatter fragrance on their faces and on their clothes and would add to their beauty and loveliness" (6792). A constant Bower of Bliss.

HIERARCHY

Paradise is not without its hierarchy, with rather exclusive quarters for the apostles. The inhabitants of the lower regions of Paradise "will look to the upper apartment of Paradise as you see the planets in the sky" (6788). The ranking in Paradise will follow the ranking on earth. "The first group of my *Ummah* to get into paradise would be like a full moon in the night. Then those who would be next to them; they would be like the most significantly glittering stars . . . then after them others in ranks" (6796).

CALVINISM

In religions where theology is supreme, moral action occupies a secondary place. A man is justified by faith; he is already one of God's elect or damned long before he is even born. Muhammad anticipates Luther and Calvin by a thousand years, "None amongst you would attain salvation purely because of his deeds," Muhammad says (6760). "Observe moderation" in your doings, he advises; but if you fail, "try to do as much as you can do and be happy for none would be able to get into paradise because of his deeds alone" (6770). It is not God's grace that wins salvation but either the atoning death of His only son or the intercessory power of His last Prophet.

GOD'S HEIGHT

Muhammad tells us the height of the inhabitants of Paradise and, incidentally, the height of Adam and even of God. The immeasurable is measured. "Allah, the Exalted and Glorious, created Adam in His own image with His length of sixty cubits. . . . So he who would get into Paradise would get in the form of Adam, his length being sixty cubits." Muhammad adds that the people who came after Adam "continued to diminish in size up to this day" (6809).

HABITATION, LAVATION

For his habitation in Paradise, the believer will have a "tent of a single hollowed pearl, the breadth of which would be sixty miles from all sides" (6805).

The inhabitants of Paradise will eat and drink but they will "neither pass water, nor void excrement, nor will they suffer from catarrh, nor will they spit" (6795). Then what will happen to the food they eat? The whole catabolic process will change. "They will belch and sweat (and it would be over with their food), and their sweat would be that of musk" (6798). "Their combs would be made of gold and the fuel of their braziers would be aloes and their sweat would be musk and their form would be the form of one single person according to the length of their father sixty cubits tall" (6796).

Spouses

The *Sahīh Muslim* allows the believers only two spouses each in Paradise, less than on earth; but they will be so beautiful that "the marrow of their shanks would be visible through the flesh" (6797).

The Qurānic Paradise

The *Sahīh Muslim* is rather niggardly in its description and promise. Let us therefore add a few more details to the scanty picture of Paradise by referring to the Qurān and some other traditions and commentaries.

The Qurān promises the believers and *mujāhids* "rivers of water incorruptible; rivers of milk whose taste does not change; rivers of wine, a joy to those who drink; rivers of honey pure and clear" (47:15). For food, "they will have fruits, any that they may desire" (56:20–21). They will be "reclining on raised thrones; and the shades of the Garden will come low over them; the bunches of fruits will hang low. And amongst them will be passed round vessels of silver and goblets of crystal; they will drink of a cup of wine mixed with *Zanjabīl* [ginger], and there would be a fountain called *Salsbīl*. And around them will be youths of perpetual freshness [*viludānum mukhaladūn*], youths of such beauty that you would think them scattered pearls; upon them will be green garments of fine silk and heavy brocade, and they will be adorned with bracelets of silver" (76:13–21). Young slaves (*ghilmān*) like "hidden pearls" will wait on them (52–54).

HOURIS

Houris are promised, houris with swelling bosoms, retiring glances; houris "unfailing and unforbidden, on lofty sofas and of a rare creation, for ever virgins, beloved and equal in age" (56:33–40).

What is denied on earth is promised in Paradise: silk dresses, wine, golden vessels. One would have thought that the believer's provision of women in this world was pretty generous, but apparently any restrictions in the matter were irksome, so he will have women galore in Paradise.

We can only mention the subject here, but for a fuller account the reader can refer to the following verses in the Qurān: 2:25, 4:13, 9:111, 10:9–10, 47:15, 52:17–24, 55:46–76, 56:15–40, 66:8, 76:12–22, and others.

OTHER TRADITIONS

Other traditions, quoted in commentaries like the *Tafseer Mazaharī*, the *Tafseer Qādarī*, and the *Tafseer Haqqānī*, and reproduced in the *Qurān Parichaya*, describe the sensual delights of the celestial region with greater abandon. For example, in every corner of the believer's tent of a single hollowed pearl, which we have already mentioned, will dwell his wives, with whom he will make love successively. According to 'Abdullah b. 'Umar, Paradise will have a bazaar for the exclusive sale and purchase of beauty and beautiful faces. A man will be able to procure any beautiful woman he desires from that market. The believers will recline on lofty couches (according to some commentators, "couches" means "women").

NUMBER OF SLAVES

According to a tradition narrated by the same authority, even the least of the inhabitants of Paradise will have one thousand slaves waiting on him. According to Anas, the number of slaves is ten thousand. According to Abū Sa'īd, "the least amongst the people of Paradise shall have eighty thousand slaves, and seventy-two women."

Number of Houris

Anas stinted on women. According to 'Abdullah b. 'Umar, every inhabitant of Paradise will have at his disposal five hundred houris, four thousand virgins, and eight thousand women who have known men. He will have the strength to have intercourse with them all.

Abū Huraira increases the number, though rather mathematically expressed, still further. According to him, every Muslim will own a mansion of pearls; every mansion will have seventy houses of rubies; every house will have seventy rooms of emeralds; every room will have seventy couches; and every couch will be covered with seventy carpets of every color, and a houri will be sitting on each carpet; every room will also have seventy tables laid out; and on every table there will be seventy dishes of seventy colors; every room will also have seventy maid-slaves. Every believer will have the capability of copulating with each of these houris and maids.

See-through Garments

According to Abū Sa'īd, these women will put on see-through dresses. Each houri will have seventy garments, but her lover will be able to look through all of them and see the marrow of the bones of her legs, and she will have a crown on her head, the meanest pearl of which would give light between the east and the west. According to another tradition, when a believer embraces any such houri, each of them will have seventy thousand boys waiting on her, holding the train of her robe. According to a tradition mentioned by Aldous Huxley, in the Muslim Paradise, every orgasm will last for six hundred years.*

*Aldous Huxley, *Moksha* (London: Chatto & Windus, 1980), p. 112.

No Similar Rewards for Women

It has been observed that faithful Muslim females are denied the analogous reward. Gibbon says that Muhammad did not give any specifics about the male companions of the female elect because he did not want to arouse the jealousy of the husbands or to disturb their felicity by inducing them to have suspicions about everlasting marriages in Paradise.

Sir William Muir makes the psychologically significant observation that Muhammad's more voluptuous accounts of heaven derive from the period when he was living in a monogamic relationship with Khadīja, a woman of threescore years and also fifteen years his senior. But as his harem swelled, the sexual delights and orgies became subdued. In the *Sūras* from this period, the houris of old are replaced by "pure wives" (Qurān 2:25, 4:57).

HELL

Muhammad's accounts of Hell are equally intimate. In caloric heat, the fire we know here on earth is only "one-seventieth part of the Fire of Hell" (6811). "There would be among them those to whom Fire will reach up to their ankles, to some up to their knees, to some up to their waists, and to some up to their collar-bones" (6816).

Stones will hurtle down on the inmates of Hell with great force. Abū Harair reports: "We were in the company of Allah's Messenger when we heard a terrible sound. Thereupon Allah's Apostle said: Do you know what is this? We said: Allah and His Messenger know best. Thereupon he said: This is a stone which was thrown seventy years before in Hell and it has been constantly slipping down and now it has reached its base" (6813).

The hunger of Hell is inexhaustible. "The sinners would be thrown therein and it would continue to say: Is there anything more?" (6825).

In Hell, "the molar teeth of an unbeliever will be like Uhud [a hill just outside Medina] and the thickness of his skin a three nights' journey" (6831). The idea of investing the unbeliever with such a thick skin is that he "should be able to suffer the torment of the Hell-Fire for a long time," as the translator explains (note 2999).

Those who tampered with the pure religion of Ishmael, the son of Abraham, the legendary progenitor of the Arabs, are severely punished. "I saw 'Amr b. Luhayy b. Cam'a b. Khinzif, brother of Banī Ka'b, dragging his intestines in Fire," Muhammad tells Abū Huraira (6838). According to Muslim thinking, 'Amr was the first Khozaite king (A.D. 200) who set up idols brought from Syria.

Similarly, Muhammad also "saw 'Amr b. Āmir al-Khuzā'i dragging his intestines in Fire." He was the first to dedicate animals to deity. There are two kinds of the animals to be dedicated: *al-bahīra*, animals which are left unmilked except for the idols; and *as-sā'iba*, animals which are not loaded and are let loose for the deities (6839).

Eternal Damnation

After the believers and the unbelievers are sifted and sent to their respective abodes, the chapter is closed forever. "Allah would admit the inmates of Paradise into Paradise and the inmates of Hell into Hell. Then the Announcer would stand between them and say: O inmates of Paradise, there is no death for you. O inmates of Hell, there is no death for you. You would live forever therein" (6829).

The Polytheists

The punishment of the unbelievers does not wait till the day of Resurrection. It begins immediately after their death. The Prophet and his Companions sighted five or six graves during a journey. Muhammad asked if anyone knew in what state their occupants had died. "As polytheists," somebody replied. "These people are passing through the ordeal in the graves," Muhammad revealed (6859).

Muhammad let the dead bodies of the unbelievers who fought and died at Badr lie unburied for three days. Then he sat by the side of the bodies, and addressing each of them by name, said: "Have you not found what your Lord had promised you to be correct?" The bodies had decayed, and 'Umar wondered how the Prophet could hold a discourse with them. "By Him in Whose Hand is my life, what I am saying to them, even you cannot hear more distinctly than they, but they lack the power to reply," Muhammad told him. Then he had the bodies (twenty-four in number) of the "non-believers of Quraish . . . thrown into the well of Badr" (6869–6870).

MUHAMMAD'S MISSION

While delivering a sermon one day, Muhammad said: "Behold, my Lord commanded me that I should teach you which you do not know and which He has taught me today. . . . Allah looked towards the people of the world and He showed hatred for the Arabs and the non-Arabs, but with the exception of some remnants from the People of the Book. And He said: I have sent thee [Muhammad] in order to put you to test and put those to test through you. And I sent the Book to you. . . . Verily, Allah commanded me to burn [kill] the Quraish. I said: My Lord, they would break my head . . . and Allah said: you turn them out as they turned you out, you fight against them and We shall help you in this. . . . You send an army and I would send an army five times greater than that. Fight against those who disobey you along with those who obey you" (6853).

VOYEURISM

There is a *hadīs*, narrated by 'Āisha, that should be of interest to Freudians. The Prophet revealed: "The people would be assembled on the Day of Resurrection barefooted, naked and uncircumcised." 'Āisha asked in alarm, or perhaps in mischief: "Allah's Messenger, will the male and the female be together on the Day and would be looking at one another?" The Prophet sagaciously replied: "Āisha, the matter would be too serious for them to look to one another" (6844).

THE RECKONING ON THE DAY OF JUDGMENT

On the Day of Resurrection, there will be two kinds of reckoning: an easy one and a thorough one. The easy reckoning is merely formal and is for the believers, whose faults Allah wants to overlook. But woe unto the unbeliever, for his accounts will be closely scrutinized. "He who is examined thoroughly in reckoning is undone" (6874).

The Qurānic Hell

As was also noted in regard to Paradise, the treatment of Hell is more detailed in the Qurān than in the *Sahīh Muslim*, and similarly the Qurānic Hell is more sizzling than the Hell of the *Hādīs*.

Though Muhammad does not refrain from holding out the threat of hellfire to his followers, hell is essentially a place reserved for the unbelievers, i.e., those who disbelieve in his apostleship and mission.

Hell has many names, and the Prophet dwells on them lovingly. The name he most loved to call it by is *An-Nār*, "the Fire." Seven other names are also frequently mentioned, and the scholars of the Qurān turned them into seven separate regions of Hell, each with its own potency, thermodegree, and inmates. Though the least of these hells would burn any man a thousand times over, that is not considered good enough punishment for many degrees of infidelity and unbelief. So hells increasingly more smoky, more blazing, and more scorching are conceived.

The Seven Regions

Curiously enough, even Muslims must go to Hell. "Not one of you but must enter it [Hell]; this is Lord's decree that must be accomplished," reveals the Qurān (19:71). In order to fulfill the letter, if not the spirit, of Allah's command, a region in Hell is conceived which is least oppressive. It is called *Jahanam*. It is Hell only in name and is in fact a purgatory for Muslims, even a passage or bridge (*sirāt*) to heaven. Muslim theologians assure us that it will be pretty cool and pleasant for Muslims unless they have committed some great sins.

The real regions of Hell and their real torments are reserved for unbelievers, infidels, and polytheists of different hues and degrees. The blazing fire of *Lazā*, which leaves nothing unconsumed, is for the Christians; the still more intense fire of *Hutamah* is for the Jews. Similarly, there is *Sa'īr* for the Sabians, *Saqar* for the Magi, *Jahīm* for idolaters, and *Hāwiyah* for the hypocrites. The last are those who saw through Muhammad and no longer believed in his mission but were afraid to admit it openly. They paid him only the prudential homage due to one who is powerful.

Muhammad is very ready to send unbelievers to hellfire, fire which "permits nothing to endure, nor leaves anything alone" (74:28). In the *Sūra Ghāshiya* ("The Overwhelming Event," i.e., the Day of Judgment), Muhammad promises a sorry plight indeed for unbelievers of all shades: Jews, Christians, polytheists, idolaters, hypocrites. "Has the tidings reached thee of the Overwhelming Event? Some faces that Day will be humiliated, toiling, weary. . . . No food will there be for them but a bitter *zarī* which will neither nourish nor satisfy hunger" (88:1–7).

Zarī is a bitter and thorny plant, loathsome in smell. In other *Sūras* (e.g., 56:52, 17:60, 44:43–46), another terrible food, the "Tree of Zaqqūm," is mentioned; in the language of the last *Sūra*, it "will boil in their [eaters'] inside like molten brass, like the boiling of scalding water."

There are other traditions in the same vein. "If the infidels complain of thirst, they shall be given water like molten copper . . . which shall burst their bowels . . . which shall dissolve everything in their bellies." According to some commentators, the water is so hot that even a drop of it is capable of melting away all the mountains of the world.

The fire in Hell knows no rival in fierceness. "It burnt a thousand years so that it became red, and burnt another thousand years till it became black and dark, and never has any light." This *hadīs* derives from Abū Huraira and is quoted in the *Tafseer Mazaharī*. According to the same commentary, the infidels will be surrounded by a wall of fire so wide that it would take forty years to traverse the distance.

The Qurān asks you to "fear the Fire whose fuel is Men and Stones, and which is prepared for those who reject Faith" (2:24). Some commentators have explained that the men and stones referred to in the verse are none other than the polytheists and the idols they worship.

Another tradition tells us that Hell will have seventy thousand jungles, each tree there having seventy thousand branches; every branch will house seventy thousand serpents and an equal number of scorpions. All these are the tormentors of the infidels and the hypocrites. The swelling of one bite of a scorpion will last for forty years.

Hell is an important limb of Islamic theology, referred to throughout the Qurān and other Islamic canonical literature. In these texts the misanthropy and hatred of Muslim theology for mankind has found a free scope.

THE LAST HOUR

The thirty-ninth book pertains to the "Turmoils and Portents of the Last Hour" (*Al-Fitan wa Ashrāt as-Sā'ah*). The subject is closely related to Paradise and Hell.

One is not sure whether by the Last Hour the Prophet means the last hour of Arabia or of the *ummah* or of the whole world. In some *ahādīs*, he prophesies the destruction of Arabia. "There is destruction in store for Arabia because of turmoil which is at hand," he said (6881). He climbed up a battlement and told the Medinans: "You do not see what I am seeing and I am seeing the places of turmoil between your houses as the places of rainfall" (6891). "Rainfall" here means "catastrophe." He prophesied for them a period "in which the one who sits will be better than one who stands and the one who stands will be better than the one who walks and the one who walks will be better than the one who runs" (6893).

THE DESTRUCTION OF THE *UMMAH*

Muhammad tells us: "Allah drew the ends of the world near one another for my sake. And I have seen its eastern and western ends." After this apocalyptical vision Muhammad asked Allah three things and, "He granted me two. . . . I begged my Lord that my *Ummah* should not be destroyed because of famine and He granted me this. And I begged my Lord that my *Ummah* should not be destroyed by drowning [deluge] and He granted me this. And I begged my Lord that there should be no bloodshed among the people of my *Ummah*, but He did not grant it" (6904, 6906).

While killing unbelievers is meritorious and wins Paradise for the believers, killing another believer is heinous and earns the punishment of hellfire. "When two Muslims confront each other with their swords, both the slayer and slain are doomed to Hell-Fire" (6899).

But this does not apply to the early Muslim heroes who engaged in internecine wars. The translator assures us: "This rule does not apply in case of the confrontation between Hazrat 'Alī and his opponents. Both the slayer and the slain are doomed to Hell-Fire only when the enmity is based on personal grudges and material interests, but in the case of Hazrat 'Alī and his opponents it was the higher ideal which actuated most of them to come into conflict with one another" (note 3009).

SOME SIGNS OF THE LAST HOUR

The great turmoil "which would emerge like the mounting waves of the ocean" (6914) will be preceded by many signs. "The Last Hour would not come unless the Euphrates would uncover a treasure of gold" (6920). It will not come "until fire emits from the earth of Hijāz which would illuminate the necks of the camels of Busra" (6935). It will not come "until the people have [again] taken to the worship of *Lāt* and *'Uzza*" (6945).

Before the Last Hour comes, the "Ka'ba would be destroyed by an Abyssinian having two small shanks" (6951). According to the translator, this refers to either the Christians or the polytheists of Abyssinia. Before this Hour *jizyā* will stop coming and the people of Iraq will "not send their *qafīz* and *dirhims* [their measures of foodstuffs and their money]" (6961).

"The last hour would not come unless the Muslims will fight against the Jews and the Muslims would kill them and until the Jews would hide themselves behind a stone or a tree and a stone or a tree would say: Muslim, or the servant of Allah, there is a Jew behind me; come and kill him." Only a very thorny tree known as the *gharqad*, which is painful to touch, will be loyal to the Jews and not reveal their identity, "for it is the tree of the Jew" (6985). Another sign of the approaching Hour will be that "the sun would rise from the West" (7039).

Dajjāl

Muhammad prepares Muslims for the coming Hour. "Hasten to do good deeds before six things happen: the rising of the sun from the West, the smoke, the Dajjāl . . . " (7039). Dajjāl is mentioned in many *ahādīs*. He is a kind of Antichrist, blind in the left eye and red in complexion, with the word *kāfir* inscribed on his forehead. He "would be followed by seventy thousand Jews of *Isfahān* wearing Persian Shawls" (7034).

Ibn Sayyād

A very interesting story is told about one Ibn Sayyād (6990–7004), who was believed to be Dajjāl by the Companions of Muhammad. He disputed Muhammad's apostleship. "Don't you bear witness that I am the Messenger of Allah?" Muhammad demanded of him. But he replied: "I bear witness to the fact that you are the Messenger of the unlettered." Then there was a competition between the two. Sayyād had to guess what was in Muhammad's mind. Sayyād could only say *dhukh* when the word in Muhammad's mind was really *dukhān* (smoke). "He only chanted *dhukh, dukh*, and the hollowness of his claim stood exposed," the translator tells us (note 3037).

According to another story, Muhammad and his Companions met Sayyād sitting in the company of some children. The children stood up but not Sayyād. Muhammad "did not like it," and he said to him: "May your nose be besmeared with dust, don't you bear testimony to the fact that I am the Messenger of Allah?" Sayyād denied this and, in fact, made the very same claim for himself, asking Muhammad to bear witness to his status. "Thereupon 'Umar b. Khattāb said: Allah's Messenger, permit me that I should kill him." Muhammad replied: "If he is that person who is in your mind [Dajjāl], you will not be able to kill him" (6990). Muhammad had many toughs at his beck and call, ready to do his bidding. That gave point to his claim.

Like the early Christians, Muhammad expected the Last Hour to come at any time. Pointing to a young boy, he told his followers: "If this young boy lives, he would not grow very old till the Last Hour would come to you" (7052).

17

Repentance (Tauba), I

We now take up the thirty-fifth book, pertaining to "Repentance and Exhortation to Repentance" (*Kitāb al-Tauba*).

Allah loves repentance in a believer. He is "more pleased with the repentance of His servant than an Arab who found his lost camel in the waterless desert" (6610–6619).

In fact, Allah loves to see the believer repent more than He hates to see him sin. "If you were not to commit sins, Allah would have swept you out of existence and would have replaced you by another people who have committed sin, and then asked forgiveness from Allah," the Prophet told his *ummah* (6620–6622). Psychologists tell us that the joys of sinning are great but the joys of repentance are even greater.

Sin is Doubly Rewarding

A man's sinning is doubly rewarding. It helps him as well as his Maker. It helps the believer to realize that he is a creature and provides an opportunity for Allah to exercise His mercy. According to Muhammad, Allah said: "A servant committed a sin and he said: O Allah, forgive me my sin, and Allah said: My servant committed a sin and then he came to realize that he has a Lord who forgives the sins. . . . He again committed a sin and said: My Lord, forgive me my sin, and Allah, the Exalted and High, said: My servant committed a sin and then came to realize that he has a Lord who forgives his sin." The servant committed yet a third sin, and Allah responded in the same way, but now He added: "O servant, do what you like. I have granted you forgiveness" (6642). Sin is doubly blessed. It blesses him who sins and Him Who forgives. It helps man to realize his creaturely nature and Allah to realize His lordly and merciful essence. It is not an accident that theologies of man's sinful nature have also sought a God of mercy.

ALLAH'S WRATH AND MERCY

Allah says: "My mercy predominates my wrath" (6626). Of this mercy, He bestows a one-hundredth part "upon the Jinn and human beings and the insects," the part with which they love one another; but He "has reserved ninety-nine parts for His servant on the Day of Resurrection" (6631). This reserve of mercy will be handy on this Day for saving the Muslims from the fire of hell, which is also needed for dealing with the infidels, or *kāfirs*. "God's wrath" is an important concept in Semitic religions.

GOOD DEEDS TAKE AWAY BAD ONES

A Muslim came to Muhammad and said: "Allah's Messenger, I sported with a woman in the outskirts of Medina . . . [and] committed an offence short of fornication. . . . Kindly deliver verdict about me." The man wanted Muhammad to impose the penalty of *hadd* (a category of punishments defined in the Qurān or in the *Hadīs*) on him. Abū Bakr and 'Umar felt that the man had committed a serious offense, but according to some traditions, 'Umar gave him the oft-repeated advice of the Prophet, which is both worldly-wise as well as pious: "Allah concealed your fault. You had better conceal it yourself also."

Meanwhile, Muhammad had a revelation: "And observe prayer at the ends of the day and in the first hours of the night. Surely good deeds take away evil deeds" (Qurān 11:115). Following this he dismissed the man, telling him: "Allah has exempted you from the imposition of *hadd*, or from your sin." Someone who was present at the time asked Muhammad whether the promise of pardon related only to that individual alone. "No, but the people at large," Muhammad said reassuringly to all the believers (6655–6661).

The two prayers mentioned are the morning and evening prayers.

The one destroys the sins of the night, and the other the sins of the day. And, presumably, after reciting them the believer is refreshed and ready for his next bout of sin. Such is human nature.

Nonbelievers as Replacements for Believers in Hell

The next five *ahādīs* (6665–6669) are very interesting. Allah does not exactly forgive the sins of the believers but visits them on the unbelievers. He punishes the unbelievers for the sins of the believers. In this way, both His wrath and His mercy are established. "When it will be the Day of Resurrection Allah would deliver to every Muslim a Jew or a Christian and say: That is your rescue from Hell-Fire," Muhammad tells his followers (6665). Allah's sense of fairness and justice is no better than that of the believers. Thus the believers create Allah in their own image.

Muhammad also promises his followers that on the Day of Reckoning, Allah will tell the Muslims: "I concealed them [your sins] for you in the world. And today I forgive them." But as for the nonbelievers, their sins will be exposed before the whole world and "there would be general announcement about them before all creation," and it will be advertised that they "told lies about Allah" (6669).

The "Necklace" Affair

The book contains a long *hadīs* which relates to a scandal involving 'Āisha, the girl-wife of the Prophet. It happened in the fifth year of the Hijra (December A.D. 626), when Muhammad was returning to Medina after defeating the tribe of Banū 'l-Mustaliq in a surprise attack and taking many prisoners, including Juwairīyya. 'Āisha, who was thirteen years old at the time, had accompanied the Prophet on the expedition, together with another co-wife, Umm Salama.

'Āisha reports: "Whenever Allah's Messenger intended to set out on a journey he cast lots amongst his wives and took one with him in whose favour the lot was cast." Luck favored her (as it did suspiciously too often), and she accompanied the Prophet on the expedition. During the last leg of the return journey, 'Āisha was left behind. In the early morning, she had gone out into the fields to relieve herself. Returning to the camp, she discovered that she had dropped her necklace, so she went back to recover it. While she was away, the caravan started for Medina. Apparently no one realized that she had been left behind because the camel carrying her *haudaj* was with the caravan. The bearers, thinking she was inside it, had placed the *haudaj* on the camel. "The women in those days were light of weight and they did not wear much flesh, as they ate less food; so they did not perceive the weight of my *haudaj* as they placed it on the camel," 'Āisha explains.

When 'Āisha returned to the camp after finding her necklace, she discovered that the caravan had left. So she waited and even slept at the same spot, calculating that they would come to fetch her once the mistake was discovered. "I was overpowered by sleep and slept," she says. Then a young soldier, Safwān b. Mu'attal Sulamī Zakwānī, who had also lagged behind for some reason, saw her, recognized her, and gave her a ride back. "By Allah, he did not speak to me a word and I did not hear a word from him except *Inna lillāhi* [*Innalillāhi wainna ilaihi rāji'ūn*, 'we are for Allah and to Him we have to return'] and I covered my head with my head-dress. He made his camel kneel down and I mounted the camel . . . and he moved on leading the camel by the nosestring on which I was riding," Āisha says.

Under everyone's gaze, Āisha and Safwān returned together. This started gossip, which soon developed into a scandal. The participants in the gossip were not merely people who were lukewarm toward Muhammad, such as 'Abdullah ibn Ubayy, a member of the Khāzrajite clan of 'Awf and a leading citizen of Medina, who had come to distrust Muhammad; they also included supporters of the Prophet, such as the poet Hassān, Hamna, the daughter of Jahsh and sister of the Prophet's wife Zainab, and Mistah, a relative and dependent of Abū Bakr, the father of 'Āisha.

Muhammad was much disturbed and perhaps had his own suspicions. He turned cold toward 'Āisha, so much so that she sought his permission to go to her father's house. The permission was given. 'Āisha's mother tried to console her, saying: "By Allah, if there is a handsome woman who is loved by her husband and he has co-wives also they talk many a thing about her."

Muhammad consulted his close relatives, particularly 'Alī and Usāma b. Zaid. Usāma said: "Allah's Messenger, they are your wives and we know nothing else about them but goodness." 'Alī advised Muhammad to divorce 'Āisha: "Allah has not put any unnecessary burden upon you in regard to your wives. There are a number of women besides her." 'Alī also suggested that 'Āisha's maid be questioned. Barīra, the maid, was sent for. 'Alī struck her (showing that the manners of the Prophet's family were quite feudal and no better than those of the unbelievers), and warned her to speak the truth. Barīra could throw no light on the incident in question but said that she had never found any wrong in 'Āisha except that "she goes to sleep while kneading the flour and the lamb eats that."

Thus a month passed. Now Muhammad went to the pulpit and reprimanded his followers for their scandalmongering. "Who would exonerate me from imputations of that person [was the reference to 'Abdullah ibn Ubayy or to Hassān the poet, another Khāzrajite?] who has troubled me in regard to my family? By Allah, I find nothing in my wife but goodness," he appealed. This touched a loyal chord in the hearts of Sa'd b. Mu'az and Usaid b. Huzair. They stood up and promised to punish any delinquent, if the Prophet so wanted it. "I defend your honour. . . . If he [the delinquent] belongs to the tribe of our brother Khazraj and you order us we would comply with your order," Sa'd b. Mu'az, the chief of the Aus, told Muhammad. A quarrel now broke out between him and the chief of Khazraj, Sa'd b. 'Ubāda, but Muhammad pacified them for the time being.

Next Muhammad went to Abū Bakr's house, determined to put an end to the matter. He again asked 'Āisha to confess if she had done anything wrong. " 'Āisha, this is what has reached me about you and if you are innocent, Allah would Himself vindicate your honour, and if accidently there has been a lapse on your part seek forgiveness of Allah," Muhammad told her. But 'Āisha maintained her innocence.

And Lo! Then and there a revelation descended on Muhammad establishing 'Āisha's innocence, even to her own great astonishment.

"I was innocent but I did not expect that Allah would descend *wahy matlu* [a Qurānic revelation] in my case as I did not think myself so much important. . . . I only hoped that Allah would in vision give an indication of my innocence to Allah's Messenger," 'Āisha says.

Coming out of his prophetic fit or trance, Muhammad announced the news: " 'Āisha, there is glad tiding for you. Verily Allah has vindicated your honour." Everybody was happy. 'Āisha's mother wanted her to get up and thank the Prophet. But she refused: "I shall not thank him and laud him but Allah who has descended revelation vindicating my honour" (6673).

God in this revelation not only vindicated 'Āisha's innocence but ordered punishment for those who spread unproved calumnies against chaste women. "And those who launch charges against chaste women, and produce not four witnesses to support their allegation, flog them with eighty stripes and reject their evidence ever after, for such men are wicked transgressors" (Qurān 24:4). And the revelation also took to task those Muslims who had given ear to the scandal. "And why did not the believers, men and women, when ye first heard of the affair, put the best construction on it in their own minds and say, 'This charge is an obvious lie?' And why did they not bring four witnesses to prove it? When they had not brought the witnesses, such men, in the sight of Allah, stand forth themselves as liars" (Qurān 24:12–13; also see 24:16).

In obedience to Allah's injunction, all the calumniators, including the poet Hassān, Abū Bakr's relative Mistah, and even Hamna, the sister of Muhammad's favorite wife, Zainab, received eighty stripes each. Zainab had not joined her sister in calumniating 'Āisha, though 'Āisha says that "she was the only lady who amongst the wives of Allah's Messenger used to vie with me [i.e., 'Āisha]" (6673).

But it was not all punishment. Perhaps to buy their silence, the punishments were judiciously mixed with rewards. A valuable castle called Bīr Hā, in the vicinity of Medina, was bestowed on Hassān the poet. Muhammad even gave Hassān a slave-girl named Shirīn, one of the two Coptic sisters sent him by the Egyptian governor as gifts, retaining the other, Mary, for his own harem.* As a result,

***Sīrat Rasūl Allah*, pp. 498–499.

the poet, who until now had been writing lampoons on Safwān, began writing verses in praise of 'Āisha's purity, slimness, and grace. 'Āisha also forgave him. " 'Āisha did not like that Hassān should be rebuked in her presence, and she used to say: It was he who wrote this verse also: Verily, my father and my mother are all meant for defending the honour of Muhammad" (6674).

After this incident Abū Bakr wanted to withdraw his support from Mistah, his indigent relative. In the language of 'Āisha, "Abū Bakr used to give to Mistah some stipend as a token of kinship with him and for his poverty and he said: By Allah, now I would not spend anything for him." But a special revelation from Allah came to Mistah's rescue. "Let not those among you who are endowed with grace and amplitude of means resolve by oath against helping their kinsmen, those in want and those who have left their homes in God's cause" (Qurān 24:22).

Regarding Safwān, the chief male character in the story, Hassān had lampooned him in a poem. In retaliation, Safwān gave him a sword wound.* Hassān's relatives captured him and in spite of Muhammad's intervention kept him as a prisoner till Hassān's wound was healed. Of course, Safwān denied the allegation hotly, and though young he died soon after. "Hallowed be Allah, by One, in Whose hand is my life, I have never unveiled any woman," he said, according to 'Āisha. She further says that "then he died as a martyr in the cause of Allah" (6674–6675). According to another tradition; quoted by Ibn Ishāq, she added that people found that Safwān "was impotent."†

Though Allah exonerated 'Āisha in this particular case, He did not refrain from administering an admonition to all the wives of the Prophet: "O Women of the Prophet! if any one of you should be guilty of unseemly conduct, your punishment would be doubled and that is easy for Allah." The system of *purdah* was also made more stringent. "And stay quietly in your houses, and make not a dazzling display, like that of the former times of Ignorance," said Allah (Qurān 33:30, 33).

*Safwān sang: "Here's the edge of my sword for you!/ When you lampoon a man like me you don't get a poem in return" (*Sīrat Rasūl Allah*, p. 498).
†*Sīrat Rasūl Allah*, p. 499.

Muhammad also instituted a more careful watch over his household after this event. For example, when he left on the expedition to Tabūk, he left 'Alī behind to keep an eye on his household in his absence. Also, we no longer find 'Āisha mentioned as accompanying Muhammad on any expedition after this affair. Apparently Umm Salama replaced her as Muhammad's companion on subsequent expeditions.

The demand for four witnesses in cases of adultery made it difficult to prove such charges in an Islamic court.

18

Repentance, II (The Self-Criticism of Ka'b b. Mālik)

We shall continue with the "Book of Repentance." In it appears a long *hadīs* entitled "The Repentance of Ka'b b. Mālik." This *hadīs*, the longest in the *Sahīh Muslim*, constitutes a very interesting psychological document. We cannot reproduce it in full here or put it to an adequately searching analysis, but the reader will do well to read it carefully and give it serious thought, for it is an illuminating story with a family likeness to the notorious "confessions" and "self-criticism" of Communist countries. Besides the usual breast-beating and protestations of loyalty to the leader, it also indicates to a discerning reader some of the psychological factors that make the members of the *ummah* or the party fall in line and keep together.

Even in Muhammad's time, Islam was not all theology, the appeal of a so-called superior monotheism against an idolatrous and superstitious polytheism, as some scholars and propagandists would have us believe. Monotheism does not have the superiority per se that fanatics often ascribe to it.* The monotheism of prophetic Islam is particularly shallow and barbarous, spiritually speaking. But from the beginning, it was combined with other, more secular appeals, negative as well as positive. The Prophet rewarded loyalty and obedience with war spoils, and visited palpable punishments of varying degrees on the lukewarm, the indifferent, and the disloyal. He used the carrot as well as the stick.

*For a fuller discussion, see our book *The Word as Revelation* (Publishers Impex India, 2/18 Ansari Road, New Delhi-110 002).

Apostasy was severely punished. The sword and its threat were frequent arbiters, but more sophisticated psychological pressures were equally in use. Social cohesion and political and ideological compliance were secured by means of social ostracism, political boycott, and ideological untouchability. The fear of divine hellfire was distant, but the fear of the strongman, the boss, the toughs of the *ummah*, or party, was ever present. In offending the Prophet, you not only offended Allah—an offense which many could take in stride—but even worse, you offended 'Umar, Talha, 'Alī, Zubair, Sa'd, 'Abdullah—the Prophet's swordsmen and hangmen. You also had to be on guard against the treacherous daggers of his assassins, Sālim b. Umayar, Muhammad ibn Maslama, Muheiasa, 'Abdullah ibn Oneis* and company, 'Amr ibn Omeya, and so on.

If one invited the Prophet's displeasure, besides inviting more concrete punishments, one also invited a pervasive social boycott. This could be a very coercive phenomenon. One's own relatives and best friends deserted one. And why? Because it was the *safe* thing to do. One had oneself played safe in the past; now others do the same in turn.

Perspicacious readers will be able to detect a close resemblance between the atmosphere described in the following *hadīs* and the more familiar (but only a little more familiar) atmosphere that obtains under the Communist regimes of our own time. But before we quote from the *hadīs*, let us provide some background information.

THE TABŪK CAMPAIGN

Muhammad planned an expedition for the autumn of A.D. 630; it was his largest and also his last, for he died soon afterward. In planning other campaigns, he used to keep the time and the target of attack to himself in order to effect the maximum surprise; in fact, sometimes he would go north when his intended destination was south. But this campaign was to be of long duration, the enemy was

*He sang: "Whenever the Prophet gave thought to an unbeliever, / I got to him first with tongue and hand." (*Sīrat Rasūl Allah*, p. 789.)

far away (300 miles to the north), and the weather was dry and hot; so this time he gave advance warning to his followers so that they could prepare and equip themselves adequately, for the expedition was to take them to the very frontiers of Arabia and might embroil them with the garrisons of the Byzantine Empire. Because of its unusually arduous nature, the Tabūk campaign was also called the "Campaign of Difficulties."

As Muhammad was planning for the biggest campaign of his life, he directed his adherents and allies and the Bedouin tribes to gather in great numbers. He collected tithes from the tribes, which were now reduced to submission, and appealed for donations and gifts from his followers, who were now rich and powerful. They had become governors, generals, contractors, and traders. They gave generously, his own son-in-law, 'Usmān, gifting one thousand dinārs, a lordly sum. These funds were used to provide mounts for the poorer soldiers. But even so, many had to be sent away for lack of funds. Though they were sent back, their spirit was considered praiseworthy, and there was even a revelation about them from Allah: "Nor is there blame on those who come to thee to be provided with mounts, and when you said, 'I can find no mounts for you,' they turned back their eyes streaming with tears" (Qurān 9:92). In the Islamic tradition, these men were subsequently remembered with honor as "Weepers."

Muhammad made an appeal to all and sundry in the Muslim world, which now included, at least nominally, the whole Arab world. His appeal was Allah's own appeal. "Go ye forth, whether equipped lightly or heavily, and strive and struggle, with your goods and your persons, in the cause of Allah. That is best for you, if ye but knew" (Qurān 9:41).

Opposition to the Campaign

Many people were lukewarm to the appeal and unwilling to undertake such an arduous and risky journey and in such hot weather, so they put forward many excuses for not going. Of such people, Allah spoke later on in several Qurānic verses: "Those who were left behind [in the Tabūk expedition] rejoiced in their inaction behind the back of the Apostle of God. They hated to strive and fight with their goods and their persons in the Cause of God: they said, 'Go not forth in the heat.' Muhammad, say to them that the Fire of Hell is fiercer in heat, if only they could understand" (9:81).

The worst offenders were the Arabs of the desert as well as the Arabs settled in neighborhood of Medina. Both were condemned by Allah in the Qurān: "The Arabs of the desert are the worst in unbelief and hypocrisy," Allah said of them (9:97). And again He warned His Prophet thus: "Certain of the Arabs round about you are hypocrites. . . . They are obstinate in hypocrisy. Thou knowest them not, but We know them. Twice shall we punish them, and in addition shall they be sent to grievous penalty" (9:101). These Arabs were not exempted from the general conscription and were forced into the march.

But there was opposition in Medina itself amongst the *ansārs* under the very nose of the Prophet, and many Medinans put forward all kinds of excuses. "If there had been immediate gain in sight, and journey easy, they would all without doubt have followed thee," Allah tells Muhammad (Qurān 9:42).

The Prophet warns these recalcitrants that "unless ye go forth, Allah will punish you with a grievous penalty and put others in your place. But Him you would not harm in the least. For Allah has power over all things" (Qurān 9:39).

But Muhammad did not leave matters with divine threats. He also took more secular measures. For example, Ibn Hishām's biography of Muhammad tells us that when Muhammad learned that certain men opposed to the expedition were meeting at the house of Suwaylim the Jew, he sent Talha with some men to burn the house. This effectively dealt with them. One of the victims, Al-Dahhāk, sang: "My salams to you, I'll ne'er do the like again / I'm afraid. He whom fire surrounds is burned."*

A LARGE ARMY GATHERED

Eventually a large army gathered and encamped in the outskirts of Medina, although many of its members were still disgruntled. Ac-

**Sīrat Rasūl Allah*, p. 783.

cording to some traditions, those who assembled but stayed back were as numerous as those who actually went. 'Abdullah ibn Ubayy, the leader of the "doubters" or "hypocrites" of the Qurān, was also there in considerable force. But eventually he did not go, probably for reasons of old age (he died a few months later). The *ansārs* too were not very numerous. According to some traditions, the expedition was thirty thousand strong, one-third of which was cavalry.

'Alī was left behind to maintain order among Muhammad's wives and possibly also to keep a watch on Medina. But some people insinuated that he was being left behind because he would have been more of a liability than an asset on such an expedition. 'Alī was angered and came out with his armor on. Muhammad pacified him by saying: "They lie. I left you behind because of what I had left behind, so go back and represent me in my family and yours. Are you not content, 'Alī, to stand to me as Aaron stood to Moses?" This satisfied 'Alī.

Some Christian and Jewish Tribes Submit

When the expedition reached its destination, it found there was not much to do, because the Byzantine army, which supposedly had been assembling on the frontiers, was nowhere in sight. So to occupy his time during the ten days he stayed in Tabūk, Muhammad accepted the submission of three Jewish settlements and two Christian princes, which was easily done with such a large show of force. To Yuhanna b. Ru'ba, the Christian prince of Ayala, he wrote the following: "Peace be on you! I praise God for you. . . . I will not fight against you until I have written thus unto you. Believe, or else pay tribute. And be obedient unto the Lord and his Prophet and the messengers of His Prophet. Honour them and clothe them with excellent vestments. . . . Specially clothe Zaid with excellent garments. . . . But if you oppose and displease them, I will not accept from you a single thing, until I have fought against you and taken captive your little ones and slain the elders. For I am the Apostle of the Lord in truth." The prince readily submitted and became a tributary.

KA'B SPEAKS

When Muhammad returned to Medina, he was determined to deal firmly with those who had failed to accompany him. Of the many who had remained behind, three were *ansārs* who had been loyal followers of Muhammad: Murāra, Hilāl, and Ka'b, the subject of our discussion in this chapter. Ka'b, who was a poet, expressed his repentance for not joining the Tabūk expedition. According to him: "I never remained behind Allah's Messenger from any expedition which he undertook except the Battle of Tabūk and that of the Battle of Badr. So far as the Battle of Badr is concerned, nobody was blamed for remaining behind as Allah's Messenger and the Muslims did not set out for attack but for waylaying the caravan of the Quraish, but it was Allah Who made them confront their enemies without their intention to do so."

Protesting his loyalty to the Prophet, Ka'b says: "I had the honour to be with Allah's Messenger on the night of 'Aqaba when we pledged our allegiance* to Islam and it was more dear to me than my participation in Battle of Badr." Ka'b tells us that in undertaking this journey to Tabūk, the "holy prophet had in his mind the idea of threatening the Christians of Arabia in Syria and those of Rome [i.e., the Byzantine Empire]"; he says the expedition was big, "more than ten thousand people." He also tells us that "when Allah's Messenger intended to set out on an expedition, he kept it as a secret." But this expedition was a different thing. "Allah's Messenger set out for this expedition in extremely hot season; the journey was long and the land [which the army had to traverse] was waterless and he had to confront a large army, so he informed the Muslims about the actual situation, so that they should adequately equip themselves for his expedition."

Ka'b had no excuse for remaining behind, neither age nor health nor lack of means. "Never did I possess means enough and my circumstances more favourable than at this occasion. . . . I had never before this expedition simultaneously in my possession two rides." Though eminently qualified to participate, Ka'b went on postpon-

*This is a reference to the second Pledge of 'Aqabah, a place near Mina in Mecca, where seventy-three men and two women of Medina took a pledge in A.D. 620 to shelter and protect Muhammad in Medina.

ing his preparations till one day he found, to his dismay, that the Prophet had departed. "I was shocked to find that I did not find anyone like me but the people who were labelled as hypocrites or the people whom Allah granted exemption because of their incapacity," he says.

Now he waited with dread for the return of Muhammad. "When this news reached me that Allah's Messenger was on his way back from Tabūk I was greatly perturbed. I thought of fabricating false stories and asked myself how I would save myself from the anger of the following day." But later, he decided to speak the truth. "Nothing could save me but the telling of truth," he said to himself.

The next day Muhammad arrived, and "those who had remained behind began to put forward their excuses and to take an oath before him and they were more than eighty persons." Their excuses as well as their allegiances were accepted. When Ka'b's turn came, Muhammad asked him what had kept him back. Was it lack of a mount? But Ka'b spoke the truth. "By Allah, I never possessed so good means . . . as I had when I stayed behind." Muhammad dismissed him, saying that he should wait till "Allah gives a decision in your case." (In the language of the Qurān: "There are others held in suspense for the command of God, whether He would punish them, or turn in mercy" [9:106].)

Later, some of Ka'b's friends came to him in sympathy. They could not compliment him for his "inability to put forward an excuse" as others did. They also told him that two other "pious" persons (Murāra b. ar-Rabīa Āmirī and Hilāl b. Ummayya al-Qāqifī) "have met the same fate as has fallen to you and they have made the same statement as you have made, and the same verdict has been delivered in their case." This comforted him somewhat.

Ka'b's Ordeal

Then the ordeal began. "Allah's Messenger forbade the Muslims to talk with three of us. . . . The people began to avoid us and their attitude towards us underwent a change and it seemed as if the whole atmosphere had turned hostile against us. . . . We spent fifty nights in this very state and my two friends confined themselves within their houses and spent most of their time in weeping." Ka'b himself went to the mosque for prayer to catch the Prophet's eye, but "he looked at me and when I cast a glance at him he turned away his eyes from me."

Even his close relatives and friends avoided him. He says: "When the harsh treatment of the Muslims towards me extended to a considerable time, I walked until I climbed upon the wall of the garden of Abū Qutāda, and he was my cousin, and I had the greatest love for him. I greeted him but, by Allah, he did not respond to my greetings." Ka'b repeatedly adjured him by Allah, and repeatedly protested his love for the Messenger of Allah, but Qutāda "kept quiet."

While he was enduring this mental torture, Ka'b received a letter from the King of Ghassān. "As I was a scribe I read that letter," Ka'b says. The letter said: "It has been conveyed to us that your friend [Muhammad] is subjecting you to cruelty and Allah has not created you for a place where you are to be degraded and where you cannot find your right honour." This communication could be very incriminating. "As I read that letter I said, This also is a calamity, so I burnt it."

When forty days had thus passed, a message came from Muhammad to Ka'b. "Verily, Allah's Messenger has commanded you to remain separate from your wife." "Should I divorce her?" Ka'b asked the message-bearer. He replied, "No, but only remain separate from her and don't have sexual contact with her." As Ka'b was young, he sent his wife away to her parents' house to be on the safe side. The same message was sent to the other two. But Hilāl's wife got the Prophet's permission to remain with her husband, as he was "a senile person." "But don't go near him," Muhammad told her. "By Allah, he has no such instinct in him. By Allah, he spends his time in weeping," she replied.

KA'B PARDONED

At last the dark days ended. On the morning of the fiftieth day, an announcer came "from the peak of the hill of Sal saying at the top of his voice: Ka'b b. Mālik, there is glad tiding for you." What other glad tiding was left for him in the world? Ka'b understood at once. "I fell down in prostration and came to realize that there was relief for me," he says. Meanwhile, other friends hurried with the glad tidings. "A person galloped his horse and came from the tribe of Aslam and his horse reached me more quickly than his voice."

Ka'b went to Muhammad in gratefulness, and the latter received him with a smiling face. Ka'b sought his permission to give away his wealth in charity in thankfulness to Allah for the new life that had been bestowed on him. The Prophet advised him to keep some for his own use. Ka'b obediently followed the advice. "I shall keep with me that part of my property which fell to my lot on the occasion of the expedition of Khaibar" (the booty won at Khaibar was quite large and considerably enriched Muhammad and his Companions), Ka'b submitted (6670–6672).

The self-abasement of the three men and their consequent pardon by Allah is celebrated in the Qurān thus: "Allah turned in mercy also to the Three who were left behind. They felt guilty to such a degree that the earth for all its spaciousness became constrained to them, and so did their souls become straitened within them. And they perceived that there is no fleeing from God and no refuge but to Himself. Then He turned to them, that they might repent. For God is easy to reconcile and Merciful" (9:118).

Permanent War

The Arabian peninsula had then come under Muhammad's sway. His followers heaved a sigh of relief. They wanted to enjoy their new wealth in peace. Some of them even began to sell their arms, saying: "The wars of faith are now over." According to Al-Wāqidī, the Prophet's biographer, when Muhammad heard this, he said: "There shall not cease from the midst of my people a party engaged in crusades for the truth, even until Antichrist appear."*

*W. Muir, *Life of Mahomet*, vol. IV, p. 201; also *Tabaqāt*, vol. I, p. 505.

THE EXONERATION OF THE PROPHET'S SLAVE-GIRL

At the end of the "Book of Repentance," there is a brief but interesting *hadīs*. Anas reports: "A person was charged with fornication with the slave-girl of Allah's Messenger. Thereupon Allah's Messenger said to 'Alī: Go and strike off his neck. 'Alī went to the person and found him in a well cooling his body. 'Alī said to him: Come out, and as he took hold of his hand and brought him out, he found that his sexual organ had been cut. Hazrat 'Alī refrained from striking his neck. He came to Allah's Apostle and said: Allah's Messenger, he has not even the sexual organ with him" (6676).

This is an interesting *hadīs* and conceals as much as it reveals. The slave-girl it mentions is none other than Muhammad's own Coptic concubine, Mary, the center of great jealousy in the harem; she was never treated with equality by the other wives of Muhammad, particularly 'Āisha and Hafza, who belonged to the Quraish blue blood. We have already mentioned the incident which caused so much commotion and scandal in the harem. Peace was eventually restored, but in order to avoid further complications, Mary was kept separately in a distant lodging in the upper quarter of Medina, with a male Coptic slave to help her in fetching wood and water. But the wives of Muhammad took their revenge by spreading rumors that the two Egyptians were having illicit relations. Muhammad felt uneasy and jealous and sent 'Alī to punish him. (Where are the four witnesses?) When 'Alī arrived on the scene with sword in hand, he discovered that the slave was a eunuch. This saved the poor man's life. (*Tārikh Tabarī,* vol. I, p. 504.)

19
Hypocrites (Munāfiqīn)

The thirty-sixth book is on the "Hypocrites, Their Characteristics and Command Concerning Them" (*Kitāb Sifāt al-Munāfiqīn wa Ahkāmihim*). It is a small book, containing only twenty-one *ahādīs*, but in some ways it is important. The Qurān refers to the hypocrites very often (twenty-five times), and there is a whole chapter, or *Sura*, named after them, called *Munāfiqīn*. Muhammad repeatedly threatens the hypocrites with blazing hellfire. The Qurānic scholars coming after him put them in the hottest region of Hell, *Hāwiyah*, a bottomless pit of scorching fire. "Allah has promised the hypocrites, men and women, and the rejecters of Faith, the Fire of Hell; therein shall they dwell. . . . For them is the curse of Allah and an enduring punishment," as the Qurān says (9:68).

The name "hypocrites" does not derive from any moral category but was applied to people who no longer believed in the prophethood of Muhammad in their hearts but were afraid to admit it openly in public. They were doubters, skeptics, men of incomplete faith, men who began to entertain questions about the apostleship of Muhammad as they came to know him somewhat better. But in the peculiar theology of Islam, such doubts were morally the most heinous. Doubting Muhammad's prophetic mission was hypocrisy. So those Muslim converts of Medina who became doubters were regarded as hypocrites.

Medinans Downgraded in Their Own City

Many Medinans had offered Muhammad and his followers refuge and protection in their city—some out of conviction, others out of chivalry, and some out of spite for the Meccans. But very soon the refugees became stronger than the citizens. Some of the citizens saw, with pain and alarm but also with increasing helplessness, that they were being reduced to a second-class status in their own hometown. Some of them murmured to each other: "See what we have done to ourselves. We have laid open our lands to them and have shared with them all that we possessed. If we had kept our own for ourselves, then by Allah, they would have gone somewhere else." The Medinans gave Muhammad and his followers an inch, and soon they seized a whole yard. It was the proverbial story of the camel and the old woman in a hut.

Now that Muhammad had been in town with them for some days, the Medinans were also able to arrive at a better estimate of him. Some of them thought that he was no better than a religious humbug. But the realization came too late. For now Muhammad was strong and they were weak. Those who no longer believed in him had come to fear him. But the result was the same: paralysis of will and action. The opposition could now be intimidated, and much of it could also be bought, for though they did not believe in Muhammad, many of them believed in war spoils.

INTELLECTUAL OPPOSITION

The opposition to Muhammad did not emanate only from *munāfiqīn*, the disillusioned converts. It also came from those who had never given up their ancestral faith or surrendered their judgment and had not been swept off their feet by the new religious fad. Some of the members of the opposition were gifted. They could put their ideas into verses. A woman poet named 'Asmā bint Marwān, belonging to the Banī Aws, appealed to the Medinan tribes of Mālik, Auf, and Khazraj in the name of their old heroes. "You obey a stranger who does not belong among you," she sang.* Abū 'Afak,

*Do you expect good from him after the killing of your chiefs / Like a hungry man waiting for a cook's broth? / Is there no man of pride who would attack him by surprise / And cut off the hopes of those who expect aught of him?" (Ibn Ishāq, *Sīrat Rasūl Allah*, p. 676).

a centenarian poet belonging to the Khazrajite clan, related to Aws Manāt, said in a poem that the different tribes of Medina were good neighbors and loyal allies, "Yet there is a rider come among them who divided them." Some of these verses are quoted by Ibn Hishām and Wāqidī and reproduced by Maxime Rodinson.*

Muhammad was much perturbed. The poets of that time were like the journalists of our age. Muhammad detested them, and lay in wait for an opportunity to deal with them effectively.

His victory at Badr in January A.D. 624 brought him the opportunity. His success against the Quraish gave him a new power in Medina. The equation with respect to both local supporters and local adversaries changed appreciably to his advantage. He seized the opportunity and struck fast. First he dealt with the poets whom he feared the most.

Assassination of Poets

"Who will rid me of this pestilential woman?" he said about 'Asmā. Omayr ibn 'Adī, a blind man and a fanatic convert from her own clan, offered to assassinate her, which he did while she was asleep with her child in her arms. "Have you slain the daughter of Marwān?" Muhammad inquired eagerly when Omayr returned from his mission. When he replied in the affirmative, Muhammad commended him to his Companions. "If you desire to see a man that has assisted the Lord and His Prophet, look ye here," he told them.†

The same fate overtook Abū 'Afak the very next month. "Who will rid me of this scoundrel?" Muhammad uttered aloud. And again there was a ready assassin at hand. Sālim ibn 'Umayr of Banī Amr, the people with whom Abū 'Afak had cast his lot and lived, stabbed the man one night while he was sleeping.

Most of the local converts, including the two assassins named above, had not fought at Badr. So they still had to prove their loyalty in action to the Prophet and to the new creed. This they did by these perfidious acts.

*Maxime Rodinson, *Muhammad* (Pelican Books, 1973), pp. 157–158.

†*Sīrat Rasūl Allah*, p. 676. Also, W. Muir, *Life of Mahomet*, vol. III, p. 132.

Hardly had six months elapsed when the blow fell on another influential half-Jewish poet, Ka'b ibn al-Ashraf. We have already mentioned his case. Muhammad made a special petition to Allah for his elimination. "Lord, deliver me from the son of Ashraf . . . because of his open sedition and verses," he prayed. "Go with the blessings of Allah and assistance from high," he told the departing assassins, and when they returned after fulfilling their task, Muhammad met them at the very gate of the mosque in welcome. One of the conspirators had received a wound by accident. Muhammad treated it in his usual way—he spat on it and it was healed.*

A NEW FEAR DESCENDS

According to ancient Arab custom, such willful murders demanded tribal vengeance. But this was not to be thought of under the new circumstances. There was something new in the atmosphere, a new apprehension, a new equation. After 'Asmā's assassination, the assassin had asked Muhammad if he would have to bear any penalty. "Not two goats shall come to blow for her," Muhammad had assured him. This turned out to be only too true. The assassin openly boasted of his act even before the five sons of 'Asmā, but nothing happened. They were too cowed. The assassin had a powerful patron.

Fear is more potent than a sentimental humanist psychology would like to believe. Fear speaks louder and strikes home quicker than many other modes of communication. "The day after Bint Marwān was killed, the men of Banī Khatma [her husband's tribe] became Muslims because they saw the power of Islam," says Ibn Ishāq.†

The same author gives us another story to the same effect. The Apostle said: "Kill any Jew that falls into your power." Thereupon Muhayyisa b. Mas'ūd, a Muslim convert, leaped upon and killed Ibn Sunayna, a Jewish merchant. The killer's brother, Huwayyisa, chided him: "You enemy of God, did you kill him when much of the fat

*Ibn Ishāq, *Sīrat Rasūl Allah*, p. 368.

†Ibid., p. 676.

on your belly comes from his wealth?" Muhayyisa answered: "Had the one who ordered me to kill him ordered me to kill you, I would have cut your head off." This was the beginning of Huwayyisa's acceptance of Islam. He exclaimed, "By God, a religion which can bring you to this is marvellous!" and he became a Muslim.*

The Demand for More Complete Submission

Muhammad took care to give the local converts no unnecessary offense in the beginning. But this period of caution did not last long. Muhammad entered Medina in April A.D. 622, and within two years he was already having his adversaries eliminated with impunity. As his power increased, he began to come out more and more openly against the lukewarm, the doubters among the local converts. Allah began to demand from them a more unquestioning submission to the authority of His Apostle and issued more frequent warnings against them. Allah told Muhammad that the "doubters" scoffed at him in private while they paid him homage in public and that they were worthless fellows. "When the Hypocrites come to thee, they say, 'we bear witness that thou art indeed the Apostle' . . . but they are indeed liars. . . . They have made their oaths a screen. . . . A seal is set on their hearts. . . . They are as worthless and hollow as pieces of timber propped up. . . . They are enemies; so beware of them" (Qurân 63:1–4).

The Opposition Divided and Demoralized

Muhammad's party had a common command, a common goal, common interests, a common ideology and passion, but the opposition was badly divided; it had no ideology but only certain grievances. Furtive in action, it said one thing and did another. Muhammad picked different groups of the opposition and struck at them one by one, now the Banū Qaynuqā, now the Banū Nazīr, now the Banū Quraizah. They had promised each other mutual help in private but withdrew when the time for this came.

*Ibn Ishāq, *Sīrat Rasūl Allah,* p. 369.

The demoralization was complete. The Qurān speaks contemptuously of the Medinans, who were promising their Jewish allies that "if ye be driven forth we will go forth with you . . . and if you be fought against we will help you. . . . But God bears witness that they are liars. If they be driven forth, these will not go forth with them; and if they be fought against, these will not help them." Muhammad also makes a keen observation about the opposition while fortifying his followers by telling them: "Ye indeed are a keener source of fear in their hearts than God. . . . Thou dost reckon them as one body, but their hearts are separated. It is because they are a people devoid of intelligence" (Qurān 59:11–15).

'ABDULLAH IBN UBAYY

There must have been many people opposed to Muhammad's growing power, but the traditions have preserved the name of Ibn Ubayy as the epitome of them all.

He was a Medinan chief of the Khazrajite clan of Awf who became an early convert to Islam. He was once the leading citizen of Medina. It is said that just before Muhammad came, his supporters were trying to make him the king of Medina. But after the arrival of Muhammad, a new force entered the scene, and his importance declined fast. But even then, because of his influence, Muhammad was advised by his best friends to treat Ibn Ubayy with circumspection.

Muslim traditions have blackened Ibn Ubayy's name, but if patriotism, independence of judgment, and loyalty are qualities, and if to save is better than to kill, he was not an unworthy man. He saved the Jewish tribe of Medina known as Qaynuqā from execution. As early as the second year of the Hijra, Muhammad besieged this tribe. When they surrendered, their hands were tied behind their backs and they were taken out for execution. But Ibn Ubayy intervened forcefully. He "thrust his hand into the collar of the apostle's robe; the apostle was so angry that his face became almost black." But 'Abdullah insisted and said: "No, by God, I will not let you go until you deal kindly with my clients [allies]. Four hundred men without mail and three hundred mailed protected me from all mine enemies; would you cut them down in one morning? By God, I am a man who fears that circumstances may change."* Ibn Ubayy was still influential in the affairs of Medina, and his appeal was also a threat. Muhammad yielded on condition that the tribe depart within three days, leaving their goods behind to the victor.

This was in February A.D. 624. Three years later, in March–April A.D. 627, when the same fate overtook another Jewish tribe of Medina known as Quraizah, the Medinan opposition had already lost its influence and Muhammad had a field day. Eight or nine hundred men were led out in groups of five or six with their hands tied behind their backs and were beheaded, and their bodies were thrown into trenches dug in the marketplace of Medina. We have already mentioned the story somewhat more fully. (See pp. 110–114.)

Dissension between the Citizens and the Refugees

Only some months after the tragedy of the Banū Quraizah was enacted, dissension had broken out between the citizens and the refugees in which it was proved that the citizens were already the losing party.

On this occasion, Muhammad was returning after looting the Banū Mustaliq, an Arabian tribe inhabiting a region about eight days' march from Medina. The booty included two hundred families, two thousand camels, and five thousand sheep and goats. On the way back, a quarrel broke out between a citizen named Sinān and a refugee named Jihjā, who was a servant of 'Umar. Jihjā struck Sinān. Tempers were frayed on both sides, and the quarrel soon spread to others. Ibn Ubayy referred to the insolence of the refugees: "This is what you have done to yourselves. You have let them occupy your country, and you have divided your property among them. . . . They are trying to outdo us seeking to outnumber us in our own land! By Allah, I think that between us and 'these vagabonds of Quraish' it is like saying 'Feed a dog and it will devour you.' But when we return to the Medina city, the stronger will drive out the weaker."†

*Ibn Ishāq, *Sīrat Rasūl Allah*, p. 363.
†Ibn Ishāq, *Sīrat Rasūl Allah*, p. 491.

Later, when confronted with this statement, Ibn Ubayy, with his usual weakness, denied it. Muhammad did not want to pick a quarrel at the time, so he accepted the denial; but it rankled in his mind, and later, at a more opportune moment, Allah confirmed it openly in a Qurānic verse (63:7–8).

THE ASSASSINATION OF 'ABDULLAH PROPOSED

'Umar counseled Muhammad to have Ibn Ubayy killed. "Command 'Abbād ibn Bishr to kill him," he advised. But Muhammad was cautious. He had an image to protect. He did not want people "to say that Muhammad kills his own followers." But though he refrained from executing the idea immediately, he gave it serious thought. Hoping to play on the rivalry between the two Medina tribes, Aws and Khazraj, he consulted Usaid b. Huzair, an Awsite chief and a staunch Muslim, about 'Abdullah, who was a chief of the Khazrajites. But even he advised Muhammad to deal with 'Abdullah gently and cautiously.

With all the proposals and consultations, the idea of 'Abdullah's assassination was so much in the air that his own son, a fanatic Muslim, also heard about it. He went to Muhammad and offered to kill his father with his own hands. Muslim traditions and histories tell this story with great pride.

But wiser counsels prevailed. Since 'Abdullah was an influential citizen, and his assassination would have unnecessarily jeopardized Muhammad's own position, he was spared. Later on, when 'Abdullah's position became weak through his own vacillation and temporizing, and he was isolated from his people and allies, 'Umar confessed the wisdom of Muhammad's decision. Muhammad replied exultantly: "If I had killed him on the day you advised me to, other Medinan chiefs would have been furious. But now they themselves would do it if I commanded them." "I know the Apostle's order is more blessed than mine," 'Umar submitted, according to Ibn Ishāq, who narrates the whole story.* The story is repeated by Tabarī too.

**Sīrat Rasūl Allah*, p. 492.

The last we hear of Ibn Ubayy is in connection with Tabūk. By this time, he had already become a back number, and he died two or three months after Tabūk. Whatever opposition was still left in Medina evaporated with him.

Now, with this background, let us turn once more to the *Sahīh Muslim*.

'Abdullah Incites the Medinans

Zaid b. Arqam reports that while returning from a journey in which they "faced many hardships" (after sacking Banī Mustaliq), they heard 'Abdullah b. Ubayy tell his friends: "Do not give what you have in your possession to those who are with Allah's Messenger until they desert him." They also heard him say that on their return to Medina, the "honourable would drive out the meaner therefrom." Zaid reported the matter to Muhammad, who questioned 'Abdullah. The latter, on oath, denied having said any such thing. Muhammad at first accepted this denial at its face value, but a revelation later descended on him (63:1) attesting that Zaid had told the truth and establishing 'Abdullah as a liar (6677).

Prayer for Dead Unbelievers Forbidden

The next two *ahādīs* (6679–6680) tell us that when 'Abdullah died, the Prophet, at his son's request, "gave him his shirt which he would use as a coffin for his father." Muhammad also came to his grave and "brought him out from that, placed him on his knee and put his saliva in his mouth." He also prayed for him even against the protest of 'Umar.

Intimidation

Intimidation of the opposition began as early as the Battle of Uhud, which took place in the third year of the Hijra (January–February A.D. 625). Zaid b. Sābit reports: "Allah's Apostle set out for Uhud. Some of the persons who were with them came back. The Companions of Allah's Apostle were divided in two groups. One group said: We would kill them, and the other one said:

No, this should not be done" (6684). Then Allah spoke: "Why should ye be divided into two parties about the hypocrites?" So the ranks of the loyal were closed, but the message was successfully conveyed to the future laggards. Thus intimidation had started quite early, and it was one of the methods of securing compliance and participation in Muhammad's "holy" wars. Either you fight for us or we fight you.

An Attempt on the Prophet's Life

According to certain traditions, when Muhammad was returning from Tabūk, certain of his opponents in 'Aqaba formed a group with the intention of killing him by throwing him over a cliff. According to Huzaifa, they were twelve men, all veiled and only half-glimpsed. Muhammad knew their identity but told no one except Huzaifa, who was forbidden to divulge the information. The Prophet cursed them all (6690). This tradition is given here in a rather garbled form.

An Outstanding Arab

Jābir gives us an interesting *hadīs*. One day Muhammad declared: "He who climbed this hill, the hill of Murār, his sins would be obliterated." Many took advantage of this divine amnesty, and "there was a ceaseless flow of persons." All were pardoned except one man, the owner of a red camel. People went to him and advised him that he too should go and obtain pardon. But the man replied: "By Allah, so far as I am concerned the finding of something lost is dearer to me than seeking of forgiveness for me by your companion [the Holy Prophet], and he remained busy in finding out his lost thing" (6691).

The *Sahīh Muslim* does not give us this man's name, but apparently he was a stout and wise soul. Was he a Zen philosopher who lived one day at a time? Sufficient unto the day is the work of the day. The hereafter will take care of itself. Other traditions identify him as Harr b. Qays, who refused to take the "pledge of the Tree," and was called a "hypocrite" by the believers.

There is also a *hadīs* which shows that those who were unacceptable to Muhammad were unacceptable to Allah even in death. A Muslim who transcribed for Muhammad "ran away as a rebel and joined the People of the Book." When he died "they dug the grave and buried him therein, but they found to their surprise that the earth had thrown him out over the surface. They again dug the grave . . . but the earth again threw him out. . . . They again dug . . . but the earth again threw him out. At last they left him unburied" (6693).

Allah both saves and kills for the pleasure of His Prophet. Jābir reports: "Allah's Messenger came back from a journey and as he was near Medina, there was such a violent gale that the mountain seemed to be pressed. Allah's Messenger said: This wind has perhaps been made to blow for the death of a hypocrite, and as he reached Medina a notorious hypocrite from amongst the hypocrites had died" (6684). According to other traditions, Muhammad was returning to Medina after his attack on the Banū Mustaliq. The man whose death the storm caused or proclaimed was Ruffaa, a chief of the Banī Qainuqā, a Jewish tribe of Medina that was one of the first tribes to suffer at the hands of Muhammad. Ruffaa had been the first to receive 'Umar and offer him hospitality when the latter came to Medina.

Description of a Hypocrite

The last two *ahādīs* of this book describe those who have neither the support of a fanatic faith nor the light of a higher philosophy and who are subject to the doubts and temptations of ordinary men. Ibn 'Umar, who had already chosen his pastures, reports Muhammad as saying: "The similitude of a hypocrite is that of a sheep which roams aimlessly between two flocks. She goes to one at one time and to the other at another time" (6696).

"THE BOOK OF COMMENTARY"

The forty-first and last book of the *Sahīh Muslim* is called the "Book of Commentary" (*Kitāb al-Tafsīr*).

The Qurān cannot be read like other scriptures, for it is very different from them in temper and subject matter. It is feverish in tone; it threatens and promises; it does not elucidate but merely lays down and prescribes. It does not deal with the "heavenly order" of the Gnostic traditions (the *rita* of the Vedas or the *Maāt* of ancient Egypt), but with the hereafter, merely an exaggerated, sensuous copy of the here.

The Qurānic verses are reputed to have come from a mind in trance, but that in itself gives them no true spiritual validity. The Yogas tell us that trance is possible at every level of the mind, but that the trances of a passionate, angry, and deluded mind (i.e., of a mind characterized by *kāma, dvesha,* and *moha*) are not to be trusted—behind them often stands a lunatic or a malevolent criminal.

The Qurān deals with "accidents"; Qurānic verses often relate to external events, individual men, incidents in the life of the Prophet. The "Book of Commentary" gives equally external information about some of these verses. It tells us about the time, the place, the circumstances of their revelation, and all such details of little larger spiritual significance. This book would have been very important if it were comprehensive and gave essential information; but in its present form it is sketchy and discusses an important subject in a superficial manner. It contains only fifty traditions.

For example, in the first five *ahādīs* of the book we are told when and where was revealed the following Qurānic verse: "This day I have perfected your religion for you, completed favour upon you, and have chosen for you *al-Islam* as your religion" (5:4). It "was revealed on the night of Friday and we were in 'Arafāt with Allah's Messenger," 'Umar reports (7154). The information throws no particular light on this revelation, which makes such a tall claim, and adds nothing essential to its subject.

The same with another Qurānic verse: "And if a woman fears ill-treatment from her husband or desertion, it is no sin for them twain if they make terms of peace between themselves" (4:128). 'Āisha tells us that "it was revealed in case of a woman who had long association with a person [as his wife] and now he intends to divorce her and she says: Do not divorce me, retain me [as wife in your house] and you are permitted to live with another wife. It was in this context that this verse was revealed'' (7165).

Who were the characters mentioned by 'Āisha? They were the Prophet himself and his wife Sauda (Tirmizī, vol. II, *hadīs* 899). Kātib al-Wāqidī also tells us in his *Tabaqāt* that Muhammad wanted to divorce his wife, then in her forties, but she went to him and said: ''I am not asking you to sleep with me, I yield my turn to 'Āisha. But I want to be there, on the Day of Resurrection, among your wives.'' Muhammad agreed. Resurrection Day was far off.

The Last Sūra

Sa'īd b. Jubair reports that *Sūra Anfāl* (''Spoils of War''), the eighth *Sūra*, was revealed on the occasion of the Battle of Badr; that *Sūra al-Hashr* (''The Gathering,'' or ''Banishment''), the fifty-ninth *Sūra*, ''was revealed in connection with the tribe of Banū Nazīr; and that *Sūra Ṭauba* (''Repentance''), also known as *Sūra Barāat* (''Immunity''), ''was meant to humiliate the non-believers and the hypocrites'' (7185). In the Qurān this appears as the ninth *Sūra*, but chronologically it is one of the last—according to Sir William Muir, the very last. This is understandable. It is entirely fitting that a *Sūra* of such bitterness, condemnation, and intention should be the last inspiration of a life that breathed such pathologic theological hatred toward the nonbelievers who constituted then, and do even now, the majority of men and women in the world.

Bibliography

HADĪS

Sahīh Muslim. English translation by Abdul Hamid Siddiqi in four volumes. Lahore: Sh. Muhammad Ashraf, 1973-1975.

Tirmizī Sharīf. Urdu translation in 2 vols. Lal Kuan. Delhi: Rabbani Book Depot, 1980.

Sahīh Bukhari. Only partial translations in English available in India. Abridged Urdu translation, *Sahīh Bukhāri Sharīf*. Churiwalan, Delhi: Kitab Khana, Ishaitu'l Islam.

Mishkātu'l-Masbīh [Niche of lamps]. Seven-hundred-year-old collection of *Hadīs*, very popular and much in use. Reprint of English translation by Dr. James Robson. Lahore: Sh. Muhammad Ashraf, 1973. Urdu translation in 2 vols.; Delhi: Rabbani Book Depot.

QURĀN

The Korān. Translation by E. H. Palmer. London, New York, and Toronto: Oxford University Press.

Glorious Qurān. English translation with the original Arabic text by Abdullah Yusuf 'Āli. Cairo: Daral-Kitab al Masri.

Qurān Majeed. Hindi and English translations with original text in Arabic; English translation by M. Pickthall. Rampur: Maktab Al-Hasnat.

BIOGRAPHIES OF MUHAMMAD

Sīrat Rasūl Allah by Ibn Ishāq. The very first definitive biography and the source of subsequent ones. English translation, *The Life of Muhammad*, translated and edited by A. Guillaume. Oxford, New York, and Delhi: Oxford University Press, 1980.

Tabaqāt Ibn Sa'd. The next most important source on the life of the Prophet and the Companions. Ibn Sa'd, popularly known as Kātib al-

Wāqidī, composed fifteen volumes on different classes (*tabaqāt*) of Muhammad's Companions and Successors, and the history of the Khalīfas up to his own time. Urdu translation in 8 vols., vols. 1 and 2, *Sīras: The Biography of the Prophet*. Karachi: Nafees Academy.

Tārīkh Tabarī, or *Annals*, by Tabarī. The first volume, *Sīrat al-Nabī*, is a biography of Muhammad. At-Tabarī died in A.H. 310 (A.D. 922), and his *Sīrat al-Nabī* is an authoritative source of Muhammad's subsequent biographies. Urdu translation in 11 vols. Karachi: Nafees Academy.

The Rauzat-us-Safa by Muhammad b. Khavendshah b. Mahmud, popularly known as Mirkhond. A fifteenth-century Persian biography which takes into account many preceding traditions. English translation under the title *The Garden of Purity*, trans. E. Tehatsek. London: Royal Asiatic Society, 1893. Now being reprinted by Idarahi Adbiyati Delhi, Delhi-6, India.

The Life of Mahomet by Sir William Muir. Scholarly and pioneering study. 4 vols. London: Smith, Elder & Co., 1861.

Mohammad by Maxime Rodinson. Scholarly. Pelican Books, 1973.

SHIAISM

Nahj al-Balāghah. Selections from sermons, letters, and sayings of 'Alī; trans. by Syed Ali Raza. Tehran: World Organization for Islamic Services.

Shiaism by S. Ghaffari. 3d ed. Tehran: Shahpur Square, 1976.

GENERAL REFERENCE

Dictionary of Islam by Thomas Patrick Hughes. 1885; reprinted, New Delhi: Oriental Books Reprint Corporation, 1976.

Encyclopaedia of Religions and Ethics, edited by James Hastings. Edinburgh and New York: T. & T. Clark.

GENERAL

The Mohammedan Controversy and Other Indian Articles by Sir William Muir. 1st ed., 1897; reprinted, Allahabad: R. S. Publishing House.

Qurān Parichaya by Deva Prakash. Hindi publication in 3 vols. The author was a great scholar of the Arabic language and Islamic religious literature. The volumes are badly printed and lack modern critical aids. Books available at Arya Samaj Dayanand Marg, Ratlam (M.P.)—India.

The Word as Revelation: Names of Gods by Ram Swarup. Among other things, discusses monotheism vis-à-vis polytheism. New Delhi: Impex India, 1980.

Index